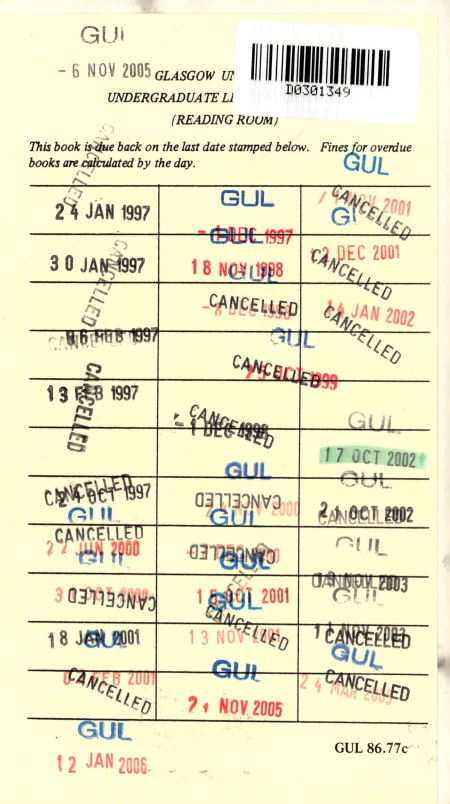

This is the first book to show how Latin American liberation theology can be applied to and can transform
pastoral care in countries such as Britain and the USA.
Hitherto pastoral care has tended to concentrate on
looking after individuals. Stephen Pattison suggests that
much of the suffering endured by individuals is actually
socially and politically caused, and so is avoidable if the
appropriate action is taken. The author argues that what
we now require is a socio-politically aware and committed pastoral care which makes an option for oppressed
and poor people and engages in practical struggle against
the forces of injustice and oppression. Focussing, as it
does, especially on mentally ill people and on women, the
book will be of interest to all those who want to broaden
their vision and knowledge of liberation theology or
pastoral care, whether theologians, pastors, students for
ministry, members of caring professions, or users of the
services they provide.

PASTORAL CARE
AND LIBERATION THEOLOGY

CAMBRIDGE STUDIES IN IDEOLOGY AND RELIGION

Religion increasingly is seen as a renewed force, and is recognised as an important factor in the moderen world in all aspects of life – cultural, economic, and political. It is no longer a matter of surprise to find religious factors at work in areas and situations of political tension. However, our information about these situations has tended to come from two main sources. The news-gathering agencies are well-placed to convey information, but are hampered by the fact that their representatives are not equipped to provide analysis of the religious forces involved. Alternatively, the movements generate their own accounts, which understandably seem less than objective to outside observers. There is no lack of information or factual material, but a real need for sound academic analysis. 'Cambridge Studies in Ideology and Religion' will meet this need. It will give an objective, balanced, and programmatic coverage to issues which – while of wide potential interest – have been largely neglected by analytical investigation, apart from the appearance of sporadic individual studies. Intended to enable debate to proceed at a higher level, the series should lead to a new phase in our understanding of the relationship between ideology and religion.

A list of titles in the series is given at the end of the book.

PASTORAL CARE AND LIBERATION THEOLOGY

STEPHEN PATTISON

Department of Health and Social Welfare,
Open University

CAMBRIDGE
UNIVERSITY PRESS

Published by the Press Syndicate of the University of Cambridge
The Pitt Building, Trumpington Street, Cambridge CB2 1RP
40 West 20th Street, New York, NY 10011-4211, USA
10 Stamford Road, Oakleigh, Melbourne 3166, Australia

© Cambridge University Press 1994

First published 1994

Printed in Great Britain at the University Press, Cambridge

A catalogue record for this book is available from the British Library

Library of Congress cataloguing in publication data

Pattison, Stephen
Pastoral care and liberation theology / Stephen Pattison.
p.   cm. – (Cambridge studies in ideology and religion)
Includes index.
ISBN 0–521–41822–4
1. Church work with the mentally ill.   2. Liberation theology.
3. Pastoral theology – Research.   4. Church work with women.
I. Title.   II. Series.
BV4461.P38   1994
259′.4 – dc 20   93–9014   CIP

ISBN 0 521 41822 4 hardback

Contents

Contents

General editors' preface

Only twenty years ago it was widely assumed that religion had lost its previous place in Western culture and that this pattern would spread throughout the world. Since then religion has become a renewed force, recognised as an important factor in the modern world in all aspects of life, cultural, economic, and political. This is true not only of the Third World, but also in Europe East and West, and in North America. It is no longer a surprise to find a religious factor at work in areas of political tension.

Religion and ideology form a mixture which can be of interest to the observer, but in practice dangerous and explosive. Our information about such matters comes for the most part from three types of sources. The first is the media which understandably tend to concentrate on newsworthy events, without taking the time to deal with the underlying issues of which they are but symptoms. The second source comprises studies by social scientists who often adopt a functionalist and reductionist view of the faith and beliefs which motivate those directly involved in such situations. Finally, there are the statements and writings of those committed to the religious or ideological movements themselves. We seldom lack information, but there is a need – often an urgent need – for sound objective analyses which can make use of the best contemporary approaches to both politics and religion. 'Cambridge Studies in Ideology and Religion' is designed to meet this need.

The subject matter is global and this will be reflected in the choice both of topics and of authors. The initial volumes will be concerned primarily with movements involving the Christian religion, but as the series becomes established movements involving other world religions will be subjected to the same objective critical analysis. In all cases it is our intention that an accurate and sensitive account of religion should be informed by an objective and sophisticated application of perspectives from the social sciences.

This is one of the most substantial and challenging contributions to pastoral theology to have appeared for some years. Pastoral care has had difficulty in relating to serious theology or developing a critical self-understanding. Liberation theology, argues Dr Pattison, can stimulate pastoral care to become more aware of its socio-political context, and more sensitive to the dangers of implicit or explicit collusion with oppressive structures and processes. These insights are of general relevance to the criticism and renewal of pastoral care, and are developed here with special relation to the pastoral care of people with psychiatric disorders, to psychiatric hospitals, and to the role of the chaplain. Dr Pattison's carefully developed argument is challenging and controversial, and has important implications for the practice of pastoral care and for a more rigorous pastoral theology.

DUNCAN FORRESTER AND ALISTAIR KEE
New College, University of Edinburgh

Preface

Like any other part of Western society, the intellectual and academic spheres have their rapidly changing fashions. In the postmodern supermarket of ideas and theories, liberation theology, which originated in Latin America in the 1960s and 1970s, may now appear to be over-familiar, even *passé*. After the triumph of capitalism and the collapse of communism in Eastern Europe, it may be thought to be well beyond its 'sell by' date. If this is the case, then this book is, in part, a protest against intellectual consumerism and trendiness. It is also an assertion that, in their haste to refresh their palates by devouring the next new idea to come along, thinkers and practitioners in the West run the risk of failing to digest the full significance and implications of ideas and movements which have a more than transitory importance.

Marxism (which heavily influenced liberation theology) is an example of a theoretical system which is presently discredited and out of favour in the academic establishment, even amongst left-wing thinkers. This is short-sighted and absurd: Marx is a giant of the intellect whose work still has much to teach us about how society works, even if we would frequently want to disagree with his theories, interpretations, and prescriptions. Similarly, there is a vast amount that we still need to learn from liberation theology, theoretically and in practice. In this book I want to argue that liberation theology provides an illuminating critique of pastoral care for the 1990s. It is not so much that liberation theology has been tried in the Western world and found irrelevant or wanting. It is more that its implications and methods have not yet been sufficiently understood and applied. Pastoral care, being a practical activity, is an obvious area in which to apply them.

In the 1970s it was thought in many countries that economies could expand indefinitely, that social consensus was here to stay, and that, while the poor might always be with us, they would become more affluent and the gap between them and the rich would continue to narrow. The demise of these assumptions means that the very practical challenge of liberation theology lies ahead not, as contemporary intellectual entrepreneurs might have us believe, behind us.

It is a great pleasure to acknowledge extensive debts in writing this work. Alastair Campbell, Una Maclean, Duncan Forrester and Peter Selby provided guiding hands and supportive criticism in initial stages. Sue Spencer agreed to read parts, and to help particularly with chapter 17 on pastoral care with women, a subject in which she has an enormous amount of practical experience and theoretical expertise. James Woodward's enthusiasm and commitment to reading speedily many chapters of the book has been the complete antidote to authorial depression and self-doubt. His willingness to compile an index is gratefully acknowledged as the act of supererogation that it is. Elaine Graham discussed pastoral care with women with me, and generously allowed me to use some of her own unpublished writing on this subject. Barbara Hayes also did the latter. Michael Bourne, John Foskett, and John Browning kindly brought me up to date on aspects of the state of contemporary mental health chaplaincy by supplying me with information. Malcolm Johnson at the Open University had the vision to appoint a practical theologian to the staff of this remarkable, interdisciplinary, secular institution and the courage to allow me to continue writing in the theological sphere. Last, but by no means least, Alex Wright of Cambridge University Press has been an honourable and exemplary commissioning editor with whom it has been a delight to work.

My chief debt is really to the patients and staff of a psychiatric hospital in the North of England where I worked as a part-time chaplain for a while. It was they who taught me what mental health services were, and could be, like, for good

and ill. The experience I gained in that setting was the concrete horizon of dialogue for the insights I was gaining from
liberation theology. It underlies the present work at all points,
even if this is not often directly apparent.

If it were appropriate to dedicate this book to an individual
I would have no hesitation in dedicating it to John Sweet, my
first theological teacher. John has given me nearly twenty years
of friendship and support, encouraging me on theological study
from very unpromising beginnings. As he approaches
retirement I take this opportunity to thank him, and to salute
him warmly and publicly from an area of theology very distant
from his own field of New Testament Studies.

Given the subject-matter of the book and the engaged,
corporately focussed response I hope it might engender,
however, I think it most appropriate to dedicate it to all those
who suffer and are oppressed, especially those who are
oppressed by what we think of as mental disorder. In this
connection I particularly remember the members of my own
family whose lives have been vitiated by severe, chronic mental
illness.

Introduction: the challenge of liberation theology

Since 1968, when Latin America's Catholic Church began to question the miserable conditions in which two thirds of the people live, over 850 priests, nuns, and bishops have been arrested, tortured, murdered, or expelled, and thousands of the Catholic laity have been jailed and killed. 'Nowadays it is dangerous ... and practically illegal to be an authentic Christian in Latin America', said Salvadorean Jesuit Rutilio Grande a month before he was shot dead by right-wing assassins in El Salvador. Two months later, in May 1977, a second Salvadorean priest, Alfonso Navarro Oviedo, was murdered in his home by a right-wing vigilante group that threatened to massacre all the Jesuits in the country. But, unlike the Catholic churches in Franco's Spain and Hitler's Germany, Latin America's bishops and priests will not be cowed. 'We will eat dirt before we betray our people', said Paraguay's Bishop Anibal Maricevich.[1]

The witness of some parts of the church against poverty, oppression and totalitarianism in Latin America over the last thirty years has been deeply impressive. In a continent marked by extremes of poverty and wealth (the latter to be found in the pockets of a tiny minority), Christian religious and lay people have added their own blood and suffering to that of the poor and oppressed. The church, particularly the Catholic Church, is experiencing ongoing martyrdom for the sake of the liberation of the people.[2]

---

[1] Penny Lernoux, *Cry of the People*. Harmondsworth: Penguin, 1982, p. 13.
[2] 'Over the past twenty years the victims of oppression have grown astronomically in Latin America, in the face of staggering inflation, cutbacks in public programs,

1

The theology of liberation (or liberation theology, as it is more commonly known) which has accompanied the church's costly contribution to social justice is equally impressive. It is committed to concrete involvement in the process of social and political liberation in Latin America (many liberation theologians live and work amongst the poor and only write and lecture as a part-time secondary activity). It is practical, contextual, and action-guiding, not remote, theoretical, and academic. It is often closely related to the life and work of the community of faith. It is intellectually innovative and rigorous in terms both of method and content. It is comprehensive, systematic, and lively, continuing to evolve and develop despite physical threats against its proponents' lives, and ecclesiastical threats of censorship to their intellects.[3]

Liberation theology is now enormously influential as a wellspring of theologies throughout the world and shows no signs of depletion or diminution after 30 years. It is here to stay:

Liberation theologies can no longer be disregarded as minor religious movements. On the contrary, they are becoming the point of reference for all other discourse about God and religion. This is because liberation theologians are posing everywhere, in many languages and modes of expression, that eternal question which we believe is *the* biblical question: What are we doing for the children of God who are left in our care, those among our sisters and brothers who are suffering unjustly and dying before their time?[4]

capital flight, environmental destruction, and the effects of runaway debt. There are beneficiaries of these conditions – the international banking system, multinational corporations, and the most competitive sectors of the national business communities. But in the meantime, the number of children irreversibly damaged by malnutrition – or simply killed – are [*sic*] on the rise. Too many people are "dying before their time"' (Otto Maduro, 'Introduction' in Marc H. Ellis and Otto Maduro, eds., *The Future of Liberation Theology*. Maryknoll, NY: Orbis, 1989, p. xvi).

[3] Compare Richard's judgement on traditional European-originated theology: 'Traditional theology is a theology that becomes more repetitive every day. It is empty, feeble, lacking in significance and – why not say so? – boring. It is a science cultivated in closed elitist academies. The world is not interested in this theology, and neither is this theology interested in the world. The cause of its sterility is that *the dominant theology has no spirituality, no God, and does not communicate God's word*. It is a theology confused by idolatry. Often it is a theology of death' (Pablo Richard, 'Liberation theology: a difficult but possible future' in Ellis and Maduro, eds., *Future of Liberation Theology*, p. 503. Emphasis original.).

[4] Otto Maduro, 'Introduction' in Ellis and Maduro, eds., *Future of Liberation Theology*, p. xvi. For more on different types of liberation and Third World Theologies see, for example, further essays in this volume and Alistair Kee, ed., *A Reader in Political*

Liberation theology as a literary genre is popular in Western capitalist democracies like Britain and the USA. Many hundreds of works have now been translated and continue to be published in English.[5] Clearly, liberation theology strikes a chord in the hearts and minds of Christians living in very different circumstances from those in which it originated.

Having said this, however, the adoption and development of positive responses to this theology has been subdued in Europe and North America. While a number of theologians, particularly in late 1970s and early 1980s, engaged in a constructive dialogue with liberation theology and it has attracted some critical attention, for the most part liberation theology has not flowered amongst Christians in the Northern hemisphere.[6,7] There have been some notable attempts to apply aspects of liberation theology such as the Methodist Mission Alongside the Poor. It is arguable, too, that its existence may have broadened the horizons of church responses on issues such as the inner city and unemployment as well as informing aspects of Christian women's struggle for liberation.[8] However, liberation theology has remained somewhat esoteric and book-fast.

Despite a decade in which the gap between rich and poor in

Theology. London: SCM Press, 1974; *The Scope of Political Theology*. London: SCM Press, 1978.

[5] The main publishers of liberation theology in English translation are Orbis books in the USA and SCM Press in the UK. A new series of books by prominent liberation theologians, 'Liberation and Theology', has been inaugurated by Burns and Oates (1987–). Only relatively few of the most fundamental foundational works of liberation theology will be alluded to in depth here, such is the scope of liberation theology now.

[6] For positive responses in the Northern hemisphere to liberation theology see, for example, Rex Ambler and David Haslam, eds., *Agenda for Prophets*. London: Bowerdean, 1980; Duncan Forrester, *Theology and Politics*. Oxford: Blackwell, 1988; Laurie Green, *Power to the Powerless*. Basingstoke: Marshall Pickering, 1987; *Let's Do Theology*. London: Mowbray, 1990; Michael Paget-Wilkes, *Poverty, Revolution and the Church*. Exeter: Paternoster, 1981; Christopher Rowland and Mark Corner, *Liberating Exegesis*. London: SPCK, 1990; David Sheppard, *Bias to the Poor*. Sevenoaks: Hodder and Stoughton, 1983; Dorothee Sölle, *Choosing Life*. London: SCM Press, 1981; John J. Vincent, *Starting All Over Again*. Geneva: World Council of Churches, 1981.

[7] For critical material on liberation theology see, for example, Alistair Kee, *Domination or Liberation?*. London: SCM Press, 1986; *Marx and the Failure of Liberation Theology*. London: SCM Press, 1990; Brian Mahan and L. Dale Rechesin, eds., *The Challenge of Liberation Theology*. Maryknoll, NY: Orbis, 1981; Edward Norman, *Christianity and the World Order*. Oxford: Oxford University Press, 1979.

[8] Cf. *Faith in the City*. London: Church House Publishing, 1985.

British and North American society has actually grown under right-wing governments, liberation theology is not widely perceived to have very much to offer Christians in advanced capitalist societies, either in theory or in practice.[9] It is revered for its provenance and scholarly voluminosity, suspected for its supposed tutelage to Marxism, and ultimately dismissed as a marginal curiosity. It now faces the final emasculation of being academically studied and examined amidst other contemporary theologies at expensive and elitist Western universities. A strange fate for a theology which one of its main originators asserts is 'rooted in revolutionary militancy'![10]

Liberation theology can be inspected and admired from afar as a fine, alien, and curious literary edifice, or it can be put to work. The latter is the intention here. Liberation theology has not been adequately attended to in the affluent countries of the Northern hemisphere, although it has substantial relevance here as well as in Latin America. That relevance needs to be exposed and explored – it is not simply apparent. An uncritical application of liberation theology without regard to difference of context would not be either relevant or faithful to this deeply contextualised theology. One place in which it can be explored in a fruitful way is in the practice and theory of pastoral care. Moreover, pastoral care in the Northern hemisphere is not only an activity in which it is appropriate to explore the relevance of liberation theology: it also badly needs the challenge of some of the insights and methods of liberation theology.

It is appropriate to examine the relevance of liberation theology to pastoral care for two main reasons. First, both pastoral care and liberation theology share a common concern for people's well being and flourishing. Secondly, both are broadly focussed on the actual practice of increasing human flourishing. One can therefore minimally assume that there

---

[9] Britain has an increasingly economically unjust, unequal society. 1988 saw the greatest rise in the gap between rich and poor for any single year in the last 200 years according to the leading authority on poverty, Peter Townsend. See further Carey Oppenheim, *Poverty: The Facts*. London: Child Poverty Action Group, 1990.

[10] Gustavo Gutiérrez, *The Power of the Poor in History*. London: SCM Press, 1983, p. 205.

are, or should be, areas of common concern which will profit from intensive critical dialogue and examination. But more than this, pastoral care actually needs the method and critique which liberation theology provides.

There are four main reasons for attempting to challenge pastoral care from the perspective of the insights and methods of liberation theology. First, while pastoral care is concerned with the totality of human well being, it mostly ignores social and political aspects which impinge on this area. The focus of modern pastoral care theory and practice has been arbitrarily and narrowly on the individual. Arguably, social injustice and inequality must be central themes in any discussion of general human welfare. They have received scant attention in contemporary pastoral care.[11] Practically, this means that, at best, pastoral care is myopic. At worst, it colludes with forces of sin, sorrow, and injustice which prevent people realising their human potential. Liberation theology challenges pastoral care to become aware of its arbitrary limitations and its involvement in the structures of injustice, in the interests of pursuing wider social and political practice in the cause of human flourishing and liberation.

Secondly, such theories and techniques which have informed contemporary pastoral care have tended to be drawn from one major domain, that of humanistic psychology.[12] While pastoral care has been committed to setting people free from the chains which bind them, these chains have been seen as essentially psychological, and so individual. The theoretical domains of sociology, politics, and social policy have not informed pastoral practice to any great extent. Again, this has had a narrowing, distorting, and possibly harmful effect in the quest for human well being. Liberation theology challenges pastoral care to broaden its scope and vision drawing on new domains of knowledge and theory.

Thirdly, pastoral care has found it difficult to develop

[11] For more detailed discussion of this see Stephen Pattison, *A Critique of Pastoral Care*. London: SCM Press, 1988, chs 1, 2, and 5. Peter Selby, *Liberating God*. London: SPCK, 1983 is still the main work on this aspect of pastoral care published in the UK.

[12] See Pattison, *Critique*, chs. 2 and 5, for critical discussion of this.

critical theories of action. Theological education still tends towards the narrowly academic; connections between this and actual practice are frequently not explored. The consequence is that pastoral or practical theology is thought of as something of a second rate after-thought, and pastoral carers find it difficult to reflect critically on their practice.[13] Not surprisingly, this often results in a kind of 'pastoral pragmatism' whereby people do what seems most obvious to them to do, and systematically fail to interrogate and change their way of acting. Emphasising liberating praxis, liberation theology challenges pastoral care to develop new practice-focussed critical methods of engagement with its task.

Finally, pastoral care has largely failed to engage creatively with contemporary trends in theology. Despite efforts in the USA by a number of pastoral theologians, pastoral care often remains divorced from theology and is not perceived to have much to contribute to it.[14] Liberation theology's assertion, that action is the starting place for worthwhile theological reflection and activity, challenges pastoral care to develop and assert its own importance within the life of the church and the generation of theological insights.

Put in this way, the challenge of liberation theology for pastoral care may sound abstract and somewhat remote. Putting it more concretely, however, my thesis is that pastoral care in the Northern hemisphere needs both to be liberated from some of its own practical and theoretical limitations and narrownesses, and to become socially and politically aware and committed to the cause of those who are oppressed. It is by

---

13 See further Paul Ballard, ed., *The Foundations of Pastoral Studies and Practical Theology*. Cardiff: Faculty of Theology, 1986; Don S. Browning, ed., *Practical Theology*. San Francisco: Harper and Row, 1983; Michael Northcott, 'The case study method in theological education', *Contact* 103, 1990, 26–32; Stephen Pattison, 'Some straw for the bricks: a basic introduction to theological reflection', *Contact* 99, 1989, 2–9; Simon Robinson, 'Mechanisms in aiding theological reflection', *Contact* 102, 1990, 23–8; Michael H. Taylor, *Learning to Care*, London: SPCK, 1983.

14 See, for example, Don S. Browning, *Religious Ethics and Pastoral Care*. Philadelphia: Fortress, 1983; *A Fundamental Practical Theology*. Minneapolis: Fortress, 1991; Seward Hiltner, *Preface to Pastoral Theology*. Nashville: Abingdon, 1958; Thomas C. Oden, *Pastoral Theology*. San Francisco: Harper and Row, 1983. Wesley Carr, *The Pastor as Theologian*. London: SPCK, 1989 is a British attempt to bridge the gap between theology and pastoral care.

looking at the practicalities of performing the latter aspect of the task that the former will be thrown into relief.

An encounter between liberation theology and the theory and practice of pastoral care will be illuminating and transforming. But this encounter must be managed and structured if it is to be meaningful.

THE STRUCTURE OF THIS BOOK

I shall assume that the reader of this work is someone who is interested in pastoral, or any kind of care, and who has some desire to learn more about, and use, liberation theology. I first encountered liberation theology when I was working as the part-time chaplain of a psychiatric hospital. The nature of this kind of publication makes it likely that many of my readers will be, like myself, white, middle class, reasonably affluent and probably conventionally educated and trained within a patriarchal environment. The basic question which underlies this work is, in what ways can liberation theology illuminate and challenge my concerns and practice in pastoral care? In trying to answer this question, I shall proceed in the following manner.

Liberation theology is diverse and pluriform with a huge literature now published in English. The purpose of the chapters in the first part of this book is therefore to outline something of the background and nature of liberation theology, as well as some of its main features. These chapters will give a broad critical account of the nature and method of liberation theology as a whole, orienting the reader in this field.

The final chapter in the first part inquires into what can be learned from liberation theology, and which of its methods and insights might most usefully be deployed in attempting to construct a critique of pastoral care. I will examine some of the objections to, and difficulties in, trying to relate this distinctively Latin American theology to pastoral care in advanced capitalist democracies like Britain, the USA, and Canada. Finally, a practical integrating and structuring methodological spiral which organises the use of the insights of liberation theology in pastoral care will be outlined. This determines the shape of the rest of the book.

The encounter with liberation theology suggests that pastoral care may have been myopic about its socio-political context, implications and biases. It has failed to recognise oppression and to analyse pastoral situations in terms of injustice and conflict of interest. A practical reorientation of pastoral care theory and practice requires recognition of this. The chapters in the second part of the book, The socio-political context of pastoral care, exemplify the analysis needed to begin to answer the questions, who are the oppressed, or the poor, how are they oppressed, what is the place of pastoral care in their oppression, and how can they be liberated? A social and political analysis of pastoral care with mentally ill people is undertaken with these fundamental questions in mind.

Mentally ill people may be perceived to be a tiny minority group whose troubles and oppression are essentially in their own minds. In fact, about one in ten people in Britain are diagnosed as clinically mentally ill at some point in their lives. The chapters dealing with their situation will show that, as a group, they are literally and metaphorically amongst the poorest and most oppressed in our society. Historically, they have been marginalised and poorly treated. They have had few choices or options. They have been allowed few resources of any kind and within the state health care system they have been deprived of facilities, abused and neglected. Community care promises little amelioration of this situation.

Arising from the analysis of the social and political context of mentally ill people is the question, 'does pastoral care with mentally ill people recognise this situation and attempt to "set the captives free", or does it tend to be blind to, or even collude with, the forces of oppression?' A detailed analysis of pastoral care with mentally ill people therefore forms the first section of the last part of the book, The politics of pastoral care. This analysis goes beyond the situation of mentally ill people, however, to pose questions concerning the politics of pastoral care in general. The need for a socio-politically aware and committed pastoral care is established, and principles for undertaking this are outlined in the penultimate chapter. These will help pastoral carers to reorient themselves if they wish to embody commitment to justice and liberation in their work. The final chapter extends and interrogates the relevance of these suggestions in relation to pastoral care with women. Women are not a minority group in our society – yet there are good reasons for thinking that they, too, have been oppressed. Lest it should be thought that liberation is only required by minorities, and that the liberationist perspective is only applicable in extreme, marginal situations of pastoral practice, this chapter examines the situation of women and how pastoral care interacts with their quest to attain their full potential.

AIMS AND HOPES

By the end of the book a number of things will have been accomplished. First, it will be seen that liberation theology presents a real challenge to the theory and practice of pastoral care in the Northern hemisphere. Secondly, it will be recognised that it is possible to use some of the insights and methods of liberation theology with integrity to illuminate and transform pastoral practice in our own context. Thirdly, readers will be conscious of the ways in which pastoral care can collude with structures of injustice and oppression. Fourthly, they will have some knowledge of the analytic tools, methods and processes needed to uncover these structures. Lastly, and most important of all, the book will hopefully have succeeded in convincing them that their own practice of pastoral care must become more socio-politically aware and committed to the liberation of the oppressed, as a matter of priority and urgency.

CRITICAL LIMITATIONS

Having outlined a structure and stated my aims and hopes, it is necessary to highlight some further features of the book. First, it is mainly a critique of present pastoral practice offering a preface to liberating pastoral care. Ceasing to do evil, or becoming more aware of the negative implications of one's actions, is actually an important preliminary to positive reconstruction and reorientation. It is a valuable ground-clearing exercise to clarify the socio-political implications and context of pastoral care as a prelude to engaging in socio-political aware and committed pastoral action.

To those who believe that if an activity is criticised it should only be done in the light of a developed positive alternative, the question may be put: do things which we come to understand as bad have to be immediately replaced? Does there have to be an alternative to slavery before we can work to abolish slavery? Does there have to be an alternative punishment for children in schools before we can call for an end to corporal punishment?[15] It is progress in itself if aspects of pastoral care are recognised as being oppressive and negative in their effects, and questioned without an immediate requirement for a better and more positive alternative, welcome though that would be. Critique is a positive contribution to pastoral care theory and practice, a staging post on the way to alternative constructive action.

My encounter with liberation theology has led me to become very aware of my own social and political position in society, and of the forces of injustice and oppression which I either resist or collude with in my pastoral practice. I believe that my action and choices are actively affected by this analysis and awareness, but in the end I have not become personally engaged in much overtly liberating activity of the kind practiced in Latin America. I remain a middle-class professional with the energy and facilities to write books. Some may feel frustrated both with my personal reaction to liberation theology, and with the fact that this book only begins to become involved with the liberation process which might produce, for example, interesting new theological insights out of liberating praxis. Others, however, may be reassured that they can learn from liberation theology without, in the first instance, selling all that they have to give to the poor, and adopting a completely new life style.

---

[15] I have developed this from Jeffrey Masson, *Against Therapy*. London: Fontana, 1990, pp. 29–30.

It is because I cannot personally claim to be directly and presently involved in liberating praxis that I choose to call the stance at which I arrive a 'socio-politically aware and committed pastoral care'. This is my own practical and theoretical response to the encounter with liberation theology. I am fully aware that it would be possible to go far beyond this and to engage with aspects of liberation theology and political engagement in many different ways.

Perhaps the main defect produced by the prefatory nature of this book is that it fails adequately to reflect the corporate and communal nature of liberation theology. Liberation theology has arisen out of secondary reflection upon liberating practice undertaken in small communities of Christian lay people – the famous and subversive base communities. It is a contradiction that a professionally trained individual in Britain should take a communally based, praxis-oriented theology and write about it in an academic mode. This might confirm some of the worst fears of the liberation theologians themselves, who have constantly inveighed against the dilution, assimilation, domestication, and trivialisation of this hard-won theology by jaded, hungry, and decadent liberal theologians in the affluent countries which keep Latin America in a state of dependency. Gutiérrez warns of the danger of abandoning 'concrete historical praxis' to 'apply the cosmetic vocabulary of "social concern", or even "liberation", to old pastoral and theological stances'.

Facile attitudes, coupled with a certain 'trendiness', or penchant for the newest vogue, have encouraged some persons simply to tack on the word 'liberation' to whatever they have always been saying anyway and go on saying it, hoping to update a sluggish old inventory by slapping a new label on obsolete goods.[16]

Assmann, similarly, states that

The theology of liberation has to stand largely on its own, and the challenge it faces is not to defraud those who expect it to be what it originally set out to be – critical and motivating reflection on faith as

---

[16] Gustavo Gutiérrez, *The Power of the Poor in History*, p. 64

the historical embodiment of liberation – by falling back on vague verbal flirtation with the idea of liberation.[17]

The danger of evacuating liberation theology of its power, challenge, and meaning is apparent here. I hope I have avoided vague flirtation with liberation theology and undertaken a serious practical engagement with it which does actually lead, at least potentially, to taking the position of the oppressed in the Northern hemisphere much more seriously in a practical way. Furthermore, there is no point in liberation theologians writing and publishing books, or allowing them to be translated, if they are not prepared for some degree of cultural assimilation and adaptation to take place in other contexts. The choice is between maintaining the pristine ideological purity of liberation theology by refusing to apply it to Christian practice in the Northern hemisphere, or engaging with it with a view to at least partially transforming perspectives and practices in relation to the oppressed. I have elected to do the latter, while trying to remain sensitive to the dangers and limitations involved in doing so.

THE NATURE OF THIS BOOK

If this book does not claim to be in itself a piece of liberation theology, how should it be regarded? First and foremost, it should be seen as an exercise in critical pastoral theology designed to bring about a reorientation in the focus and practice of pastoral care.[18] Pastoral care needs to be liberated from its psychological and individualistic captivity.

Although the nature of the subject matter and the intentions

---

[17] Hugo Assmann, *Practical Theology of Liberation*. London: Search Press, 1975, pp. 118–19.

[18] For more on the nature of pastoral theology see Ballard, ed., *Foundations*; Hiltner, *Preface*; Browning, *Religious Ethics*; A. O. Dyson, 'Pastoral theology: towards a new discipline', *Contact* 78, 1983, 2–8. For present purposes, pastoral theology may be regarded as critical action-guiding theology which focusses on practical pastoral issues and practice (i.e., is 'operation-centred', to use Hiltner's term) and within which pastoral thought and action can be situated.

underlying this work are practical, it has a significant theoretical contribution to make. This consists in providing a practical methodology, derived from Latin American liberation theology, which alerts pastoral care to its socio-political context and its part, actual or potential, in structures of injustice and liberation. The methodology is potentially applicable to many kinds of situations; it provides a springboard for new ways of seeing and practising pastoral care.

The book can also be seen as contributing to transcultural hermeneutics. My task has been to take a body of written Christian theological texts originating in one cultural context and partially to interpret its significance and meaning for another.[19] I have never visited Latin America, nor have I read liberation theology in its original Portuguese and Spanish. Paradoxically, there may be a certain utility in this lack of first-hand experience. The virtue of it is that I have had to interpret liberation theology by means of encounter with translated texts. If my efforts can be regarded as fruitful, the possibility of this kind of interpretative exercise, the strength and fecundity of liberation theology in its written form in itself, and the validity of others attempting to do likewise in different areas of Christian life and thought, will have been demonstrated. Thus liberation theology may escape its literary captivity in weighty unread tomes on the bookshelves of the affluent North to reveal its continuing capacity to transform action and behaviour, theory and ideology outside its original context.[20]

---

[19] For more on hermeneutics and interpretation see, for example, Robert M. Grant and David Tracy, *A Short History of the Interpretation of the Bible*. London: SCM Press, 1984; David Tracy, *Plurality and Ambiguity*. London: SCM Press, 1987; Frances Young and David F. Ford, *Meaning and Truth in 2 Corinthians*. London: SPCK, 1987. On translation and inculturation of ideas see, for example, Robert J. Schreiter, *Constructing Local Theologies*. London: SCM Press, 1985.

[20] Young and Ford write, 'You cannot make a text mean anything you like, and the author's intention has some primacy in determining meaning. But meaning is not limited to the author's intention [or context] and how the reader reads it also bears on the question of meaning. The text has the potential to transcend the intention of the author. But it is equally possible that the reader's limitations will reduce perception of meaning' (Young and Ford, *Meaning and Truth*, p. 87).

DEFINITIONS

Pastoral care has been variously defined and discussed.[21] For preliminary purposes in the present work a slightly modified and augmented version of Campbell's definition will be used.[22] Thus, Christian pastoral care may be broadly understood as

that activity within the ministry of the Church which is centrally concerned with promoting the well-being of individuals and of communities. The ultimate aim of pastoral care is that of ministry as a whole, i.e. to increase love between people and between people and God. Its specific functions are healing, sustaining, reconciling, guiding and nurturing.

Liberation is a concept which will be discussed in more detail later. For present purposes, liberation may be taken broadly to mean 'the social emancipation of the oppressed'.[23]

Justice is a complex concept. At least three basic, and to some extent conflicting, core principles can be found within the concept of social justice. There is a 'conservative' principle which advocates distribution to people according to their means; an 'ideal' principle which advocates distribution according to deserts; and a 'prosthetic' principle which advocates distribution according to need.[24] In this book I adopt the so-called prosthetic view of justice. By implication injustice occurs when people's basic needs are not met. The concept of basic need is also problematic. Here I shall take a commonsensical view that basic needs are defined in relation to a particular social context, but that everyone needs adequate food, shelter, health care, and housing, together with the means to develop their full physical and intellectual potential and parti-

---

21 See Pattison, *Critique*, ch. 1.

22 Alastair V. Campbell, 'Pastoral care, nature of', in Alastair V. Campbell, ed., *A Dictionary of Pastoral Care*. London: SPCK, 1987.

23 Leonardo Boff and Clodovis Boff, *Salvation and Liberation*. Maryknoll, NY: Orbis, 1984, p. 116.

24 David Miller, *Social Justice*. Oxford: Oxford University Press, 1976, ch. 1. Cf. also D. D. Raphael, *Problems of Political Philosophy*. London: Macmillan, revised edn., 1976, ch. 7.

cipate as fully as they are able in their own society and destiny.[25]

Power is another complex concept which has multiple usage. Following Lukes, I shall define power by saying that A exercises power over B when A affects B in a manner contrary to B's interests.[26] This definition is equally appropriate when talking of the power of individuals, or of the power of groups or nations.

CONCLUSION

Liberation theology represents one of the most important theoretical and practical challenges to pastoral care today. For too long this challenge has been ignored. It is possible, and tempting, to continue ignoring it, to stick to pastoral pragmatism, to remain individualistic in one's pastoral concerns, or, like the rich young man in the gospels, simply to go away sorrowful because of the burdens of one's limitations, vested interests, and wealth. It is more purposeful and useful, however, to take courage, to hear the challenge and respond to it to the extent that one can. 'There is one, and only one, theology of liberation', insists Leonardo Boff. 'There is only one point of departure – a reality of social misery – and one goal – the liberation of the oppressed.'[27] If something of the practical and theoretical relevance of this assertion for pastoral carers in the advanced democracies of the Northern hemisphere is demonstrated in this book, it will have accomplished its purpose.

---

[25] For a more detailed discussion of need see, for example, Raymond Plant, Harry Lesser, and Peter Taylor-Gooby, *Political Philosophy and Social Welfare*. London: Routledge and Kegan Paul, 1980.

[26] Steven Lukes, *Power*. London: Macmillan, 1974, p. 34.

[27] Boff and Boff, *Salvation*, p.24.

PART I

Liberation theology

CHAPTER I

The background to liberation theology

The two chapters which follow this one introduce some of the main features and methods of liberation theology. The literature of liberation theology in English is now extensive and can seem complex and off-putting. It is important, therefore, to provide some critical orientation in this area before moving on to see what insights and methods from liberation theology might be applicable to pastoral care in chapter 4. Necessarily, I shall have to generalise and be selective in my use of sources drawing mainly upon classic early texts which set out the basic principles of liberation theology. There are many other works, some referred to in the accompanying notes, which can be usefully explored.

Liberation theology regards itself as historical and contextual, so it is appropriate to begin by spending some time considering its social, historical and ecclesiastical background, before going on to examine its content and methods.

SOCIAL AND HISTORICAL BACKGROUND TO LIBERATION THEOLOGY

For affluent Western Christians who have not visited Latin America, it is difficult to imagine the reality within which liberation theology has arisen. Latin America (including Central America) is a vast continent with huge material resources, a growing population, and extremes of wealth and poverty.

Something of the scale and scandal of injustice and poverty can be gleaned from Brazilian liberation theologian Leonardo Boff:

in Brazil, 75 percent of the people live in relative economic margina-
lization; 43 percent are condemned to a minimum salary in order to
survive. A worker from Sao Paulo, Manuel Paulo, says it best: 'What
I earn is so little that it only proves that I am still alive.' And his wife,
Helena, adds: 'This is no life for anybody.' Once one of the most
promising countries in the world, Brazil serves as an appropriate
example: 40 percent of all Brazilians live, work, and sleep with
chronic hunger; there are 10 million who are mentally retarded due
to malnutrition; 6 million suffer from malaria; 650,000 have tuber-
culosis and 25,000 suffer from leprosy.[1]

A similar picture emerges in this picture of life in Colombia
written by a North American journalist, Penny Lernoux, a
long-standing resident of Latin America:

As everywhere in Latin America, the violence in Colombia can be
traced to the land. Because of the physical and economic insecurity in
rural areas, millions of peasants and small farmers migrated to the
cities during the 1950s. Today (1980), with 93 percent of the arable
land occupied by 25 percent of the the farms, the rural exodus
continues. By the end of the century the majority of Colombians will
live in cities.

Lernoux continues,

The same trend can be observed on the entire continent: by the year
2000 two thirds of the projected Latin American population of 630
million people will be crowded into megalopolises, nearly half their
areas given over to slums. Or 210 million people living in tin and
cardboard shacks with no running water, no electricity, no schools,
no jobs – with nothing to hope for and nothing to lose.[2]

The situation and main problems of Latin America can be
summarised thus:

Latin America exists in a state of economic dependence on
the affluent nations of the Northern hemisphere which
conquered the continent from the fifteenth century
onwards and have continued to exploit its resources (the
recent debt crisis, whereby it has become apparent that
many Latin American countries are indebted to European
and American banks in such a way that all their earnings

[1] Leonardo Boff, *Church: Charism and Power*. New York: Crossroad, 1985, p. 22.
[2] Lernoux, *Cry*, p. 365.

must go to servicing the debt, is the latest example of this dependency).

External economic dependency is mirrored by internal economic dependency within Latin American countries whereby a minority of wealthy land-owners, bankers, and business people, allied with foreign capitalist interests, own or control most of the national wealth and means of production at the expense of the vast majority who experience extreme poverty and oppression.

The continent is experiencing a massive population explosion.

Many of the poorest people, hitherto agriculturally dependent, are moving to the cities to find work. Urbanisation continues apace.

Lessening production combined with unequal distribution of wealth, the growth in population, and increased urbanisation, leads to permanent and explosive social and political instability – hence the need for enormous forces of governmental and military repression which perpetrate violence against the population.

There is economic, informative, and cultural colonialism, backed up by military aid and force to right-wing regimes perpetrated by the USA and its allies in Latin America in the interests of maintaining exploitative economic opportunities and warding off the 'communist threat'.[3]

---

[3] This is drawn from Emilio Castro, *Amidst Revolution*. Belfast: Christian Journals Limited, 1975, pp. 14ff. For more on the social, economic and historical situation of Latin America see, for example, Philip Berryman, *The Religious Roots of Rebellion*. London: SCM Press, 1984, especially chs. 1–3; José Míguez Bonino, *Revolutionary Theology Comes of Age*. London: SPCK, 1975, especially chs. 1–3; Enrique Dussel, *History and the Theology of Liberation*. Maryknoll, NY: Orbis, 1976; Gustavo Gutiérrez, *A Theology of Liberation*. London: SCM Press, 1974, especially chs. 2, 6, 7, and 8; J. Andrew Kirk, *Liberation Theology*. London: Marshall, Morgan and Scott, 1979, ch. 1. For material on political conditions and philosophy and the influence of the USA in Latin America see, for example, José Comblin, *The Church and the National Security State*. Maryknoll, NY: Orbis, 1979; John Eagleson, ed., *Christians and Socialism*. Maryknoll, NY: Orbis, 1975; Paul Gallet, *Freedom to Starve*. Harmondsworth: Penguin, 1972; Lernoux, *Cry*.

The Latin American experience since the fifteenth century, when the Spanish and Portuguese *conquistadors* first arrived and subdued or eliminated the native populations, has been one of conquest and exploitation by European and North American powers. (Gutiérrez, however, notes, 'From the very beginning of the *Conquista* the native American peoples rebelled against their dominators ... Indians, blacks and *mestizos* who had received the gospel found reasons in it for resisting the oppression to which they were subjected.'[4]) After the *conquistadors*, who took and redistributed the land, came the nineteenth-century industrialists. Latterly, the USA has been the main exploitative and colonising influence, supporting many unjust and oppressive situations in the continent by financial and other means. Gutiérrez writes, 'External dependency and internal domination are the marks of the social structures of Latin America.'[5] The cost of this to poor and oppressed people in terms of poverty, violence, injury, and loss within unjust totalitarian regimes is enormous. Most of the population of Latin America has had no sense of agency and power in their own lives. Those who 'die before their time' have no voice in their own history.

Until about 1960, there was a mixed attitude to this situation of injustice and dependency. Fatalism combined with some optimism led to the hope that modernisation would lead to development and greater prosperity for all. However, the dream of development did not materialise. After the successful 1959 Cuban revolution, the language of development and evolutionary change gave way to that of popular revolution and liberation. Realisation dawned that, if things remained as they were, there could be no end to the poverty and injustice of Latin America. The liberal–modernist project, with its pseudo-promises, was cast aside by radicals in favour of fundamental, sometimes violent, social change along socialist lines.

Latin American misery and injustice go too deep to be responsive to palliatives. Hence we speak of social revolution, not reform; of liberation not development; of socialism, not modernization of the prevailing system.[6]

[4] Gutiérrez, *Power of the Poor*, p. 189.   [5] Ibid., p. 45.   [6] Ibid.

In some places since 1960 there has been intermittent successful radical social change. There have been periods of socialist rule in Chile and Nicaragua, for example. However, these changes have not proved permanent. The liberation struggle against exploitation and vested interests is destined to continue, often violently, for years to come.

THE RISE OF LIBERATION THEOLOGY

Some 90 per cent of the population of Latin America is Christian. Most are at least nominal members of the Roman Catholic Church. Historically, that church has been an influential and conservative force in Latin American society. Despite the prophetic witness of a few courageous priests and religious, like Bartolomé de Las Casas, a sixteenth century Dominican who denounced the oppression of the native people in the new colonies, the church has been overwhelmingly on the side of the powers that be. Its various theologies down the centuries have largely reflected this stance.

After an early period of 'prophetic theology' lasting from 1511 to 1553, when Las Casas and others denounced the oppression of the Amerindians, there was a lengthy era of 'the theology of colonial Christendom' (1553–1808) which largely provided an ideological justification for colonial oppression. This theological era gave way to a 'political theology of emancipation' which reflected the struggle of Latin American countries for independence (1808–31). It was succeeded by a conservative 'neocolonial theology' (1831–1930) and then by the moderately progressive 'New Christendom' mentality (1930–62).[7]

New Christendom thinking recognises the importance of the state and the political realm, but regards these things as subsidiary and inferior to religious life.[8] It is important that lay Christians should implement their Christian principles in the

---

[7] This typology of theological eras comes from Alfred T. Hennelly, ed., *Liberation Theology: A Documentary History*. Maryknoll, NY: Orbis, 1990, pp. xvi–xvii.

[8] Christendom and other typologies of church–state relations are explored in Gutiérrez, *Theology of Liberation*, chs. 4 and 5; Alfredo Fierro, *The Militant Gospel*. London: SCM Press, 1977, ch. 2.

everyday life of social institutions, thus Christianising them, but the hierarchy and clergy of the church should have nothing directly to do with the ordering of political life.

This kind of standpoint suffered a reversal when some people in the Catholic Church began to realise that, far from being a divine and spiritual entity which was above the ways of the world, the church was actually firmly entrenched in the exploitative structures of Latin America. In its putative neutrality, it gave support to those structures, while reinforcing a sense of fatalism and inevitability amongst the poor. The church was not using the state for its own ends, but was being used by the state for its own ends. In forging good relationships with the ruling elites to retain its own peace, influence, and privileges, the church had defended the exploiters against the exploited. It was playing an ideological role, legitimising and sacralising the existing social order, thereby implying that a humanly created unjust order was actually a reflection of the will of God. The alternative to playing this legitimating role was to consciously adopt the liberation struggle of the oppressed.

The theology of liberation, which accompanied the increasing commitment of a minority of church leaders and religious to social and political struggle gradually emerged in the 1960s and 1970s, stimulated by a combination of factors.

One important precursor of liberation theology was the pioneering educational work of Paulo Freire, a Brazilian lawyer. During the 1960s Freire began a programme of adult education and literacy known as 'conscientization' with groups of illiterate people around the Latin American continent. The programme aimed at equipping people with a critical reflective knowledge of reality which would enable them to discern their true situation, and so lead to historical commitment and action to change dehumanising social structures.[9]

---

[9] See further Paulo Freire, *Pedagogy of the Oppressed*. Harmondsworth: Penguin, 1972; 'Conscientizing as a way of liberating', in Hennelly, ed., *Liberation Theology*. Lernoux describes conscientisation thus: 'In contrast to the rote method, conscientization encourages the student ... to understand the meaning of words, particularly such key words as "hungry", "barefoot", "land", and "rich". The aim is to make people aware of themselves and their environment, to learn to think. And once people learn

Methods like those of Freire were used in the now famous 'base communities' (*comunidades eclesiales de base*), another important precursor to fully-fledged liberation theology. These communities are small, tightly knit, lay-led local groups of ordinary people with similar incomes, jobs, education, problems, and aspirations who come together to worship, read the Bible, and take action to help each other. They have formed a springboard for liberating action around the continent of Latin America, and now number many thousands. It is from these communities that many of the fundamental new theological perceptions recorded by 'educated' religious and priests in works of liberation theology have come.[10] They are both the main source and a practical exemplification of liberation theology.

A further factor was a growing concern amongst religious intellectuals that both governments and churches were using ideological tools to legitimate the inhuman conditions of many of the people of Latin America. Highly trained intellectuals, like Gutiérrez and Segundo, began to apply the methods of Marxist suspicion and analysis to their own situations, radicalising their commitment to improving the condition of the people.

The second Vatican Council of the Catholic Church in the early part of the 1960s had a considerable impact on the emergence of liberation theology. This event, *inter alia*, affirmed the role of lay people in the church, emphasised the importance of the church working as a sign of the kingdom in the world (rather than a separate enclave of exclusive salvation), and proclaimed the central importance of human rights and dignity. This last point was given great prominence

---

to think, they ask questions. They want to know why their village has no running water, for example, and what they can do about it. That is the seed of civic participation, making Latin Americans reflective agents for change instead of "objects to be rescued from a burning building", as Freire phrases it' (Lernoux, *Cry*, p. 40).

10 For more on base communities see Leonardo Boff, *Church: Charism and Power*; Berryman, *The Religious Roots of Rebellion*, especially ch. 1; Hennelly, ed., *Liberation Theology*, pp. xviii–xix. For an example of critical theological reflection which has emerged from base communities see, for example, Ernesto Cardenal, *Love in Practice: The Gospel in Solentiname*. London: Search Press, 1977.

in a subsequent papal encyclical, *Populorum Progressio* (1967), a 'ringing plea for social justice and fundamental changes for the impoverished masses of the Third World'.[11] Effectively, this encyclical and its predecessors, *Mater et Magistra* (1961) and *Pacem in Terris* (1963) provided a manifesto for Latin American Catholics to amplify their engagement with the structures of injustice.

The British critic, Alistair Kee, attributes the rise of liberation theology to the creative interaction between the theology and philosophy of Vatican II, and the presence of the Cuban revolution in the continent of Latin America. It was the success of the latter which began to make real social change seem possible. It acted as a lodestar for Christian activists seeking justice for the poor throughout Latin America, and forms the last important predisposing factor for the emergence of liberation theology.[12]

Some of the tiny minority of individual Christian leaders and religious who adopted the cause of the poor in the 1960s are well known by name. Helder Camara, archbishop of Recife in Brazil was an important figure, as was the 'revolutionary priest', Camilo Torres, who died in armed guerrilla conflict in his native Colombia in 1966.[13] With the continuing worsening of social conditions, many more priests and prelates were prepared to move in this direction when liberation theology

---

[11] Hennelly, ed., *Liberation Theology*, p. 41.

[12] See Alistair Kee, *Marx and the Failure of Liberation Theology*. London: SCM Press, 1990, p. 131. There may have been a further factor contributing to liberation theology's emergence and ecclesiastical involvement of the oppressed. There is some evidence that the church faced a crisis of relevance at the beginning of the 1960s, with many people no longer being baptised or having access to priests (cf., for example, Lernoux, *Cry*, ch. 2; Juan Luis Segundo, 'The future of Christianity in Latin America', in Hennelly, ed., *Liberation Theology*). Could it be that the engagement of liberation theologians with the cause of the poor stemmed not only from genuine ethical and religious concern for their plight, but also from a need on the part of 'progressive' clergy and religious to ensure the long-term significance of the institutional church? If so, liberation theology's rise can be seen as in some ways a power play to retain influence with the masses. Or is this particular interpretation taking the 'hermeneutics of suspicion' too far?

[13] See further, for example, Helder Camara, *Church and Colonialism*. London: Sheed and Ward, 1969; M. Zeitlin, ed., *Father Camilo Torres: Revolutionary Writings*. New York: Harper and Row, 1972.

first proclaimed itself as such at the second general conference of Latin American bishops at Medellín, Colombia in 1968.

The Medellín conference completed the preparatory phase of liberation theology and began its formative phase.[14] It was here that the concept of 'liberation' first gained currency, together with concepts like 'participation' and 'institutionalised violence'. The upshot of the conference, whose proceedings were heavily influenced by theologians later well known as 'liberation theologians', like Gustavo Gutiérrez, was formally to commit the Catholic churches in Latin America to the cause of the poor and to provide theological undergirding for this.[15]

Although by no means all Catholic prelates, priests, and religious are committed to social and political liberation, and there has been something of a backlash since 1968 whereby more conservative bishops have been appointed in Latin America, liberation theology, and the liberation struggle itself, show no signs of diminishment. The present pope, like his predecessor, has not condemned the commitment of many priests and religious to the cause of justice in Latin America, even if he has reservations about direct political action and the use of Marxism. An attempt by the conservatives to reverse the general direction taken by the church at Medellín was defeated at the Puebla conference in Mexico in 1979.[16] Attacks by the Vatican on individual theologians like Leonardo Boff and Gustavo Gutiérrez have, if anything, fanned the flames of commitment to liberation and liberation theology.[17] Liberation theology is here to stay.

Before moving on to consider the nature, content, insights and methods of liberation theology in greater detail, it is

[14] Gibellini suggests that liberation theology has had three main phases to date: (a) a preparatory phase 1962–8; (b) a formative phase during which the seminal theological studies were published 1968–75; and (c) a systematising phase from 1975 onwards in which methods have been reflected upon and major themes in theology have been reworked (pp. 1–2). See Rosino Gibellini, *The Liberation Theology Debate*. London: SCM Press, 1987.

[15] For an account of the conference see Lernoux, *Cry*, pp. 37–47. See also Hennelly, ed., *Liberation Theology*, for a brief account and documents emanating from the conference.

[16] See further Lernoux, *Cry*, ch. 11.

[17] See Hennelly, ed., *Liberation Theology*, parts 5 and 6 for these and more recent developments.

appropriate to deal in a brief and preliminary way with three important questions: What is liberation? What is liberation theology? and, Who are the liberation theologians?

'Liberation' is a difficult term to define exactly. Several key elements are, however, contained within it when it is used in general terms. First and foremost, it denotes activity which frees people from all that shackles them and stops them from living full human lives in which their potential can be realised. Thus understood, liberation is the activity which frees people from domination and oppression. It has connotations of both negative freedom *from* that which inhibits and oppresses, and more positive freedom *to* find new areas of development once oppression has been overcome. In Latin America, in practical terms liberation struggle is clearly directed towards the demise of inequality, injustice and poverty. It takes the form of active, corporate, social and political struggle, rather than being an individual or therapeutic activity, as it might be in the Northern hemisphere:

> In liberation, the oppressed come together, come to understand their situation through the process of conscientization, discover the causes of their oppression, organize themselves into movements, and act in a coordinated fashion.[18]

While liberty or freedom is a bourgeois ideal which may not have concrete content, liberation is understood as present action which has no meaning apart from activity. Liberation must precede liberty when subjugation or oppression of any sort prevails.[19]

On the part of the liberation theologians, Leonardo Boff defines liberation as 'action delivering a captive to liberty and calling for a humanistic commitment'.[20] Liberation needs to take place at different levels: on the social level where collective

---

[18] Leonardo Boff and Clodovis Boff, *Introducing Liberation Theology*. Tunbridge Wells: Burns and Oates, 1987, p. 5.

[19] For discussion of 'liberation', see further, Gustavo Gutiérrez, *A Theology of Liberation*. London: SCM Press, 1974, p. 27; M. Merle, 'Liberty and liberation', in René Metz and Jean Schlick, eds., *Liberation Theology and the Message of Salvation*. Pittsburg: Pickwick Press, 1978.

[20] Leonardo Boff and Clodovis Boff, *Salvation and Liberation*. Maryknoll, NY: Orbis, 1984, p. 15.

oppression, exclusion, and marginalisation occur; on the individual level, where there is injustice and the denial of human rights; and on the religious level where social sinfulness takes place.[21] It must be undertaken by the poor themselves, as they seek to become the subjects of their own history. It cannot be done on their behalf, although people from other social classes can opt to join the poor in their struggle to bring about change.

It is at this point that liberation theology becomes relevant. As we shall see, liberation theology is complex, subtle, and pluriform. At its base, however, it is relatively easy to identify and define. All liberation theology is theology done from a position of active involvement with the oppressed in their struggle for liberation. Liberation theology starts with an *a priori* commitment to the liberation struggle and option for the poor. In Gutiérrez's graphic terms, it is theology done from the perspective of the 'underside of history' where the poor are attempting to become subjects of their own destiny.[22] It is a second order activity which accompanies and reflects upon the experience of the struggle for liberation in the light of faith – action and commitment first, theological reflection afterwards. Its purpose is to fortify, inspire and inform Christian action within the overarching liberation struggle of the poor. It is thus severely practical theology.

Reflecting on the basis of practice, within the ambit of the vast efforts made by the poor and their allies, seeking inspiration in faith and the gospel for the commitment to fight against poverty and for the integral liberation of all persons and the whole person – that is what liberation theology means.[23]

A sense of the practical, action-oriented and poor-centred nature of liberation theology can be gained from considering briefly the third question raised above, i.e. who are the liberation theologians? One answer to this question is that the poor people of Latin America who struggle for liberation are the true liberation theologians. It is they alone, in their communi-

---

[21] Cf. Boff and Boff, *Introducing Liberation Theology*, p. 3 for this typology.
[22] See further Gutiérrez, *Power of the Poor*, pp. 169ff.
[23] Boff and Boff, *Introducing Liberation Theology*, p. 8.

ties of action and reflection, who have the right to interpret God's action in the world today. This is, however, a somewhat naive answer, because we would probably know little of liberation theology unless it had been interpreted, written down, and published by the literate, educated people who spring to mind when liberation theology is mentioned. Such people are Gustavo Guttiérez, a Peruvian priest, the Boff brothers, Clodovis and Leonardo, priests in Brazil, Jean Luis Segundo, a Uraguayan priest and Jon Sobrino, a Jesuit teaching and working in El Salvador. Nearly all the liberation theologians are men, most are Catholics (Rubem Alves and José Míguez Bonino being conspicuous as Protestants), many of them are priests or in religious orders (therefore celibate) and all are extremely well educated, mainly within the paradigm of European theology (many of them have studied in Europe). However academically high-powered, all liberation theologians reckon to spend much of their time doing practical work with the oppressed striving for liberation. They live out the option for the poor in their works as well as in their words – hence much of the power and credibility of this theology. Gustavo Gutiérrez, one of the most prominent liberation theologians, actually works most of the time as pastor of a poor area of Lima and writes his theological works in his 'spare time'![24]

Latin America is a vast continent, and different liberation theologians have different contexts and concerns. Liberation theology is not a monolithic entity, but a complex mixture of themes and ideas. There are common features which can be highlighted for the purposes of the present work, which is essentially a critical essay on pastoral care, rather than a book about liberation theology as such. Working at a high level of generalisation in this way, however, does not do justice to the subtlety of liberation theology. With these caveats in mind, it is appropriate to look now at the nature, character, content, and methods of this theology.

[24] Biographical notes on some liberation theologians can be found in Rosino Gibellini, ed., *Frontiers of Theology in Latin America*. London: SCM Press, 1980. Detailed studies of particular theologians include Robert McAfee Brown, *Gustavo Gutiérrez: An Introduction to Liberation Theology*. Maryknoll, NY: Orbis, 1990; Alfred T. Hennelly, *Theologies in Conflict: The Challenge of Juan Luis Segundo*. Maryknoll, NY: Orbis, 1979.

CHAPTER 2

The nature and content of liberation theology

The main features of the nature and content of liberation theology can be anatomised under a number of broad headings.

A committed theology

Above all, liberation theology is a theology of active and concrete commitment, specifically to the struggle of the oppressed people of Latin America as they try to throw off the yoke of poverty and economic dependency. 'The theology of liberation is rooted in revolutionary militancy', writes Gutiérrez.[1]

Definitions by liberation theologians of their own theological activity reflect their paramount concern for the liberation struggle and their practical involvement in it. In contrast to European theology, the theology of liberation receives its challenge not from atheism, rationalism, or secularisation, but from the dehumanisation of ordinary people in Latin America. The challenge to theology

does not come primarily from the man [sic] who does not believe, but from the man who is not a man, who is not recognised as such by the existing social order . . . the question is not how . . . to speak of God in an adult world, but how to proclaim him as Father in a world that is not human.[2]

---

[1] Gutiérrez, *Power of the Poor*, p. 205.
[2] Gustavo Gutiérrez, 'Liberation, theology and proclamation', *Concilium* 6, 1974, 57–77, at pp. 68–9.

It is the inhuman situation of many of those living in Latin America which conditions definitions of theology itself, such as this one: 'Theology will be a critical reflection from and about the historical praxis of liberation in confrontation with the word of the Lord lived and accepted in faith.'[3] Most succinctly, Gutiérrez defines theology as 'a critical reflection on praxis (meaning liberating activity – SP) in the light of the Word.'[4]

A practical theology

'Liberation theology is far from being an inconclusive theology. It starts from action and leads to action ... "Back to action" is a characteristic call of this theology.'[5] Flowing from its preferential option for the concrete liberation struggle of the oppressed is a strongly practical emphasis on the importance of liberating action, or praxis. Praxis is a concept which finds its fullest expression in Marxism where it denotes integrated thought and action for revolutionary change. Truth and knowledge are not to be found in intellectual abstraction, but in action. This assertion is embodied in Marx's famous eleventh thesis on Feuerbach: 'The philosophers have only interpreted the world in different ways; the point is to change it.'[6] Any valid knowledge must be discovered in, and related to, the liberation process. Only in action can the meaning of love and compassion be revealed. This theology points out that Christian knowledge of God is in fact derived from God's concrete revealing action shown forth in practical liberating events such as the Exodus.[7]

The emphasis on concrete historical praxis as the starting point for theological understanding means that liberation theologians frequently have scant respect for the apparently academic theologies found in the Northern hemisphere. Such theologies are over-concerned with classical texts, abstract

---

[3] Ibid., p. 70.   [4] Ibid., p. 57.
[5] Boff and Boff, *Introducing Liberation Theology*, p.39.
[6] T. B. Bottomore and Maximilien Rubel, *Karl Marx on Sociology and Social Philosophy*. Harmondsworth: Penguin, pp. 82–4. Cf. Gutiérrez, *A Theology of Liberation*, p. 9.
[7] See, for example, Raul Vidales, 'Methodological issues in liberation theology', in Gibellini, ed., *Frontiers of Theology in Latin America*.

philosophical problems and orthodoxy, i.e. right believing and thinking, when they should be concerned instead with orthopraxis, i.e. correct action in accordance with the contemporary will and purposes of God who desires to set the captives free.[8] Criticisms of liberation theology on a conceptual level from a position which lacks concrete commitment to the oppressed are seen as 'radically irrelevant'! 'Liberation theology responds to such criticism with just one question: What part have *you* played in the effective and integral liberation of the oppressed.'[9] Orthopraxis alone establishes the validity of theological reflection and insights.

An ideologically self-aware theology

The liberation theologian's suspicion is that 'anything and everything involving ideas, including theology, is intimately bound up with the existing social situation in at least an unconscious way.'[10] The concept of ideology is a complex one.[11] Here, following Marxist usage, it is understood to denote any form of thought which has been invaded by the vested interests of the ruling classes and which is then used (albeit unconsciously) to obscure the true nature of reality, in this case the reality of oppression.

Accepting the Marxist tenet that ideas are basically determined by the material sub-structure, and therefore primarily reflect the interests of the dominant classes in any particular society, liberation theologians have tried to expose the ideological nature of theology and the uses to which it has been put.[12] They also try to be explicit in showing from which vantage point ideologically their own theology is written.

---

[8] For more on orthopraxis see Gutiérrez, *A Theology of Liberation*, p. 10. For a critique of orthodoxy, see Jóse Comblin, 'What sort of service might theology render?', in Gibellini, ed., *Frontiers of Theology in Latin America*.

[9] Boff and Boff, *Introducing Liberation Theology*, p. 9.

[10] Cf. Juan Luis Segundo, *The Liberation of Theology*. Dublin: Gill and Macmillan, 1977, p. 8.

[11] See further, for example, Karl Mannheim, *Ideology and Utopia*. London: Routledge and Kegan Paul, 1936; John Plamenatz, *Ideology*. London: Macmillan, 1971.

[12] 'What else does the history of ideas prove, than that intellectual production changes its character in proportion as material production is changed? The ruling ideas of

The theologians of liberation accept that theology is essentially human language about God which is conditioned and moulded by its specific social context:

Theology is now learning that it is only human discourse after all . . . Theology is not what mediated the faith, and it is not the theory of Christian practice. Manipulating or using the words of which God made use in the Bible for our own discourse does not confer the qualities of God's word on our human discourse . . . As human utterance, theology belongs to this world. It is wholly conditioned by the portion of the world in which it itself is immersed. Far from trying to protect itself from all analysis by the human sciences, it should be completely open to such analysis.[13]

By ignoring the essentially human nature and socio-political context of theological discourse, much theology mistakenly regards itself as a politically neutral 'divine' science. This disguises the fact that theology actually serves the interests of those who are dominant in the social order. Because of this unwitting, unconscious bias, the voice and interests of the oppressed are hidden.[14] Thus, sacramental theology helps to devalue historical endeavour; an emphasis on universality and ecumenism helps to conceal class conflict; and the passive god of Greek philosophy supplants the active, historically involved God of the Bible.[15]

A biassed theology

Since all theology is human discourse, and all human discourse is conditioned by the socio-political nature of reality, all theology must be regarded as being biassed. In the case of liberation theology this bias is conscious and overt:

each age have ever been the ideas of its ruling class' (Karl Marx and Frederick Engels, *Manifesto of the Communist Party* in Karl Marx and Frederick Engels, *Selected Works in One Volume*. London: Lawrence and Wishart, 1968, p. 51). While not adopting a Marxist position, some Western theologians have acknowledged the impact and significance of the underlying social order for the production and usage of theological ideas. See further, for example, Robin Gill, *Social Context of Theology*. London: Mowbray, 1975.

[13] Comblin, 'What sort of service might theology render?', p. 66.
[14] See especially Comblin, *The Church and the National Security State*, ch. 1 for a critique of the way in which theology has failed to serve the interests of the oppressed.
[15] See further Segundo, *Liberation of Theology*, especially ch. 2.

Liberation theology consciously and explicitly accepts its relationship with politics. First of all, it incorporates into its own methodology the task of ideological analysis ... and in so far as direct politics is concerned, it is more concerned about avoiding the (false) impartiality of academic theology than it is about taking sides and consequently giving ammunition to those who accuse it of partisanship.[16]

Liberation theology is biassed in two main ways. Practically and theoretically it is biassed in terms of its support for the revolutionary struggle of the oppressed. It is written from 'the underside of history', from the perspective of 'non-persons', i.e. those who are not considered human by the present social order, the exploited classes, marginalised ethnic groups, and despised cultures.[17] It is among the poor, struggling to become subjects of their own history and to find their own voice that the activity of the biblical God is discerned:

the poor are the ones who change the course of history into a more humane and universal one ... the kingdom grows and finds expression in the struggles to humanize the world which the poor and lowly initiate with their lives.[18]

Analytically, liberation theology is biassed in adopting Marxist methods for understanding the Latin American situation and its own social position. Since all analytic tools are biassed because of their basic presuppositions, liberation theology opts for

those analyses, postulates and diagnoses which are more closely in line with the goal of discerning and achieving a social order in which human beings can live as true adults, as 'new persons' after the ideal of Jesus Christ.[19]

While rigid Marxist orthodoxy, dogmatism, and ultimate solutions are largely rejected, the categories and tools of Marxist

---

[16] Ibid., p. 75.   [17] Cf. Gutiérrez, *Power of the Poor*, p. 193.
[18] Alejandro Cussianovich, *Religious Life and the Poor*. Dublin: Gill and Macmillan, 1979, p. 88. Cf. also Enrique Dussel, *Ethics and the Theology of Liberation*. Maryknoll, NY: Orbis, 1978, ch. 2.
[19] Vidales, 'Methodological issues', p. 42. Cf. Segundo, *Liberation of Theology*, ch. 2; Bonino, *Revolutionary Theology*, pp. 34ff.

class analysis are those selected as best suited to understanding the situation of the poor in Latin America.[20]

A historical theology

'The theology of liberation is a theology of salvation in the light of the concrete history and political conditions of the present day.'[21] The description of liberation theology as a historical theology denotes not a preoccupation with the past, but a dominant concern for God's action in the world of the present. History is the place where God is revealing himself in the liberating activity of the oppressed. To quote Gutiérrez, 'history is a process of the liberation of man [sic]'.[22] In this perspective, 'faith becomes no more or less than man's historical activity', and humankind continues its process of self-creation in response to the grace of God, liberating itself from all that dehumanises.[23]

It follows that liberation theology needs to understand present historical events and processes as fully as possible:

Instead of using only revelation and tradition as starting points, as classical theology has generally done, it [liberation theology] must start with facts and questions derived from the world and from history.[24]

This in turn implies the need for the use of the social and political science in order to understand what questions are being posed and what facts there are available. The social sciences enable liberation theology to read 'the signs of the times'.[25] Theology and faith themselves have no suitable tools or programmes for social and political analysis and prescription. Liberation theology, therefore, presupposes the voice of

---

[20] Cussianovich writes, 'Change can only come from a view centred on social class . . . This class-oriented view enables us to grasp the exploited, marginalized and alienated character of the people. It also highlights the interests of the dominant class which are at work' (Cussianovich, *Religious Life*, p. 96).

[21] Gustavo Gutiérrez, 'Liberation praxis and Christian faith', in Gibellini, ed., *Frontiers of Theology in Latin America*.

[22] Gutiérrez, *A Theology of Liberation*, p. 32.

[23] Assmann, *Practical Theology*, p. 35.

[24] Gutiérrez, *A Theology of Liberation*, p. 12.   [25] Ibid., p. 8.

the social sciences in particular, as its first or preliminary theological word.[26]

While contemporary history is primary in liberation theology, future and past are not ignored. Present history is seen as being dynamised by God's eschatological promises whose fulfilment lies in the future, but whose effect is felt even now. 'The commitment to the creation of a just society and, ultimately, to a new man, presupposes confidence in the future.'[27] This future hope does not devalue the contemporary struggle for human liberation. The liberation theologians have been very critical of the way in which the biblical promises for the future have been privatised, individualised, and deprived of any critical historical potential for the present. However, they are also aware of the dangers of identifying any present action or ideology with the totality of God's coming kingdom. While they maintain the absolute importance of committed Christian action in the present and see the liberation struggle as the concrete project of God's salvation now, they also maintain that there is a radical discontinuity between the present and God's ultimate future purposes.[28] Thus it can be said that the importance of history and historical commitment in particular situations is absolute, while no one ideology, social programme or social order is absolutised.[29]

Turning to the past, liberation theologians have been very active in trying to de-ideologise Christian tradition and the Bible so that they can yield their liberating potential. In particular, they have attempted to rescue the 'Jesus of history' who challenges and cannot be manipulated from the amorphous, malleable 'Christ of faith' who can be co-opted to any cause.[30]

[26] Vidales, 'Methodological issues', p. 44.

[27] Gutiérrez, *A Theology of Liberation*, p. 213.

[28] Cf. Gutiérrez, *A Theology of Liberation*, p. 168. Juan Luis Segundo, 'Capitalism versus Socialism: crux theologica', in Gibellini, ed., *Frontiers of Theology in Latin America*, argues that the absolute must be found in the relativity of the present rather than the present being relativised.

[29] See José Miguez Bonino, 'Historical praxis and Christian identity', in Gibellini, ed., *Frontiers of Theology in Latin America*, where a model of continuity and discontinuity between the present human liberation struggle and God's ultimate eschatological action and purposes is proposed.

[30] See, for example, Leonardo Boff, *Jesus Christ Liberator*. London: SPCK, 1980; Jon Sobrino, *Christology at the Crossroads*. London: SCM Press, 1978.

Rediscovering key parts of the Bible has also been important in recovering the historical God of the Bible who is revealed in his liberating acts.[31] The Bible provides a source of motivation for the liberation struggle. It bears witness to a God who desires justice and seeks the liberation of the oppressed, to Jesus' own preferential option for the poor and his condemnation of the rich (cf. Matthew 25. 31–46), and to the Apostles' ongoing care and concern for the poor in their community.[32]

Liberation theology is a historical theology, principally concerned with identifying and co-operating with God's salvific acts in the 'Bible of the present'.[33] But it is also involved in a critical, dialectical relationship with the traditions of the past and the promises of the future.

A relative theology

In liberation theology any claim to absolute unchanging knowledge of the truth is denied. Since any theology is a socially influenced product, it cannot have the eternal and universal validity that traditional European theologies have seemed to claim. The latter, it is argued, have 'absolutised an aspect of the present world situation', in this kind of claim, thus performing an ideological function in covering up rather than uncovering the nature of reality.[34] Dussel describes European theology as 'totalised', by which he means that it is a theology closed to the in-breaking of the theological perceptions of non-Europeans, and to questions which emanate from the periphery rather than the 'centre' of the theological world. Thus, theology follows colonial patterns of exploitation.[35]

[31] Boff and Boff, *Introducing Liberation Theology*, pp. 34ff. lists books of the Bible favoured by liberation theologians including Exodus, the Prophets, the Gospels, the Acts of the Apostles and Revelation.

[32] Cf. Boff and Boff, *Introducing Liberation Theology*, pp. 44ff.

[33] Vidales, 'Methodological issues', p. 40.

[34] Cf. Dussel, *Ethics and the Theology of Liberation*, p. 150. Cf. Mannheim, *Ideology*, p. 78: 'the absolute which was once a means of entering into communion with the divine, has now become an instrument used by those who profit from it, to distort, pervert, and conceal the meaning of the present'.

[35] US theologian Robert McAfee Brown describes his own realisation of this colonial mentality in 'Reflections of a North American', in Ellis and Maduro, eds., *The Future of Liberation Theology*.

Liberation theology wishes to avoid becoming another totalised system, unresponsive to the needs of the present and those
who are oppressed in a non-European situation. It is therefore
prepared to see its content, concerns and methodologies as
radically provisional. It is an evolving, changing theology that
sees itself as only partly reflecting the totality of God's word
and truth. It has no desire to standardise, to gain conformity,
or to reflect the concerns of those outside Latin America.
Liberation theologians manufacture a theology of the periphery, while calling upon the centralised Catholic Church to
recognise the need for theological pluralism which encompasses the need for different kinds of contextual theology.[36]

Liberation theology continues to develop, evolve and
change. It does not expect to be a permanent, static activity
which becomes fossilised into universalisable dogma. It pre-
dicts its own passing – and welcomes the prospect!

A complete theology

It perhaps appears paradoxical in the light of liberation theology's avowed relativity and relativism that it also claims to be a
complete theology, unlike many other contemporary theologies. Segundo writes,

What is designated as 'liberation theology' does not purport to be
merely one sector of theology, like 'theology of work' or the 'theology
of death'. Liberation theology is meant to designate and cover theology as a whole. What is more, it does not purport to cover theology
from one of many possible standpoints. Instead it claims to view
theology from the standpoint which the Christian fonts point up as
the only authentic and privileged standpoint for arriving at a full and
complete understanding of God's revelation in Jesus Christ.[37]

---

[36] See further, for example, Enrique Dussel, 'Historical and philosophical presuppositions for Latin American theology', in Gibellini, ed., *Frontiers of Theology in Latin
America*.

[37] Segundo, 'Capitalism versus Socialism', p. 241. This assertion is illuminated by
Mannheim's observation that, 'it is certain that there is a wide range of subject-
matter which is accessible only either to certain subjects, or in certain historical
periods, and which becomes apparent through the social purposes of individuals'
(Mannheim, *Ideology*, p. 150).

One of the major differences between liberation theology and other social and political theologies which have sprung up contemporaneously with it in Europe and elsewhere is that liberation theology is not merely a segment of, or the practical application of, a corpus of dogmatic theology. Traditional theologies have tended to treat social and political awareness and action as the arena of applied Christian ethics, deduced from fundamental doctrinal principles.[38] These different Christian social theologies have been fragmented and deductive in method. They have not sought to add to, or illuminate, basic thinking about the nature of God, Christ, and the other central themes of Christian theology.

Liberation theology rejects this traditional position. It claims to be a way of approaching the whole of theology which must be recast from the standpoint of the option for the poor. From this position, it is argued, the whole method and content of theology must be reassessed. If all language and ideas are human creations and reflect specific social and political conditions, then a change in these conditions, new practical commitments, and the perspectives derived from them require the growth of a whole new way of looking at, and understanding, Christian theology. All the major doctrines, ideas and texts of the Christian tradition must be reexamined and evaluated from the viewpoint of the oppressed. Inductive methods must be used to ascertain whether the tenets of dogma reflect or deny the concerns and insights of the oppressed. All aspects of theology must be completely remade.

This awareness is gradually leading to the emergence of a complete theology of liberation which reclaims and reinterprets doctrines and traditions from the perspective of the poor. Christology, the nature of God, soteriology, ecclesiology, and

---

[38] For similarities and differences between liberation theology and other kinds of social and political theologies see, for example, Alfredo Fierro, *The Militant Gospel*. London: SCM Press, 1977; Kee, ed., *The Scope of Political Theology*; Bonino, *Revolutionary Theology*, pp. 145ff; Jürgen Moltmann, 'An open letter to José Míguez Bonino', in Hennelly, ed., *Liberation Theology*.

the nature of revelation are amongst the areas of doctrine which are receiving new and critical accounts.[39]

A political theology

Liberation theology is political in two ways. First, it focusses upon, and gives, primacy to the political dimension of human existence. Secondly, it is a politically mediated theology.[40] It is this second dimension of political mediation which makes liberation theology fundamentally different from classical Christian theology and social ethics. For it is not merely a theology concerned about politics or with applying Christian ideas within the political arena. It is a theology which actually arises from fundamental political engagement, and which must use the language and concepts of politics to perform its theological task.

In common with some other contemporary political theologies, liberation theology regards the political dimension of existence as the most important and fundamental:

The construction of the 'polis' . . . is a dimension which encompasses and severally conditions all of man's activity . . . Everything has a political colour. It is always in the political fabric that a person emerges as a free and responsible being, as a person relating to other people, as someone who takes on a political task.[41]

The primacy of the political dimension of existence is complementary to the liberation theologians' rejection of 'privatisation' and individualism, so prevalent in traditional European theologies:

[39] See further, for example, Antonio Pérez Esclarín, *Atheism and the Liberation*. London: SCM Press, 1980; Jon Sobrino, *Christology at the Crossroads*. London: SCM Press 1978. For a comprehensive liberationist approach to classic elements of theology see Juan Luis Segundo, *A Community Called Church*. (1973); *Grace and the Human Condition*. (1973); *Our Idea of God*. (1974); *The Sacraments Today*. (1974); *Evolution and Guilt*. (1974) (Maryknoll, NY: Orbis).

[40] See further Fierro, *Militant Gospel*, pp. 28ff. For the concept and meaning of 'mediation' see, for example, Boff and Boff, *Introducing Liberation Theology*, ch. 3.

[41] Gutiérrez, *A Theology of Liberation*, p. 47. Politics in this connection is defined as 'the sphere for the exercise of a critical freedom which won down through history'. Politics as an 'orientation to power' is to be seen in this perspective.

The Christian message is not simply a word whispered to individuals in their isolated lives as lone persons. It is also a public proclamation to society, uttered in the face of its concrete structures and the prevailing system.[42]

All theologies need to deprivatise themselves to speak to socio-political realities and structures. Sin must be seen in its corporate and social dimensions, and tackled theologically in the same way ('Sin has become a very private affair', writes Dussel, 'But the great historic and communitarian sins of humankind pass unnoticed by all.'[43] Traditional theologies have been 'saturated to the point of nausea with existentialist and personalist themes'[44]).

This brings me to the second aspect, the political mediation of theology. In every generation, theology adopts and adapts the language and concepts which enable it to understand its own context and speak meaningfully within it. In the past theology has used many different thought and language systems to reinterpret and reformulate its message. Aquinas, for example, used Aristotelian philosophy.[45] Bultmann and Tillich utilised existentialist concepts to discuss aspects of faith in a mid-century Northern hemisphere context. It follows that where politics lies at the heart of the human condition, political concepts and language must also be central in theological discourse and understanding. Because of the primacy of political action and understandings in the construction of liberation theology, that theology is filled with social and political concepts relevant to the Latin American situation. Politics is an integral part and stage of the theological process.

In the case of liberation theology, the political language and analysis of Marxism is particularly prominent. This is defended by the liberation theologians on the grounds that 'after Marx

---

[42] Vidales, 'Methodological issues', p. 62.

[43] Dussel, *Ethics and the Theology of Liberation*, p. 27.

[44] Comblin, 'What sort of service might theology render?', p. 74. Liberation theology accepts the individual's importance. Assmann writes, 'Politicizing private life doesn't mean threatening its precious inner core of personal intensity, but making it conscious of its true historical character' (Assmann, *Practical Theology*, p. 32.) For discussion of the political, practical, public and critical nature of theology see Fierro, *Militant Gospel*.

[45] See further on this point, Gutiérrez, *A Theology of Liberation*, p. 5.

our way of conceiving and posing the problems of society will never be the same again.'[46] In much the same way that we live in a post-Freudian age, and many of Freud's concepts are now basic to our self-understanding and theology, we live in a post-Marxian age in which Marxist concepts and methods must form an important part of our ways of analysing and thinking theologically.[47] If all theology is historically and contextually conditioned and mediated, then liberation theology must be politically mediated within its own particular sociopolitical situation.

A universalistic theology

In liberation theology there is a strong tendency to affirm the consonance, if not the complete identity, of Christian salvation and the liberation struggle of the oppressed. Gutiérrez, for example, clearly affirms the single destiny of humanity and the universality of God's salvific will and intent:

> The idea of the universality of the salvific will of God, clearly enunciated by Paul ... has been established ... There is only one human destiny, irreversibly assumed by Christ, the Lord of history. His redemptive work embraces all the dimensions of existence and brings them to their fullness. The history of salvation is the very heart of human history.[48]

The implications of this affirmation of the unity of God's saving action and human history are manifold. First, there is no separate, distinct, or privileged 'church history' or salvation history which excludes people who are not Christians. God is publicly at work in history creating a kingdom of heaven for everyone, not just for the chosen few.

Secondly, the church is no longer the primary place where salvation is concretised; it is to be found amongst the poor and

[46] Segundo, *The Liberation of Theology*, p. 35, n. 10. See also Fierro, *Militant Gospel*, p. 78f.
[47] For the use of Marxism see, for example, Pedro Arrupe, 'Marxist analysis by Christians', in Hennelly, ed., *Liberation theology*; Kee, *Marx and the Failure of Liberation Theology*; Arthur F. McGovern, 'Dependency theory, Marxist analysis, and liberation theology', in Ellis, and Maduro, eds., *The Future of Liberation Theology*.
[48] Gutiérrez, *A Theology of Liberation*, pp. 150, 153.

oppressed in their engagement in human history in general.[49] The church is a sign, a sacrament, and a community of witness and hope which proclaims and works towards the kingdom of God through liberation. But it is not solely, or even mainly, the place where salvation is to be worked for and obtained. And it most certainly does not exist for the maintenance or furtherance of narrow ecclesiastical interests and purposes:

This new way of being Church understands that it does not exist for itself; it is to be a sign of Christ for the world and the place where the Spirit is explicitly active. A sign does not exist for itself but for others. The Church as sign is *from* Christ *for* the world . . . This Church is . . . a Church involved in the working world and living out the meaning and joy of the resurrection in the heart of the secular world.[50]

Thirdly, basic theological concepts are given concrete, this-worldly meanings. Thus, conversion ceases to be an individualistic experience and becomes a turning to the poor neighbour: 'Conversion means leaving one's own way . . . and entering upon the way of the other, the neighbor, and especially of the poor in whom we encounter the Lord.'[51] Grace is not primarily an a-social experience of the metaphysical, but a call into communal action: 'Grace impels human beings toward a process of liberation from those dimensions that are hostile to the saving encounter and it tends to establish a new situation: the freedom of the children of God.'[52] And liberative activity on the part of the oppressed itself becomes salvific activity.[53] Finally, faith is manifested as human political activity in history: Assmann baldly declares, 'Faith is no more or less than man's [sic] historical activity' (which is essentially political)![54]

This kind of unifying and universalising thinking presents some problems. It can, for example, be seen as an attempt to resacralise the world by making all action of any kind, however

---

[49] Cf. Bonino, *Revolutionary Theology*, ch. 6; Gutiérrez, *A Theology of Liberation*, ch. 12.
[50] Boff, *Church: Charism and Power*, p. 62.
[51] Gustavo Gutiérrez, *The Truth Shall Make You Free*. Maryknoll, NY: Orbis, 1990, p. 5.
[52] Leonardo Boff, *Liberating Grace*. Maryknoll, NY: Orbis 1979, p. 148.
[53] See Gutiérrez, *A Theology of Liberation*, p. 159f.
[54] Assmann, *Practical Theology*, p. 35.

unconscious, Christian.[55] It can also lead to the dilution and evacuation of Christian faith and language, so that it has no distinctiveness, no relative autonomy, and no useful or creative function. Liberation theology must, therefore, find a way of affirming the worldly liberation struggle while preserving some Christian distinctiveness.

The most satisfactory model for doing this has been suggested by Bonino.[56] He advances a model of continuity – discontinuity based on Paul's theology of the body. In this model, human activity in 'secular' history is essential to the concretisation of the kingdom of God on earth. However, salvation can never fully be realised on earth. There is, therefore, continuity and discontinuity between present human action for salvation and God's ultimate eschatological purposes. In the light of this, Christians must take the present time with absolute seriousness and avoid futuristic uncreative and unrealistic idealism. But they must also realise the relativity of human action and the fact that not all human action will in the end be deemed to have been in accord with God's purposes. This model leaves room for a distinctive Christian faith and commitment, while not devaluing earthly commitment to the relative.[57]

At the centre of liberation theology is a very distinctive theological method. It is to a description and consideration of this method that we now turn.

---

[55] See Fierro, *Militant Gospel*, pp. 339ff. for a discussion of this problem.

[56] See Bonino, 'Historical praxis and Christian identity'.

[57] Further discussion of the identity and separateness of the liberation and salvation is to be found in Boff and Boff, *Salvation and Liberation*.

CHAPTER 3

The methods of liberation theology

The treatment given to methods here will be quite brief. Certain issues arise from the outline of methods which follows, for example, the use of Marxism and the Bible in liberation theology. These receive a little consideration towards the end of the chapter.

The task of liberation theology

It has already been noted that the essential task of liberation theology is 'a critical reflection on Christian praxis in the light of the Word'.[1] Its purpose is to help Christians to understand their liberating praxis and to modify and suggest practical courses of action: 'The theology of liberation tries to enlighten and guide the church toward pastoral practice, and geo-politics, and a strategy of liberation'.[2] Such a theology must be 'inductive, pluralistic, experiential, partial and related to (its) environment in order to be relevant'.[3] Its basic methodological characteristic is that it is 'an inductive science ascending from the ground up. It does not start from basic principles and then draw conclusions from them'.[4]

---

[1] Gutiérrez, *A Theology of Liberation*, p. 13.
[2] Comblin, *The Church and the National Security State*, p. 216.
[3] Hugo Assmann, 'The power of Christ in history: conflicting Christologies and discernment', in Gibellini, ed., *Frontiers of Theology in Latin America*, p. 134.
[4] Luis G. del Valle, 'Towards a theological outlook starting from concrete events', in Gibellini, ed., *Frontiers of Theology in Latin America*, p. 85.

The place of liberation theology in the liberation struggle

Theological reflection is not seen as a primary part of the liberation struggle itself, even by the liberation theologians. Theirs is but a secondary activity which flows from the primary action of Christian commitment to the struggle. Apparently paradoxically, as Forrester points out, despite its context within primary concern for, and commitment to, liberation for all the oppressed, 'Liberation theology sees itself as more a "Church theology" than most other contemporary theology.'[5] The church referred to here is not the ideal or institutional church, but rather the symbolic community which strives for liberation and manifests the first-fruits of new and just ways of living, witnessing to God's redemptive will for all people. None the less, this theology stems from, and is addressed mainly to, those who would see themselves as directly members of the Christian community, not just the human race in general. As the church serves the world in seeking liberation, so liberation theology serves the church. Liberation theologians thereby become 'friendly critics' in critical solidarity with the church. At this level liberation theology might be seen as quite some distance away from the general struggle of the poor in history in Latin America.

Liberation theology is secondary to active commitment. It is also a secondary 'word' following the first 'word' of the social sciences. These are used to expose the situation and conditions in which the poor live, as well as the reasons for their oppression. The human sciences provide analytic tools for an understanding of society – the locus of God's saving activity – which are not available within theology itself. Thus, theology is regarded by liberation theologians as

a second act in relation to the first act of Christian commitment, and the second word in relation to the first word of the human sciences, especially those whose analyses and diagnoses impinge directly on oppression-liberation.[6]

[5] Forrester, *Theology and Politics*, p. 130.
[6] Raul Vidales, 'Some recent publications in Latin America on the theology of liberation', *Concilium* 6, 1974, 127–36, at p. 130. See also Assmann, *Practical Theology*, p. 38; Boff and Boff, *Introducing Liberation Theology*, pp. 24ff.

The 'locus theologicus'

Where is it possible to do authentic theology in Latin America? Where does one need to situate oneself to see God's contemporary action revealing his nature? The answer to these questions for liberation theology is that the *locus theologicus* is amongst the poor struggling for liberation.[7] The *sine qua non* and starting point for liberation is the pre-theological response of faith represented by commitment to the poor. It is from this perspective only, that the word of God, both past and present, can be rightly discerned and understood.

The *locus* for theology exists in space and time. Liberation theology finds its primary *locus* in the present and amongst the poor. While the historic resources of the Christian tradition such as the Bible are important witnesses to God's activity in the past, they are inevitably conditioned by their own historical and social contexts. They can, therefore, only act as secondary resources for God's people involved in contemporary liberation.[8] It is the present which must first be understood and acted upon. Only then can the Christian tradition be appropriately rediscovered, interpreted, and understood.

The tools of liberation theology

Christian theology in and of itself has no cognitive or analytical tools for understanding contemporary social reality. Liberation theology needs to discern the nature of that reality, as well as becoming aware of its own place within it. It must, therefore, use the tools provided by the social sciences, particularly those which relate clearly to oppression-liberation. It has to

accept the mediation of a new type of scientific rationality to which it has not been accustomed. This new line of reasoning is the contribution of the human sciences, of the social sciences specifically.[9]

---

[7] See Vidales, 'Some recent publications', p. 129.
[8] See further, for example, Assmann, *Practical Theology*, p. 60f.
[9] Vidales, 'Methodological issues', p. 38. Cf. Assmann, *Practical Theology*, pp. 38, 59ff.

To fashion a language which meaningfully reflects the experience of faith and commitment within a context of social and political oppression, theology must start with social analysis. Thus, the first stage of liberation theology is what is described as a 'socio-analytical mediation'.[10]

The most important usage of the social sciences is to understand the situation of liberation-dependence in Latin America. But they have also been essential in freeing Christianity and its tradition from an ideological bondage to the dominant classes and the unjust *status quo* in society. Socio-political analysis of aspects of church life and tradition has exposed its unseen biases and interests, as well as bringing liberative strands and 'dangerous memories' to the fore.[11] Perhaps the most controversial example of social and political analyses showing up the ideological captivity of Christian institutions and traditions is Leonardo Boff's, *Church: Charism and Power* which subjects the Catholic Church to a Marxist analysis revealing many vested interests, a means of production which is controlled by a clerical minority, and much oppression. This led to Boff being disciplined by the Vatican in the mid-1980s.[12]

While the social sciences have been the main analytical tools associated with liberation theology, literary sciences, such as those associated with modern biblical scholarship, have also been important. There is an increasing number of biblical studies undertaken from the liberationist perspective.[13] José Miranda in particular seems to believe that correct and rigorous study of scripture using modern scholarly literary methods

[10] Boff and Boff, *Introducing Liberation Theology*, pp. 24ff. In the Boffs' methodological description, the 'socio-analytical mediation' is followed by a 'hermeneutical mediation' in which the oppression-liberation process is examined in the light of faith requiring critical interrogation of the Christian resources and tradition. Finally, the 'practical mediation' produces recommendations and strategies for liberative action.

[11] The concept 'dangerous memory' is from the European, Metz, whose thought has influenced liberation theology. See Johannes B. Metz, *Theology of the World*. London: Search Press, 1969.

[12] See Leonardo Boff, *Church: Charism and Power*.

[13] See, for example, Juan Luis Segundo's volumes in the series, 'Jesus of Nazareth Yesterday and Today' (Maryknoll, NY: Orbis, 1984–); George V. Pixley, *God's Kingdom*. London: SCM Press, 1981. See Rowland and Corner, *Liberating Exegesis*, for what is available here.

will produce dangerous memories which will confirm and amplify the liberationist position. Clearly presupposing a Marxist analysis of society, Miranda tends to assume that there is little contradiction between a Marxist view of present reality and the biblical text exposed to appropriate biblical critical methods.[14]

The verification principle

In liberation theology, as in Marxism, the truth and value of knowledge must always be evaluated within the praxis of modifying the world. Only if knowledge appears to reflect reality as it is discovered in the process of trying to change the world can it be regarded as true. Biblical truths and the historic traditions of Christian revelation must be evaluated with primary reference to the reality of the liberation struggle.[15] Truth is verified in loving action – to do is to know.

Truth, for the contemporary human being, is something **verified**, something 'made true'. Knowledge of reality that leads to no modification of that reality is not verified, does not become true ... The praxis that transforms history is ... the matrix of authentic knowledge and the acid test of the validity of that knowledge. It is the place where human beings re-create their world and shape themselves. It is the place where they know the reality in which they find themselves, and, therefore, know themselves as well.[16]

The dialectical method

The dialectical method is a central feature of the process of liberation theology. Having analysed present social and political reality and de-ideologised the church and Christian tradi-

---

[14] See José Miranda, *Marx and the Bible*. London: SCM Press, 1977; *Being and the Messiah*. Maryknoll, NY: Orbis, 1977; *Marx Against the Marxists*. London: SCM Press, 1980; *Communism in the Bible*. London: SCM Press, 1982.

[15] See Segundo, *Liberation of Theology*, p. 39 and Assmann, *Practical Theology*, pp. 74ff. for the necessity for liberation theology to be 'praxiology', not de-contextualised thought.

[16] Gutiérrez, *Power of the Poor*, p. 59. Gutiérrez writes elsewhere: 'Practice is the locus of verification of our faith in God, who liberates by establishing justice and right in favor of the poor ... To believe is to practice ... Only from deed, can the

tion, Christians actively involved in the liberation struggle can enter into a critical dialogue with that tradition. This dialogue serves to both encourage and modify Christian praxis, since the tradition contains its own liberative content and so presents its own challenges.

The dialectical process may be seen as a circle whereby ideas, understandings and traditions, on the one hand, and actual practical action, on the other, continually enter into dialogue, stimulating and modifying each other. The concept of praxis contains this twofold essence of reflection-action within it. Dialectical method within a praxis orientation is most clearly seen in Segundo's now-famous treatment of the 'hermeneutic circle'.[17]

The hermeneutic circle is defined by Segundo as 'the continuing change in our interpretation of the Bible which is dictated by the continuing changes in our present day reality, both individual and social.[18] The circle has four stages. First comes 'our way of experiencing reality, which leads to profound ideological suspicion'. This arises from Christian commitment to the liberation struggle which arouses suspicion that ideas and institutions, including religious ideas and institutions, may in the past have been ideologically determined and interpreted to obscure issues of liberation-domination. Secondly there is 'the application of our ideological suspicion to the whole ideological superstructure in general and to theology in particular'. At the third stage, 'there comes a new way of experiencing theological reality that leads to exegetical suspicion, that is to the suspicion that the prevailing interpretation has not taken important pieces of data into account'. Lastly, 'we have our new hermeneutic'.

The hermeneutic circle does not close here, however. The 'circle' is, in fact, a 'spiral' which requires that the process should be continually repeated and modified to take into

proclamation by word be understood. In the deed our faith becomes truth, not only for others, but for ourselves as well' (*Power of the Poor*, p. 17).

[17] See Segundo, *Liberation of Theology*, pp. 8–9 for description and discussion of the hermenuetic circle. Segundo acknowledges a debt to Bultmann for this device; it would also be derivable from Hegelian–Marxist theories of dialectic.

[18] Segundo, *Liberation of Theology*, p. 8.

account the changing situation of social and political context and reality. It should also be noted that when the fourth stage is reached, the Christian tradition is able to speak with integrity and to influence and inform the contemporary situation, posing questions for action and modifying it, not simply being determined by it: 'Every new reality obliges us to interpret the word of God afresh, to change reality accordingly, and then go back and reinterpret the word of God again, and so on.'[19]

This kind of hermeneutic method has many strengths and attractions. It is fluid and progressive, not static. It allows for the interaction of belief and action, of the present and of the past, without confusing the autonomy of these different realms. It could be applied to other aspects of Christian ideology and practice, not just to using the Bible and the Christian tradition, to allow their liberative potential to emerge. Later I will suggest that a modified version of this circle or spiral is the key to integrating some of the insights and methods of liberation theology into pastoral care in the Northern hemisphere.[20]

Controversial issues

In this outline of liberation theology I have not presented a critique of the genre, and I do not intend to provide one here. My purpose has been to give a clear account of some of the main features, insights, and methods of this theology with a view to applying it critically to the situation of pastoral care in the Northern hemisphere. It will be necessary to make critical comments about the strengths and limitations of the liber-

---

[19] Ibid., p. 8.

[20] Boff outlines a similar methodological or hermeneutic spiral to that of Segundo. Less clearly expressed in terms of stages, it still embodies the praxis-oriented dialectical model outlined above. Boff starts his spiral from an ethical, i.e., theoretical commitment. He writes of the theological method of liberation theology: 'It begins with indignation at the poverty experienced by God's children ... [T]his poverty is seen as a religious experience for the poor in whom the Suffering Servant is present. The second step is the investigation of the ways that produce such wanton misery on one side and scandalous wealth on the other. Here, the historical, social, political and economic analyses are brought into play. Third, this reality of misery ... is read with the eyes of faith and theology, discerning the paths of sin ... Finally, pastoral activity is developed that enables the Church and all Christians to help in the process of complete liberation' (Boff, *Church: Charism and Power*, p. 20).

ationist perspective as we proceed through the rest of this work. These will be particularly pertinent in the next chapter where the relevance and plausibility of the insights and methods of liberation theology for pastoral care in Britain and other parts of the developed world will be assessed.

However, it would be disingenuous to disguise the fact that sharp criticism has been directed at this theology. Liberation theology is a perception-changing theology which puts itself at the service of a liberating gospel of which the poor themselves are the messengers. This gospel is a stumbling block and a scandal: 'it is no longer "presentable" in society. It will not sound nice and it will not smell good'.[21] It would be disappointing if such a theology failed to arouse criticism and controversy. Mention must be made of some critical points here.

The use of Marxism in liberation theology has provoked anxieties and criticisms. Liberation theologians do not discuss properly their use of Marxism, leaving it to their readers to work out how far, and in what ways, this perspective informs their work. It is also argued that the liberation theologians not only use Marxist methods of social analysis, but also implicitly take on Marx's atheism and prescriptive social vision of communism, putting themselves at odds with the theistic Christian vision of the kingdom of God.[22] In opposition to the last point, some argue that liberation theology has not applied Marx's critique of religion to itself vigorously enough, and that this is something it should do if it wishes to situate itself more fully alongside the poor.[23] At a more pragmatic level, while liberation theologians constantly talk of undertaking historical

[21] Gutiérrez, *Power of the Poor*, p. 22.

[22] See, for example, Norman, *Christianity and the World Order*.

[23] See Kee, *Marx and the Failure of Liberation Theology*. Liberation theologians themselves remain implicitly committed to the idea that the church can be a sign of hope and liberation. Kee argues that one of the main points of a Marxist analysis is that social institutions reflect the material substructure and can only change for proletarian liberation when the substructure is changed. Thus churches, which Marx deemed to represent a manifestation of human alienation, are historically conservative and ideological institutions which cannot liberate human beings until historical and material circumstances change. They cannot be seen as independent enclaves of the new age if a historical and material analysis is rigorously and consistently applied. Marx could not, and would not, exempt them from fundamental critique.

materialist analysis of the social and political situation in Latin America, there are few examples of this actually being done systematically in their writings. This makes it difficult to see exactly what is meant by such analysis, at what level it should be undertaken, or what its actual results might be.

A major emphasis of liberation theology has been on rediscovering the liberative message of the Bible and its bias of privilege to the poor and oppressed. The scriptures, liberation theologians would argue, 'have been used too long to comfort the afflicted; the Scriptures are also meant to afflict the comfortable'.[24] Many theologians in the Northern hemisphere would question the selectivity of texts used, especially the dominance of the Exodus story. Within the interpretation of the texts, selected liberation theologians ignore uncongenial or countervailing themes (what, for example, is to be made of the mass slaughter of innocent Egyptian men and women or the genocide of the Canaanites by the 'chosen people' in the Exodus story?). There are many biblical themes and narratives which counter-balance that of the liberation of the oppressed (Romans 13 where Paul talks of the powers that be being ordained by God being an example). It can also be argued that there are many valid standpoints for interpreting the Bible, and that the poor have not privileged access to its 'true' meaning. Lastly, the liberation theologians are accused of mistakenly conflating the poor of the Bible with the Marxist notion of the contemporary revolutionary proletariat, so distorting and confusing the real historical situation of the biblical writings and their production with the present day.[25]

Particularly in its early stages, liberation theology asserted its autonomy and separateness from historical and contemporary European-type theologies, even political theologies. One look at the writings of, say, Gutiérrez with its extensive references and footnotes, makes it quite clear that liberation theology owes a great deal to European theology. Barth, Bonhoeffer, Bultmann, Cox, Metz, and Moltmann, together with the theological teachings of the Catholic *magisterium*, have all quite

---

[24] Scharper in Lernoux, *Cry*, p. 372.

[25] For a critique of liberation theology's use of the Bible see Andrew Kirk, *Liberation Theology*. London: Marshall, Morgan and Scott, 1979.

clearly constituted important dialogue partners for the (European-trained) liberation theologians, and have contributed insights and methods to their theology.[26] Jürgen Moltmann has, with some justified frustration, accused liberation theologians of effectively writing European theology.[27]

Liberation theology does not want to be a theology in the classic mode, ie, abstract, theoretical, and ahistorical. But this raises the question, is it usefully regarded as theology in any conventional sense of the word at all? It is often difficult to see in what sense it is language about God rather than about the human situation. Similarly, it frequently looks like an ethic or code of human practice. It is perhaps this sense that liberation theology does not look 'religious' enough which has led liberation theologians to emphasise the spiritual origins and aspects of the commitment to liberation.[28] With its concentration on social and political analysis in the first socio-analytical mediation, and its emphasis on finding human solutions to the problems of oppression, it is tempting to enquire in what way liberation theology can think of itself as distinctively theological enquiry.[29]

Again, the relative absence of rigorous, rational, critical activity on the level of meta-language, where theological concepts are interrogated in traditional theological discourse, appears to question the appropriateness of seeing liberation theology as theology in the hitherto accepted sense of the word.

[26] Gustavo Gutiérrez, *The Truth Shall Make You Free*. Maryknoll, NY: Orbis, 1990 has an account of Gutiérrez's doctoral discussions in 1985 – at the French Catholic Institute of Lyons! Having spent a lifetime of criticising the sort of theology done at this kind of Institute, Gutiérrez sought legitimation from a European source. Can this incident be seen as a commentary on the reality of liberation theology's relation to Europe – and to the poor? Even one of his examiners described the discussions as 'playing the university game' (p. 19.). This is a curious event in liberation theology's history.

[27] Jürgen Moltmann, 'An open letter to José Míguez Bonino' in Hennelly, ed., *Liberation Theology: A Documentary History*.

[28] Boff suggests this theology starts with spirituality, the experience of the spirit of life, the experience of grace, and the silence of contemplation: 'We are absorbed by the gratuitousness of God and by God's saving and liberating plan. This . . . is not the silence of closed eyes that we find in some . . . mystics but the mysticism of eyes open on the world' (Leonardo Boff, 'The originality of the theology of liberation' in Ellis and Maduro, eds., *The Future of Liberation Theology*, p. 40). For spiritual aspects of liberation theology see Gustavo Gutiérrez, *We Drink from Our Own Wells*. London: SCM Press, 1984; *On Job*. Maryknoll: Orbis, 1987.

[29] See further Kee, *Marx and Failure*, p. 228.

Some critics, therefore, argue that it should be regarded as pre-critical theological utterance which makes direct symbolic assertions about God arising from praxis, 'the direct and spontaneous expression of a politically involved and committed faith, not second-stage critical reflection on that direct expression'.[30] This easily leads to confusion and contradiction, both within liberation theology itself, where different writers might be writing at different levels, and in dialogue with other, more critical and reflective, theologies which have elaborated theories and methods, and which feel themselves constrained to conduct themselves more strictly within the canons of rational discourse.

To these major critical themes others can be added. There may be a danger of 'experiential fundamentalism' within liberation theology, whereby it is assumed that because something is true in the contextualised praxis of Latin American Christians it must be true for all Christians everywhere. Again, there is a real danger of liberation theology becoming parochial, provincial, and rigidly separatist, thus depriving itself of external critique and relevance (it would be ironical if a theology which has accused others so effectively of having 'totalised' world views which exclude 'the other' were itself to become totalised). Finally, there is the danger that liberation theology may be too concerned to vindicate itself academically and theoretically in the eyes of its critics, and so become verbose, over-technical, complicated, abstract, and obscure. This would be a sad fate for a theology which springs from the situation of the ill-educated poor, and aims to stimulate lively liberating action, not stultifying literary production.[31]

---

[30] Fierro, *Militant Gospel*, p. 317.

[31] The liberation theologians are aware of some of these criticisms. The Boffs list seven 'temptations' to which this theology might be prone. These are: disregard for mystical roots (for example, prayer and contemplation) from which commitment to liberation springs; overstressing the political aspect of questions to the exclusion of other aspects, for example, friendship; subordinating faith to societal considerations; absolutisation of liberation theology, downgrading other forms of oppression, for example, of women; overstressing differences between liberation theology and other forms of theology and ethics; lack of concern for dialogue with other churches or types of theology; failure to make liberation theology intelligible to the church (Boff and Boff, *Introducing Liberation Theology*, pp. 64–5.).

Conclusion

Liberation theology is not unproblematic. It is full of complexities, obscurities, and contradictions. To put it in more positive terms, it is rich, lively, and controversial with much power to confront, challenge, and annoy on many different levels. In this short introduction to the genre, I have necessarily been schematic and selective. I hope that I have said enough to convince readers that this theology of reversal and subversion from the underside of history has more than enough within it to merit response in the Northern hemisphere. In the next chapter, I shall move on to examine what the nature of this response should be in relation to pastoral care. What are the questions which liberation theology poses most forcefully for our practice of pastoral care? Is it possible to use with integrity some of the insights and methods of liberation theology? If so, which insights and methods should they be, for we are unlikely to be able to cope with all of them?

CHAPTER 4

Putting liberation theology to work

In the Introduction, I suggested that this book could be seen as an exercise in transcultural hermeneutics in which the significance of a set of texts is critically interpreted in another, different cultural setting. This can be thought of as a critical conversation, in this case between the texts of Latin American liberation theology and the theory and practice of pastoral care in the Northern hemisphere.[1] Here the insights and methods of the former are allowed to interrogate or question the latter. The aim is to see whether pastoral care theory and practice can learn anything from liberation theology, or needs to be changed in any way. The overarching question is, What can pastoral care learn and make use of from liberation theology? What can a theology which describes itself as a pastoral theology in so far as 'it is the theology that sheds the light of the saving word on the reality of injustice so as to inspire the church to struggle for liberation', offer to our kind of pastoral care?[2]

From liberation theology it is possible to identify a number of other critical questions at different levels and of varying significance. These invite pastoral care to consider, develop, change and grow in theory and in practice. Amongst the most

---

[1] For the model of critical conversation used here see, for example, Pattison, 'Some straw for the bricks'; Taylor, *Learning to Care*; Browning, *Fundamental Practical Theology*; Tracy, *Plurality and Ambiguity*.

[2] Boff and Boff, *Introducing Liberation Theology*, p. 17. For the liberation theologians' comprehensive view of pastoral action which goes beyond ministry to individuals see, for example, Juan Luis Segundo, *The Hidden Motives of Pastoral Action*. Maryknoll, NY: Orbis, 1978. Pastoral activity tends to include *all* the church's practical activity, not merely individual care.

important emerging from my own encounter with liberation theology texts are the following:

Do we see pastoral care too narrowly, for example, as an individually focussed activity, to the exclusion of social and political factors?

Is it appropriate to see pastoral care as a social and political activity, or, as having these dimensions?

What would it mean to give primacy to the social and political dimension in pastoral care?

Does pastoral care in the Northern hemisphere collude with forces of injustice and oppression?

Is pastoral care implicitly or explicitly on anyone's 'side'; does it serve the interests of any particular social groups?

Is social and political 'liberation' a concept which has any practical or critical value for people in the Northern hemisphere and/or for pastoral care?

Are there oppressed and poor people in our society; are they seeking liberation?

Is pastoral care with any people who might be thought of as being oppressed liberating or oppressive?

To whom do pastoral carers seek to make themselves neighbours – to the poor or to the powerful?

Rather than pursuing each of these questions individually here, I will outline a methodological spiral informed by all of them which integrates the questions and insights arising from liberation theology and provides a systematic structure for the rest of the book. I shall then give an account of some of the assumptions, insights, and methods drawn from liberation theology which will inform the ensuing examples of the analysis of pastoral care theory and practice. It is problematic to transfer insights and methods developed in one culture to another one, so the chapter concludes with brief discussions of some of the problems which might be encountered in applying some of the insights and methods arising from liberation theology in the context of pastoral care in the Northern hemisphere. Such problems include, for example, the nature and class structure of advanced capitalist society, the existence of 'the poor' in that society, and the relevance and applicability of Marxist social analysis to it.

INTEGRATING THE METHODS AND INSIGHTS OF LIBERATION THEOLOGY: A METHODOLOGICAL SPIRAL

A revised and adapted version of Segundo's hermeneutic circle, described in the last chapter, can be used to integrate the insights and methods of liberation theology into pastoral care theory and practice. Here I outline a methodological spiral which structures the critical hermeneutic conversation with liberation theology, giving direction for the analysis of pastoral care which follows. In doing the latter, it will shape the remainder of the book. This methodological device is designated a spiral as this implies a continuing process of movement and analysis through time as opposed to a single, episodic activity which is not necessarily repeated.

The proposed methodological spiral has five main stages. It starts with the insights and methods of liberation theology. This basically theoretical starting point can be designated stage A. The insights and methods of this theology lead to questions and concerns that pastoral care theory and practice in the Northern hemisphere may have failed to see its social and political context, implications, and biasses. This is stage B of the spiral. The concern and suspicion leads on to a third stage, C, where it becomes necessary to undertake social and political analysis using the 'tools of suspicion' (for example, Marxist social analysis) of the pastoral situation to see whether there are inequalities, injustices, and conflicts of interest implicit in it.[3] The next stage, D, requires that the practice, theory,

---

[3] The 'hermeneutics of suspicion' is a relatively common term in scholarly discourse. Nietzsche, Darwin, Freud, and Marx are associated with looking behind the superficial in social, intellectual, and institutional life to see the distorting, ideological content of ideas and organisations. Going beyond the face value of any phenomenon to see in what way it embodies undeclared interests and assumptions is a fruitful critical activity, exemplified, for example, by feminist analyses of Christianity which

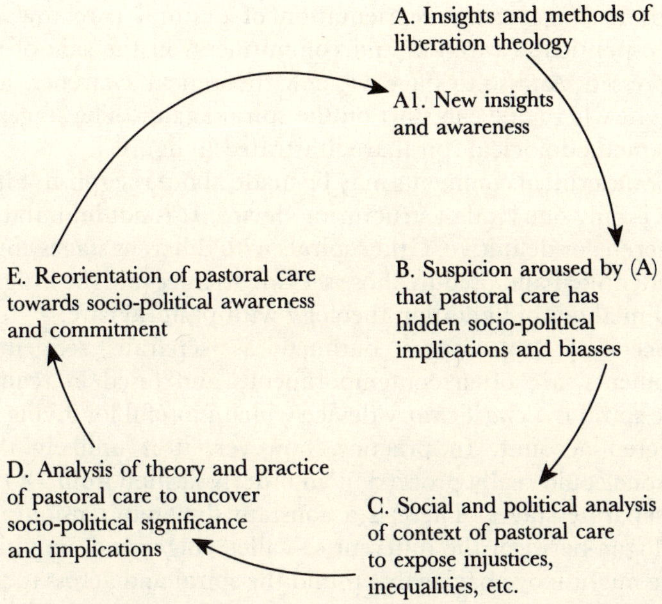

A. Insights and methods of
liberation theology

A1. New insights
and awareness

E. Reorientation of pastoral care
towards socio-political awareness
and commitment

B. Suspicion aroused by (A)
that pastoral care has
hidden socio-political
implications and biasses

D. Analysis of theory and practice
of pastoral care to uncover
socio-political significance
and implications

C. Social and political analysis
of context of pastoral care
to expose injustices,
inequalities, etc.

Figure 1   A diagrammatic representation of a methodological spiral
integrating some of the insights and methods of liberation theology with
pastoral care

and theology of pastoral care are analysed to uncover their socio-political significance and implications. Awareness of this leads to stage E, the reorientation of pastoral care towards socio-political awareness and commitment on the side of the oppressed. And so to stage A1, new theoretical awareness and insight where one can start on the spiral again.[4] The stages of this methodological spiral are illustrated in figure 1.

Some critical comments may be made about the spiral. First, this is only one kind of structuring device. It is not immutable, concrete, or definitive. Other spirals with different stages could be identified and used by those seeking to integrate the insights and methods of liberation theology with pastoral care.

Secondly, the stages outlined as separate sequential 'moments' are often contemporaneous and fused in reality. The spiral is a clarificatory device which is useful for giving an ordered account. In practice, however, it is unlikely that anyone could really proceed in an orderly fashion from A to A1 in separate stages. There is a constant dynamic tension and dialogue between the different so-called stages and activities. One might move backwards round the spiral and across it, not simply forward in an orderly manner. I have simplified into apparently independent 'moments' or progressive stages a rather diffuse, simultaneous, and complex dialogical process (It would be more accurate in this sense to draw a diagram which had lines of connection from each discrete stage to every other stage. To pursue the metaphor of conversation, however, to do this would be to suggest that what is going on is a muddled cacophony rather than an ordered dialogue – which is, of course, much closer to real life!).

Thirdly, this spiral is dynamic and progressive. It does not stand still, nor is it ever finally completed. The purpose of using it is not to find a static end point, but rather to spiral in a complex process of continuing action, critique, and reorientation. The systematised spiral structures and makes overt the

show its (unwitting) enthralment to patriarchal assumptions, institutions, and ideas. For discussion of the term see, for example, Tracy, *Plurality and Ambiguity*, especially ch. 4.
[4] This spiral is developed from Segundo, *Liberation of Theology*, ch. 1.

dynamics of something most of us do, regardless of any interest we might have in liberation theology.

Having recognised some limitations of this useful heuristic device, something must be said about the spiral's strengths and advantages. Its use allows both continuity and discontinuity between the insights and methods of liberation theology and the practice, theory, and theology of pastoral care in the very different context of the Northern hemisphere. A dynamic relationship is created between pastoral care and liberation theology, allowing dialogue while avoiding simple imitation or dubious synthesis. There is thus the possibility of working towards a socio-politically aware and committed pastoral care in our own context which is certainly indebted to, and informed by, liberation theology, but which is not enslaved to it, and which can develop its own distinctive features and directions. Preserving a degree of distinction between these two areas of practice and discourse is necessary if the integrity of each is to be respected, and matters of particular context are to be taken seriously.

The spiral's use also opens up fruitful interaction between the theory and practice of pastoral care, social analytic methods, and a particular kind of theology. Furthermore, the structure provided by it will actually make apparent the real meaning of a concrete social and political analysis of the pastoral situation. One of the surprising features of liberation theology is that, while social analysis is much talked of, and the voice of the social sciences is supposed to be a prominent 'first voice' in theological method, there is very little concrete exemplification of this approach in practice. Following the stages of the methodological spiral through to the examples of specific actual pastoral situation shows what social analysis might involve in practice and how useful it might be.

For the liberation theologians themselves, their methodological spiral starts with ethical indignation at the situation of the poor. This leads sequentially to liberating praxis alongside the poor, then to the suspicion that theology needs to be reinterpreted in new ways requiring a critical reexamination of theology for liberating themes, which eventually proceeds to a reframing and practical reengagement with the liberation struggle.

In the present case, the spiral starts with the insights and methods of liberation theology which have been considered. These arouse concern that pastoral care may have ignored the poor and possess hidden social and political biasses. This suspicion can only be tested by analysing concrete examples of pastoral situations. In the remainder of this book, the situations of women and mentally ill people are examined in detail. This analysis leads on to the examination of pastoral responses to these groups, together with their underlying biasses and presuppositions. When this critical exploration is complete it should be possible to see to what extent the liberationist approach has practical value and the necessity of reorienting pastoral care in the direction of social and political awareness and commitment. First it is necessary to make overt the assumptions and insights drawn from the corpus of liberation theology, and to discuss some of the objections which might be made to them.

ASSUMPTIONS

The working assumptions to be adopted below from liberation theology, can be grouped under three headings. First, assumptions concerning the nature of reality and social existence; second, assumptions concerning theology; and, finally, assumptions concerning pastoral care.

Assumptions about the nature of reality and social existence

The most fundamental assumption to be made here is that the economic, social, and political dimensions of human existence are of primary importance. The social and political dimension of existence is primary; it is also an arena of conflict and inequality. Power, wealth, and privilege are differentially distributed to the advantage of some and the extreme disadvantage of others. It is possible to see social groups as comprising two main different classes composed basically of those who have and those who have not. The interests and needs of these classes are often in direct conflict with each other. There is direct relationship of dependence between the power and wealth of some and the disadvantage of others – it is not an accident, or fate, which decrees that this is so. It is possible to analyse the nature and causation of the material and ideological forces which sustain injustice and inequality in being with a view to bringing about fundamental change. This is an important task if appropriate socio-political action for liberation is to occur.[5]

Theological assumptions

One of the most basic theological assumptions to be adopted here is that the material, social, and political dimensions of existence are of fundamental theological concern. The social and political realm is the primary arena of divine concern and Christian response. Religion is not just personal, and there is no separate 'secular' political realm in which Christians have no part or interest. The political and material are of spiritual and theological concern. Working from this basic assumption, several others can be added. So, for example, sin must be regarded as a social and corporate matter which has to do with the erection and maintenance of oppressive and unequal social structures. God's concern is with this kind of disorder; it is not confined to the church or to the faithful. God's will to liberate people is universal; all sorts of people contribute to the progress of liberation salvation whereby people free themselves to develop their own potential and that of their fellows in community to the maximum. God is a God of justice who longs for social justice and makes a preferential option for the poor.

[5] These assumptions are basically Marxist in nature, though they are not labelled as such because, although liberation theologians have been heavily influenced by Marxist analytical techniques and assumptions, their relationship with Marxism is unclear. It is possible to hold Marxist-like assumptions like these without being a professed Marxist, and to envisage people arriving at them other than by reading Marx, especially in societies where gaps between rich and poor are so extreme that it is very difficult not to think in terms of there being two 'classes'. For the question of whether Marxist-like analysis fits advanced capitalist societies such as Britain see below.

They have a privileged and important place in understanding the will of God and in initiating the process of liberation. He works not by transcendent intervention from on high, but by human action for liberation from below. It is from the margins of society where the poor are confined that God breaks in to the present social order. He reveals himself in their liberating action. In this context salvation primarily means this-worldly deliverance from the powers of social and political oppression. It takes place in present history and is the human work of the poor and those who identify with their aspirations, responding to God's promises of hope. Historical liberation, as witnessed to in many parts of the Bible and Christian tradition, is the primary manifestation of salvation.

Ecclesiologically, the assumption is made that, while the church can be sign and symbol of God's liberating purposes and activity, it has no privileged position. As an organisation composed of human beings situated within a social context, it must be wary of its own complicity with forces of injustice and inequality. Similarly, the literary and historical resources of the church are relativised by the contemporary struggle of the poor for liberation. The church must pay attention to 'the Bible of the present' i.e., the social and political nature of reality, to situate itself alongside the poor in seeking radical social change. It must engage in praxis – detailed social and political analysis and action contributing to the liberation struggle. In this connection, orthopraxis is more important than orthodoxy – truth is discerned in liberating action which accords with the will of God, not in abstract, ahistorical theoretical reflection. Commitment to socio-political analysis and action is an integral part of theological method, not an optional extra.

Assumptions about pastoral care

The assumptions made about pastoral care hereafter flow from, and complement, the assumptions included under the previous two headings. The primary assumption to be made, therefore, is that the social and political realm of existence should be of primary concern in pastoral care theory and practice. Pastoral care should be aware of structures of injustice. Ministry has social and political implications. It is important to be aware of differences of power, wealth, status, and the identification of 'the poor' in any pastoral situation. It is necessary to analyse how pastoral practice fits in to the wider social order and the ways in which it challenges or affirms structures of injustice. It should be recognised that pastoral care has helped to make the poor invisible and been complicit in maintaining injustice. Pastoral care should be open to the voices of the powerless on the margins, recognise its own implicit and explicit biasses, and adopt a preferential option or bias towards the poor and marginalised with a view to helping them attain their own liberation. If fundamental social change is required to ameliorate a situation, then pastoral care must work towards this. It must commit itself to action and develop a prophetic, challenging dimension oriented towards social and political liberation against oppression. In all this, pastoral care needs to use the mediation of some of the insights and methods of the social and political sciences to understand the nature of the present human social context and appropriate social action for liberation.

METHODS

Following the liberation theologians themselves, I will use a broadly Marxist perspective in the sociological and political analysis of the context and practice of pastoral care which follows (stages c and d of the methodological spiral). As far as is possible, Marxist understandings and frameworks will be used to inform my analysis. It should be noted that the use of this organising perspective for analysis does not necessarily imply the acceptance of specifically Marxist social and political solutions. However, the Marxist perspective offers several advantages.

First, using this perspective preserves continuity with the type of social analysis used by the theologians of liberation. Secondly, commitment to a particular perspective allows greater analytic clarity. The Marxist perspective is especially useful in this connection because it is comprehensive, providing a structure for understanding the whole of society and human relations. Furthermore, it is overt and conscious of its own methodological presuppositions and biasses. This makes it both easier to use and to criticise than using a mixture of perspectives or using perspectives which are not overt about their concealed presuppositions (the liberation theologian Bonino writes: 'A neutral science of society does not exist.'[6]) Lastly, Marxist analysis is one of the most complete and effective tools of social investigation so far developed. In terms of trying to expose the nature of relationships in society, to expose where injustice and inequality lie, it may well have no equal. David Jenkins, bishop of Durham, writes:

Marxist diagnoses and intuitions about certain central features and forces of present social reality are the most appropriate, challenging and creative that are available to us . . . The Marxist critique seems to be the most powerful pointer to our sharpest present human contradictions and sources of inhumanity.[7]

And from a sociological viewpoint Bottomore defends the Marxist perspective on the grounds that,

no other general theory has shown anything like the same power to define and analyse significant problems in the development of societies, to formulate quasi-causal connections, and to provoke argument on fundamental theoretical issues.[8]

A Marxist, or materialist, approach to the kind of sociopolitical analysis to be undertaken below will allow us to relate an overall view of social functioning to the particular position of pastoral care in our society. But what is meant by the Marxist or materialist perspective?

Jenkins summarises the central features of the Marxist analytic perspective succinctly and well:

1 Members of all human societies (other than the most primitive) fall into two categories – the ruling class and subject class or classes.

6 Bonino, *Revolutionary Theology*, p. 34.
7 David Jenkins, *The Contradiction of Christianity*. London: SCM Press, 1976, p. 32.
8 Tom Bottomore, *Marxist Sociology*. London: Macmillan, 1975, p. 75.

2 The dominance of the ruling class is explained by their control of the means of economic production. This dominance is consolidated politically by the ruling class's control over military force and over the production of ideas.

3 The ruling class and the subject classes are in conflict. The developments in this conflict are influenced primarily by technological changes affecting the methods and means of production.

4 Modern capitalist societies make the class conflict clearer because they promote a polarization of wealth and power over against poverty and dependence.[9]

A Marxist perspective relates the entirety of the social and political phenomena and organisation of society to the material technological base of production. Social organisation is basically dependent upon the means of production and the relation of people to this.[10] At the heart of Marxist socio-political analysis lie the concepts of class and class conflict. Within capitalist society there are two main social classes. The relatively small capitalist class with its power elite is the dominant class. It is effective and cohesive and can be described as dominant because it has control (which may involve ownership) over the main means of economic activity, over the means of state administration and coercion, and over the means of communication and persuasion.[11] The working class of advanced capitalist countries is composed of the majority of people, those

whose main, and usually exclusive, *source of income*, is the sale of their labour power, or transfer payments by the state [e.g., welfare benefits], or both; whose *level of income* places them in the lower and lowest income groups; and whose individual *power* at work and in society at large is low or virtually non-existent.[12]

[9] Jenkins, *Contradiction of Christianity*, pp. 32–3.

[10] For more on the Marxist perspective see, for example, Schlomo Avineri, *The Social and Political Thought of Karl Marx*. Cambridge: Cambridge University Press, 1968; T. B. Bottomore and M. Rubel, *Karl Marx on Sociology and Social Philosophy*. Harmondsworth: Penguin, 1963; Ian Gough, *The Political Economy of the Welfare State*. London: Macmillan, 1979; G. Lichtheim, *Marxism*. London: Routledge and Kegan Paul, 1964; David McLellan, *The Thought of Karl Marx*. London: Macmillan, 1971.

[11] Ralph Miliband, *Divided Societies*. Oxford: Oxford University Press, 1989, p. 27.

[12] Miliband, *Divided Societies*, p. 23. Emphasis original. This definition encompasses a much wider group of people than traditional industrial workers.

There is a fundamental conflict of interests between these two classes because the dominant ruling and controlling class seeks to maximise the exploitation of the working class to increase capital, while the underclass resists this as best it may to seek its own good.

Stated thus baldly, these key Marxist ideas may sound crude and improbable. It is important, therefore, to add that Marxist social critics develop a very subtle and nuanced analysis from this basic starting point. So, for example, they acknowledge the plurality, diversity, and complexity of the main social classes. They do not see the dominance of the ruling class as being expressed in one monolithic, easily identified form or as using only one particular means. Nor is it assumed that the overall dominance of that class means that the working class has no power or influence in society (the class struggle is characterised by ongoing conflict and tension, not by the hidden and final defeat of the working class by the ruling class). The existence of intermediate classes such as small business owners (the 'petty bourgeoisie') is recognised. It is also acknowledged that ordinary people in capitalist society may not themselves perceive themselves to be class members and that conflicts of interest between the main classes may often be disguised or covert so far as most people are concerned.[13] None the less, there is a fundamental class struggle which revolves around, and illuminates fundamental issues of distribution of power, property, privilege, and position in capitalist societies characterised by structures of domination and exploitation. Miliband argues that 'class struggle has constituted the central fact of social life from the remote past to the present day'.[14]

The subject matter of class analysis is the nature of this struggle, the identity of the protagonists, the forms which the struggle assumes from one period to another and from one country to another, the reasons for the differences in these forms and the consequences which flow from these differences; and class analysis is also concerned with the ideological constructs under which the struggle is conducted, and with the ways in which class relations in general affect most if not all aspects of life.[15]

---

[13] See further, for example, Miliband, *Divided Societies*.
[14] Ibid., p. 3.   [15] Ibid., p. 3.

The Marxist perspective, which focusses on class struggle in all its many forms throughout the social order, usefully highlights issues of differential distribution, power, and conflict, as well as connections of dependency, socio-economic context and the place of ideology. It enables vigorous, sharp and demystifying analysis of social phenomena and institutions to take place over a wide range. However, this organising analytical perspective has its critics and problems. Some people have argued, before and especially since the collapse of communism in Eastern bloc countries, that Marxism is no longer relevant to the world. This objection can be countered by pointing out that communism as a social and political programme can be distinguished from the use of Marxist analytical techniques. Bottomore, for example claims:

Marx's conceptions were capable of giving rise in one direction to a broadly positivist sociology, and in another direction to a style of thought which has generally been referred to as 'critical philosophy'.[15]

A more serious objection is that modern advanced capitalist societies such as those of Britain and the USA really do not fall into the analytic categories which Marxism proposes. In particular, it is argued that the class structure of advanced societies is different and more complicated than that identified by Marx in the last century.[16] So, for example, while a century ago in Britain there was a large working class involved in wage labour in industrial concerns and a very small ruling or capitalist class, it is asserted that this major class division has been modified. There are now many social classes, including a large middle or managerial class and a class of people who have nothing directly to do with the means of production because they are unemployed (Marx would have identified this latter group as the *lumpenproletariat* who had no significant place in his social theory). Furthermore, it might be objected that the kind of radical class inequalities of wealth, status, and power which gave impetus to the Marxist notion of fundamental class

---

[16] Tom Bottomore, *Marxist Sociology*, p. 11.

[17] 'Classes ... are formed socially out of the division of labour. They make up more or less cohesive and socially conscious groups from those occupational groups and their families which share similar work and market situations' (A. H. Halsey, *Change in British Society*. Oxford: Oxford University Press, new edn. 1985, p. 28).

struggle have been considerably eroded over the course of the present century.

There is much debate about the nature and significance of class position for social theory. Analysts standing in the Weberian sociological tradition, for example, reject the idea that all social inequality can be explained by reference to direct relationship to the means of production and ownership thereof, i.e. by class. They argue that status and power are important independent variables in social structure and that these are not fundamentally dependent on social class, though they may be significantly related to it.

The debate about the nature, significance and putative centrality of class in analysis of contemporary society is a complex one, and cannot be discussed in detail here. However, there is a good deal of evidence to suggest that there is still a fundamental dichotomy of socio-economic interest in advanced capitalist societies. Convincing arguments can be advanced to show that there has been little real redistribution downwards of wealth and power over the last century.[18] Despite overall improved standards of living throughout society, it can still be maintained that there is a rift between classes. This manifests itself in great inequality in property, power, privilege and position. The rise of the middle class and embourgeoisement of the working class can be seen as misleading secondary phenomena disguising the continuing class divide.[19]

There are good *prima facie* grounds for maintaining that there are two main social classes whose material interests continue to be in opposition to each other, when a statement like the following from A. H. Halsey is considered:

In Britain now the richest 5 per cent still own 41 per cent of all marketable wealth. Income is less unequally distributed, but here again the richest 1 per cent take home about the same amount as the poorest 20 per cent.[20]

[18] See especially, John Westergaard and Henrietta Resler, *Class in a Capitalist Society*. London: Penguin, 1976.
[19] See further Miliband, *Divided Societies*; Tom Bottomore, *Classes in Modern Society*. London: George Allen and Unwin, 1965; Anthony Giddens, *The Class Structure of Advanced Societies*. London: Hutchinson, 1973; Halsey, *Change in Modern Britain*; Graham Room, *The Sociology of Welfare*. Oxford: Basil Blackwell, 1979.
[20] Halsey, *Change in British Society*, p. 38.

Halsey concludes his statement, made in 1985, with the comment, 'These are quite spectacular inequalities.' Since 1985, fundamental inequalities have increased so that more wealth is concentrated in the hands of the upper or ruling classes while the poor have actually become poorer, experiencing more unemployment and cuts in state benefits. Peter Townsend, an expert on poverty, claims that 1988 saw the greatest increase in inequality between rich and poor in British society for 200 years.[21] Another observer of British fiscal policy in the 1980s notes that of the total tax cut of £6 billion made in 1988 one-third went to the top 5 per cent of taxpayers and further claims that, 'Stripped of rationalization and rhetoric, the government's tax policies are part and parcel of a major programme of upward redistribution of income.'[22] Marxists like Miliband expect this gap and the centralisation of power and wealth to continue to increase in the next decade and beyond.[23]

There is, then, an important debate about whether or not materialist analyses based on the primacy of class relations are valid in Britain today. The debate remains unresolved, but at least allows the continuing possibility of this particular organising perspective being used in advanced capitalist societies. Marxist analyses of such societies which take class and material interest as fundamental categories continue to be instructive and fruitful in exposing power relationships and inequalities.[24]

A further objection brought against adopting a Marxist

---

[21] Peter Townsend, talk at conference on Poverty and Health, Birmingham, November 1990.

[22] Ramesh Mishra, *The Welfare State in Capitalist Society*. Hemel Hempstead: Harvester Wheatsheaf, 1990, p. 31.

[23] Miliband, *Divided Societies*.

[24] Gooby-Taylor and Dale argue that 'materialist methods offer the most useful theories of the welfare state advanced to date (Peter Gooby-Taylor and Jennifer Dale, *Social Theory and Social Welfare*. London: Arnold, 1981, pp. 121–2). 'Marxism appears to us to offer the most fruitful approach because it makes it possible to unite an account of social structure resting on the notion of mode of production with an account of human action resting on a theory of ideology' (ibid., p. 127). Interesting examples of the Marxist analytic approach to welfare and social analysis can be found in, for example, Gough, *The Political Economy of the Welfare State* (Gough argues that materialist analysis permits an integrated approach to the social sciences which have become compartmentalised over the last century); Chris Phillipson, *Capitalism and the Construction of Old Age*. London: Macmillan, 1982; Peter Leonard, *Personality and Ideology*. London: Macmillan, 1984.

position in social analysis is that it is 'gender blind'.[25] Classical
Marxist social theory has failed to take note of the particular
situation of women in society and their relationship to the
means of reproduction as well as to those of production, contributing thereby to the invisibility of women and to their oppression in patriarchal society by subsuming them under general
class analysis. This is resisted by feminists who assert that the
primary oppression experienced by women is caused by patriarchy, not just by capitalism, and who therefore call for a
revision of Marxist analysis. Gender relationships must be
analysed, as well as those of class, they assert. This is an
important criticism, as is the perception that Marxist analysis
has been largely blind to issues of racial oppression. It will be
important in the analysis which follows to remain aware of this
feminist critique within the general Marxist perspective.[26] In
general I accept as a working hypothesis Miliband's assertion
that class position is primary for understanding oppression.
Race and gender are important dimensions of stratification,
but they cannot be separated from class location. Women and
people of colour may be super-exploited and super-oppressed
groups within the working class, but generally they still share
the interests of that class.[27]

The final problem with using an overarching Marxist perspective is that not very much of the relevant research on the
socio-political situation of mentally ill people or women adopts
this perspective. While some kinds of research, for example, on
the relationship between social class and mental disorder, is
fairly easily assimilable within a Marxist framework, other
kinds, for example, on the relationships between professionals
and individuals are not easily compatible in this way. The
Marxist perspective is a macrosocio-political one: the closer

[25] Jennifer Dale and Peggy Foster, *Feminists and State Welfare*. London: Routledge and
Kegan Paul, 1986, p. 54.
[26] For discussion of the relationship between Marxist and feminist perspectives see
Dale and Foster, *Feminists and State Welfare*, ch. 3; Alison Jaggar, *Feminist Politics and
Human Nature*. Totowa, NJ: Rowman and Allanheld, 1983; Miliband, *Divided
Societies*, ch. 4; Fiona Williams, *Social Policy: A Critical Introduction*. Cambridge: Polity
Press, 1989.
[27] Miliband, *Divided Societies*, pp. 100ff.

one gets to local situations and individuals, the less easy it is to integrate insights into the larger whole. It must be acknowledged that, in situating many different kinds of social and political research within a Marxist framework, there is a real danger of distorting or warping their original methods and intentions. It is important not to violate the integrity of a particular approach by forcing it willy nilly into a Marxist mould. However, it seems legitimate, wherever possible, to draw out the implications of any research findings for a Marxist perspective of the topic under consideration. In the analyses which follow of the socio-political context of pastoral situations, close attention will be paid to trying to extrapolate and underline factors which bear upon class, class conflict, power, exploitation, inequality, and ideology.

Despite the very significant problems involved in using a Marxist analytical perspective to examine the socio-political context of pastoral situations, this perspective will be adopted here. Marxist approaches to social analysis are biased and one-sided, a way of not seeing, as well as a way of seeing. However, they provide a methodologically self-aware way of proceeding which can highlight in a very clear way some of the main concerns of this book – injustice, inequality, conflict, domination, exploitation, etc. This is a corrective to, for example, psychoanalytic perspectives on the pastoral situation which largely fail to recognise these elements. I will assume hereafter that society is divided into two main classes whose relationships and interests are determined by their position in relation to the means of production; that status and power are distributed unequally broadly according to people's position in the class structure; that there is a conflict of interests between the two main classes in society; that all social relationships and institutions reflect this class conflict and are biased in favour of those who have social and economic power, i.e. the ruling and upper classes who own and control the means of wealth production in late capitalist society.

OBJECTIONS AND PROBLEMS

Consideration of the problems of using a Marxist socio-political perspective in analysing the context of pastoral situations brings me to looking at some of the problems in relation to working towards a socio-politically aware and committed pastoral practice inspired by a hermeneutic conversation with liberation theology.

One area of legitimate concern which might be raised is to do with the differences between Latin American society and our own. In Latin America most people are of a peasant class, live in absolute poverty, and are clearly oppressed. In the UK, however, there is a higher standard of living for everyone, most people live in cities having very little to do with the land or agriculture, very poor people are a minority, not many people live in absolute poverty, and class conflicts are much less clear and sharp in a pluralistic democratic system. This poses questions like, are there really oppressed people in Britain? and, is it appropriate to use the prism of socio-political analysis in the UK as opposed to using it in the very different cultural and economic situation of Latin America?

The answer to the latter question specifically is implicit in what follows: only as a Marxist oriented social and political analysis of the context of pastoral care unfolds will it be possible to judge whether this kind of activity is useful and appropriate. The former point, however, deserves more attention. A common and comforting assumption which is often made in advanced capitalist systems is that wealth, equality, and dignity are being more evenly distributed. Everyone is getting richer, therefore there is no real socio-economic oppression, as there might be in Latin America.

Actually, this is not the case. Although few people are in conditions of absolute poverty, many are very poor and 'have a standard of living so low that it excludes people from the community in which they live'.[28] About 13 million Britons (around 24 per cent of the total population) lived on or below

---

[28] David Donnison, *The Politics of Poverty*. Oxford: Martin Robertson, 1982, p. 7

the Government's very low poverty line in 1987.[29] Further-more, the gap between rich and poor seems to be growing rather than diminishing: 'Between 1979 and 1987 the poorest tenth of the population saw their incomes rise by just 0.1% in real terms (after housing costs) while the average rose by 23%.'[30] Amongst the poor are unemployed, elderly, and disabled people, as well as sick people and those from ethnic minorities.[31] Relative material deprivation is accompanied by lack of opportunity, hardship, ill health, poor housing, and sheer human misery. While it may be that oppression and hardship in advanced capitalist societies is not constellated in the same way as it is in Latin America, it cannot be argued that there are no oppressed or marginalised groups, or that they are just a tiny minority. We have our own poor and oppressed people with us always; as we shall see, many men-tally ill people come from the poorest and most oppressed social classes.

From a distinctively religious, theological point of view a number of concerns might be expressed. First, conducting a socio-political analysis of the situation of mentally ill people using the tools of the 'secular' human and behavioural sciences does not seem to have much to do with theology or church life. However, it should be recalled that this stage of social and political analysis actually forms part of a *theological* method derived from liberation theology. Theology and the church have no tools available to them for understanding the present social and political context other than those provided by disci-plines like sociology. The end towards which this apparently secular activity is directed is to understand the text of the present for theological and pastoral reasons.

Some Christians might have reservations about using a Marxist analytical perspective in this social analysis, on the grounds that Marxism has historically been seen as inimical to the practice of religion. It is true that Marx saw religion as a sign of human alienation and oppression which would eventu-ally wither away with the advent of the communist utopia. In

---

[29] Oppenheim, *Poverty*, p. 19.   [30] Oppenheim, *Poverty*, p. 19.
[31] See further Robert Holman, *Poverty*. Oxford: Martin Robertson, 1978, pp. 28ff.

this sense Marxism is indeed hostile to religion.[32] In the present context, however, the Marxist perspective is only used as a descriptive analytical tool of wider social reality. Its anti-religious prescriptive programme is being put to one side, as it is by the liberation theologians.[33]

Another aspect of the liberationist project which might cause anxiety is the choice of a conflictual, class-based model for understanding society. Reconciliation, unity, and peace-making have been important themes in Christianity from the earliest times. It may seem arbitrary, even faithless, to adopt a conflictual model of human social relations. However, it is no part of the Christian tradition to actively ignore conflict if it actually exists. Reconciliation is a more demanding and com-plicated matter than simply pretending that conflicts do not happen. The point is to face conflict and recognise its causes with a view to effecting just reconciliation. It is perhaps useful to recall the prophetic tradition of the Old Testament which condemns the glossing over of conflicts and injustices, pro-claiming woe on those who cry 'Peace! Peace!' when there is no peace (cf. Jeremiah 6. 14.).[34]

There are similar and more practical problems associated with the conflictual perspective on social relations when we come to the nature of the church and its bias towards the oppressed. Christians often think of the church community as being a place which should be available to, and accepting of, all people, irrespective of their background or social status. The sociological identification of the oppressed matched with the call to actively side with them may seem an unacceptable position. It is important to remember, however, that for all its

---

[32] For the relationship between Marxism and Christianity see Nicholas Lash, *A Matter of Hope*. London: Darton Longman and Todd, 1981; Jan Milic Lochman, *Encounter-ing Marx*. Belfast: Christian Journals Limited, 1977.

[33] This is problematical for some critics: Kee believes that liberation theology is wrong to use Marxism as a critical tool for understanding wider society while not applying its insights to the church. Liberation theology ignores its more radical responsibili-ties and implications, failing to use Marxism in a way which respects its integrity. See Kee, *Marx and Failure*.

[34] For discussion of just reconciliation versus unjust conciliation and of the need to recognise conflict see, for example, J. G. Davies, *Christians, Politics and Violent Revolution*. London: SCM Press, 1976.

rhetoric of inclusion, socio-political neutrality and universal acceptance, the institutional church has often been perceived by the poor and oppressed as being actively on the side of the rich and influential. Perhaps it is time to try and actively redress this balance. It is certainly appropriate to try to see the place and position of the church from the perspective of those who have hitherto felt alienated and excluded by it.

Turning to the perspective of pastoral carers in particular, there may be concern that all this talk of socio-political analysis, Marxist perspectives and methodological spirals seems a long way from the everyday practice of pastoral care. Much pastoral care is devoted to the healing, guiding, sustaining, reconciling, and nurturing of individuals. It might be felt that more focus on the essential nature of individual pastoral encounters would be more relevant than the kind of complex social and political analysis proposed here. This book is directed towards extending the contextual awareness and perspectives used in pastoral care beyond a focus on individuals. Sin, sorrow, and well-being do not start or end with individual people.[35] If pastoral care is to promote human well-being and growth, it must be prepared to take a broader view on its activities.

A reading of liberation theology has suggested that it is necessary to apply the tools and analyses of socio-political suspicion to pastoral care. Following the methodological spiral outlined above it is now time to turn centrally to examples of pastoral care to ask what socio-political factors bear upon them, and how, basically from a Marxist perspective. The main example to be considered in this book is pastoral care with mentally ill people. In the next few chapters, an analysis of socio-political factors bearing upon the situation of mentally ill people is examined.

---

[35] For discussion of the pastoral care's focus see Pattison *Critique*, especially chs. 1 and 5.

PART II

The socio-political context of pastoral care

CHAPTER 5

The socio-political context of mental disorder

> Some student of human society has observed that one half
> of mankind [*sic*] does not know how the other half lives.[1]

Mental disorder, mental illness, madness, insanity, lunacy, or
whatever you care to call it, is not uncommon in our society
but few people give it much attention. Although 11 per cent of
men and 17 per cent of women are diagnosed as being ill
enough to be hospitalised at some point during their lives,
mental disorder and mentally disordered people occupy little
space in the interests of most of us. Often it is as if they were
actually invisible. Most of us will have family or friends who
have had some kind of severe mental disorder at some time, yet
we probably devote little attention to this subject.

If we think about mental disorder at all, we probably regard
it as a disease of the mind. It is a personal misfortune afflicting
unfortunate individuals like any other disease. With any luck,
they will receive appropriate medical treatment from well-
intentioned doctors who will do their best to cure disorder with
basically physical remedies. Of course, we know that the hospital and community facilities in which mentally ill people are
treated and accommodated are not as good as they might be,
but then what part of the National Health Service does offer
ideal conditions? On the whole, therefore, mentally disordered
people do not fare too badly, getting quite a lot of the sort of
help they need. And perhaps we should be glad that they are
getting this help at all.

---

[1] 'Warmark', *Guilty but Insane*. London: Chapman and Hall, 1931, quoted in Roy
Porter, ed., *The Faber Book of Madness*. London: Faber and Faber, 1991, p. 1.

The caricature view expressed in the last paragraph will be problematised in this part of the book by a socio-political analysis of the context of mental disorder. Using the social scientific insights and methods related to the basic Marxist analytic perspective it will be shown that social and political factors impinge on what is called mental illness to a very significant extent. This analysis exposes the situation of mentally ill people as being broadly one of injustice, exploitation, powerlessness, and oppression in society as a whole, and within the various contexts in which they are 'cared' for. Those regarded as mentally disordered (a substantial, if often unnoticed, minority in the population) can be seen as the poor in our society. They should be regarded as among the poorest of the poor. It will further be seen that this situation is integrally linked to the nature and structure of our society. There are links between the social order and the situation of mentally ill people today. Mental disorder is not an arbitrary personal affliction. The context and care which surround it are also integrally linked to wider social factors.

The analysis to be undertaken considers the following main topics:

(a) Who comes to be mentally ill in our society?
(b) What socio-political factors bear upon mentally ill people who are hospitalised?
(c) What socio-political factors are relevant to the situation of mentally ill people who are discharged into or continue to live in community settings, now the preferred place for looking after them?

I will first outline some key topics and concepts, looking briefly at the place of the state in Marxist thought (including the place of welfare services within it), and then at the concept and nature of social control as it applies to welfare, and especially psychiatric, services.[2]

---

[2] See further Richard Warner, *Recovery from Schizophrenia: Psychiatry and Political Economy*. London: Routledge and Kegan Paul, 1985, p. 7.

MARXIST ANALYSIS, THE STATE AND WELFARE

The lives of everyone, including those who are mentally disordered, in Western capitalist democracies are lived in, and intimately affected by, the undergirding social order shaped by the state (which is in turn fundamentally shaped by the historical material circumstances of capitalism). Furthermore, the source and locus of care for many mentally disordered people is the various welfare services provided by the state. The critique of the socio-political situation within which pastoral care of mentally ill people occurs therefore starts by outlining a broadly Marxist view of the state and the implications of this for welfare services provided by it.

Within a historical–materialist perspective, the social order and all social institutions are shaped and influenced by the fundamental conflict of interests between the capitalist and working classes. This is determined by the historical and material relationship of these classes to the means of production. The state, the most important single social institution in advanced capitalist society, reflects an ongoing tension between serving the interests and needs of the capitalist class and those of the working class.

The very existence of an identified dominant class implies that the state is likely to reflect and maintain the interests of the owners and controllers of capital. Some Marxists argue that the state is essentially the capitalist class in government pursuing the interests of that class alone (Marx and Engels saw the state as an idealised illusion which glossed over the class divisions of capitalist society and acted as 'a committee for managing the common affairs of the whole bourgeoisie'.[3]) A more moderate view, however, accords the state some relative autonomy and power: the state can act independently of the capitalist class and sometimes against its immediate interests (thus, it can sometimes serve the interests and needs of the working class).

This more 'liberal' Marxist view, exemplified in the work of

---

[3] Marx and Engels, *Manifesto of the the Communist Party*, p. 37.

thinkers like Miliband, should not be allowed to obscure the fact that basically the state serves as promoter and protector of the interests of capital. Miliband argues that the governments of most advanced capitalist countries

have mostly been composed of men who beyond all their differences and diversities have at least had in common a basic and usually explicit belief in the validity and virtues of the capitalist system ... and ... have ... shared a quite basic and unswerving hostility to any socialist alternative to that system.[4]

There is an effective partnership between corporate capitalist power and state power based on common interest. This is embodied in ideological, economic, personal, and other ties between these entities. Members of the dominant corporate class in the private sector and the power elite in the state share background, interests, etc. in common, and enjoy access to power in a similar way.[5] They do not wish to see fundamental changes in the present social order.

In the interests of capital, the state enforces the structure of the social order. It also defends that order from internal and external threats (by force if necessary), and helps to legitimise it by the appearance of democratic equality between citizens. The state regulates and curbs some of the worst excesses of capitalist practice, thus ensuring its continuing viability. Most important for present purposes, the state formulates and implements social policy. Social policy includes all aspects of national economic life, regulatory functions in relation to capital, and the determination, provision, and administration of welfare and human services.[6] Key amongst welfare functions are employment policies, universal services for meeting basic needs, and measures for preventing and relieving poverty. Specific functions include the provision of housing, health care, education, employment and training.

In all these areas of welfare provision, Marxist critics argue,

[4] Ralph Miliband, *The State in Capitalist Society*. London: Quartet, 1973, p. 65.
[5] See further, for example, Miliband, *Divided Societies*, ch. 2. 'The ascent of British man', *The Economist* 325; 7790, 1992, 21–2, records that 66 per cent of holders of the top 100 jobs in Britain went to public schools, 54 per cent were Oxbridge graduates, and 96 per cent were men.
[6] Miliband, *Divided Societies*, p. 131ff.

one will find the underlying tectonics of class conflict and class interest reflecting the wider class struggle. On the one hand, the state uses welfare provision as an instrument of containment and control, seeking to limit, contain, and 'buy off' working class pressure and discontent, and to nurture conformity to the values and practices of capitalism. Social welfare and legislation is used to 'protect the system of class relations existing at any one time'.[7] It represents part of the price that capital pays for continuing domination and legitimacy. Capital tries to pay the minimum for this, so there is pressure on the state to cut down on, or minimise, welfare provision. On the other hand, welfare provision reflects some of the interests and needs of the working class whose demands have been (unwillingly) responded to by the state. Its existence can give limited, but valuable, benefits to working people in the form of universal health and education services. Thus,

the welfare state exhibits positive and negative features within a contradictory unity ... It simultaneously embodies tendencies to enhance social welfare, to develop the powers of individuals, to exert control over the blind play of market forces; and tendencies to repress and control people, to adapt them to the requirements of the capitalist economy.[8]

The Marxist approach to the contradictions, ambiguities, and conflicts within the state and state welfare provision, dominated by the economic and political interests of capital and the ruling class, can be historically exemplified. The infamous Poor Law Amendment Act of 1834 which forced people to suffer institutional confinement in workhouses, unless they supported themselves by selling their labour, can be regarded as a measure to ensure a plentiful supply of cheap labour to industry which directly benefitted the capitalist class. The advent of national insurance and state-supported health services at the beginning of this century, can be seen as a way of responding positively to working-class discontent, and to the needs of capital for a healthy work- and fighting force. The cuts

[7] Vic George and Paul Wilding, *Ideology and Social Welfare*. London: Routledge and Kegan Paul, 1976, p. 91.
[8] Gough, *The Political Economy of the Welfare State*, pp. 11–12.

in state welfare provision in the 1980s can be read as a clear attempt to restore wealth to the dominant class during a time of recession, when working class power is diminished by fragmentation and high unemployment.[9]

It is within this overall perspective on the state and the Welfare State that a socio-political analysis of the situation and care of people perceived to be mentally disordered must be situated. It is within this perspective, too, that the concept and function of social control, which forms an important focussing prism for analysing the situation of this group of people, must be considered.

SOCIAL CONTROL

Social control is 'the means by which society secures adherence to social norms; specifically, how it minimizes, eliminates or normalizes deviant behavior'.[10] For any society to function efficiently, its members need to share common values and behave in socially approved, useful ways. If people fail to conform, social life and enterprise are jeopardised. Societies therefore evolve implicit or explicit means of exacting a reasonable degree of conformity.

One way of doing this is by positively rewarding conformity with power, wealth, prestige, and praise; but it is also possible to extract it by physical coercion (for example, punishment by death, forcible confinement), or the threat of it. A subtle, widespread means, which is more difficult to detect, is to use a range of ideological, medical, and welfare means which may be presented as 'care' to ensure desirable behaviour and attitudes amongst the population. 'Social control' is a much disputed concept, but in the present context it is used to include and

---

[9] For more on these examples see Derek Fraser, *The Evolution of the British Welfare State*. London: Macmillan, 1973; J. Saville, 'The welfare state – an historical approach' in M. Fitzgerald, P. Halmos, J. Muncie and D. Zeldin, eds., *Welfare in Action*. London: Routledge and Kegan Paul, 1977; Vicente Navarro, *Class Struggle, the State and Medicine*. London: Martin Robertson, 1978; Mishra, *Welfare State in Capitalist Society*.

[10] Peter Conrad and Joseph W. Schneider, *Deviance and Medicalization*. St Louis: Mosby, 1980, p. 7.

examine all these mechanisms of encouraging, inducing, or maintaining conformity.[11]

Social control is a part of any society. However, in a capitalist society, with its unequal distribution of power, the norms and values that are affirmed and the sanctions which are used are basically congruent with the norms of the market economy. Amongst the deviants who are identified in this kind of social order are those who do not contribute to, or who disturb or protest against, the economic order. Such persons might be designated mad (i.e. ill, thus needing help or care) or bad (i.e. wilfully disruptive, thus needing punishment). According to the category of designation chosen, they might receive the attentions of the health care system or of the criminal justice system. Those who work in these systems can be seen as society's agents of social control and 'gate-keepers' of different kinds of means used to exercise it. Thus, sociologists have suggested that medicine in general, and psychiatry in particular, can appropriately be regarded as part of the means of social control in its caring or therapeutic aspect which is designed to constrain, eliminate, or rectify a particular kind of undesirable behaviour.

There is a radical critique of medicine's role in social control. Rather than seeing it as a morally neutral, benevolent, scientific pursuit it can be regarded as a value laden part of the social control apparatus which implicitly promotes the interests of the dominant social order in its theories and actions. Zola notes,

Medicine is becoming a major institution of social control, nudging aside, if not incorporating, the more traditional institutions of religion and law. It is becoming the new repository of truth, the place where absolute and often final judgements are made by supposedly morally neutral and objective experts. And these judgements are made, not in the name of virtue or legitimacy, but in the name of health.[12]

---

[11] For discussion of uses of this concept see, for example, Stanley Cohen and Andrew Scull, eds., *Social Control and the State*. Oxford: Blackwell, 1983; C. Ken Watkins, *Social Control*. London: Longman, 1975.

[12] Irving K. Zola, 'Medicine as an institution of social control' in John Ehrenreich, ed., *The Cultural Crisis of Modern Medicine*. New York: Monthly Review Press, 1978, p. 80.

The 'medicalisation' of many aspects of life, and the permission granted to allow a particular group in society to define and treat a specific group of deviants, is directly related to the socio-political context and order. What proper deviance control is, and who the appropriate control agents should be, are essentially political questions which need the tacit assent or even formal legislative permission of the state. Thus it can be argued that 'Medical designations are social judgments, and the adoption of the medical model of behaviour [is] a political decision.'[13] With its technology, collaboration with other social control agencies, and its ideology which conceptualises deviance in medical terms, medicine has been called, 'the most powerful extralegal institution of social control in our society'.[14]

Although what we now regard as mental illness has often presented a direct social control problem historically, it was not always regarded as mainly the province of medicine and doctors. For many centuries, mental disorder was regarded as primarily a theological problem. In the nineteenth century, it became mainly a legal one.[15] So, what are the advantages of regarding perceived socially disruptive or non-conforming behaviour as 'mental illness' and 'treating' it by medical means within the contemporary social order?

There are some advantages to the individual designated as ill. She is not perceived as malicious, blameworthy, responsible for her own situation, or eligible for punishment. She is given help by prestigious medical professionals who will aim to restore her to a position of usefulness and respect in the community. On the other hand, there may be several disadvantages. These might include a lack of meaning in her 'illness', a failure to place it within a wider framework of cause and effect, a difficulty in refusing offers of 'help' due to wider social pressure and expectations (help or care is much more

---

[13] Conrad and Scheider, *Deviance and Medicalization*, p. 35.   [14] Ibid., p. 241.
[15] See further, for example, Andrew T. Scull, *Museums of Madness*. London: Allen Lane, 1979, especially chs. 4 and 5; Kathleen Jones, *A History of the Mental Health Services*. London: Routledge and Kegan Paul, 1972; Roy Porter, *A Social History of Insanity*. London: Weidenfield and Nicholson, 1987; *Mind Forg'd Manacles*. London: Athlone Press, 1987.

difficult to evade than punishment or control), and the diminishment of social rights and expectations (sick people are relieved of such responsibilities as work in society, but they are accorded a sub-adult status and are frequently deprived of various rights and of influence).[16]

Perhaps most significantly of all, mental illness is notoriously vague as a concept, and its scope can be vast (consider the fact that homosexuality, masturbation, and pregnancy outside wedlock have all been regarded as symptoms of mental illness in the past). It may be relatively easy for someone to be diagnosed as mentally ill, but it can then be very difficult to shake off the consequences and stigma of this diagnosis. To be confined to prison a person must be found guilty of an offence in a public court of law. A prison term is of defined length and, when completed a person can return to society. Within the parameters of psychiatry, however, it can be very easy to be diagnosed as mentally ill, to be confined against one's will for an indeterminate period of time, and then to live with the stigma of mental disorder for the rest of one's life; all this without the benefit of public trial or much protection from the law. These points can be illustrated by a fictional example which is drawn from aspects of real life:

Mr X was a disruptive adolescent and was taken by his parents to see what he thought was a career guidance worker. It turned out, to his surprise, that this person was a psychiatrist. X was told that he had a serious psychotic illness; to his horror and against his will, he was hospitalised in a large old hospital some distance from his home for a few months. He had to stay there because the doctor had legally detained him. He did not know how long this would be for. When he got out of hospital after nearly a year he tried to pick up the threads of his life, applying for teacher training. Although he had the right qualifications for entry, his application was turned down because the college medical officer thought he would not be able to manage the course as a result of his mental condition. Now, twenty years later, and with no recurrence of the 'illness' which took him into hospital in the first place, X believes his life was ruined by this early event. He is unemployed and feels that employers do not consider his applications

---

[16] Cf. Conrad and Schneider, *Deviance and Medicalization*, pp. 246ff; Thomas S. Szasz, *Law, Liberty and Psychiatry*. London: Routledge and Kegan Paul, 1974.

seriously because of his supposed history of mental illness. The irony is that another psychiatrist told him recently that his initial diagnosis must have been incorrect as he would not now be in a suitable condition to even apply for jobs if the first diagnosis was accurate. X has tried to get his records changed in the hope of expunging the stigma of mental illness from his life. His efforts to do this have been unsuccessful. For him, what was intended as a helpful intervention has been massively destructive.

The medical model of social control for mentally disordered people has several advantages to the state in capitalist society. A powerful control method can be exerted over people who do not conform to the social order, but who refuse to break the law. It provides a broad catch-all category for deviance identification and control. It allows the state to present itself as benevolent and caring in its provision of services rather than coercive and controlling. At the same time, radical treatment procedures can be used on mentally ill people which could not be used on other groups, such as prisoners without grave public concern (Electro-Convulsive Treatment (ECT) is one example of this). The concept of illness presupposes that unorthodox and undesirable behaviour originates within the physiology of the individual, thus drawing attention away from any social causes, values, or meanings, for example, those of poverty and protest, which might be attached to that behaviour; pathology is thus individualised and privatised. The state can form an alliance with a powerful upper class group deemed to be scientific, professional, and neutral i.e. doctors, giving them enormous power, and deriving legitimacy in its dealings with deviants while confident that such people are unlikely to challenge the social order in their modes of operation and treatment. Last, but not least, the use of medical techniques such as drugs to treat mental illness can help to support a flourishing and highly profitable private pharmaceutical industry.[17] Conrad and Schneider write: 'defining deviance as disease allows behaviour to retain its negative judgement, but

---

[17] See further Lucy Johnstone, *Users and Abusers of Psychiatry*. London: Routledge, 1989, ch. 9.

medical language veils the political and moral nature of this decision in the guise of scientific fact.'[18]

Of course, there are costs or disadvantages to the state in supporting a medical model of mental disorder. It must try to be seen to care for ill people, and it must be prepared to absorb pressure from health care workers seeking more funds and resources. However, because of the relative weakness and small size of the 'mental illness' constituency, these pressures are relatively insignificant. They can be largely resisted or managed, as will be seen below.

The medical model of mental disorder can be defined thus:

In the narrowest version (sometimes also called the 'disease model') it is assumed that the origins of the problem in question lie in some process inside the individual – an 'illness' or 'disease' – which, although it may be initiated by external or genetic causes, can be regarded as autonomous once it is in existence. In the broadest sense, the 'medical model' may be taken to include any approach that defines the locus of the problem as within the individual.[19]

In contemporary capitalist society it gives a basis for effective and far-reaching social control within and beyond the law. This appears benevolent and morally neutral to many of its recipients and to the citizenry in general, while it remains consonant with the fundamental values and structures of the capitalist social order. With its emphasis on individual rather than class, cure rather than prevention, and disease rather than social structure, the medical model aids and abets the cohesion of the prevalent social order as it is, ignoring for the most part its injustices, class conflicts, and pathogenic effects.[20]

This kind of understanding informs the views of the Marxist

[18] Conrad and Schneider, *Deviance and Medicalization*, p. 249.
[19] David Ingleby, 'Sanity, madness and the welfare state' in Michael Wadsworth and David Robinson, eds., *Studies in Everyday Medical Life*. London: Martin Robertson, 1976.
[20] For political and social control aspects of the medical model in capitalist society see, for example, Lesley Doyal, *The Political Economy of Health*. London: Pluto, 1979, ch. 1; Johnstone, *Users and Abusers of Psychiatry*; Peter Sedgwick, *PsychoPolitics*. London: Pluto, 1982, ch. 1; Howard B. Waitzkin and Barbara Waterman, *The Exploitation of Illness in Capitalist Society*. Indianapolis: Bobbs-Merrill, 1974; Howard Waitzkin, *The Politics of Medical Encounters*. New Haven: Yale University Press, 1991.

psychologist David Hill. Hill argues that there is little or no scientific basis for diagnostic constructs used in psychiatry, that there is a substantial component of social and political bias in the identification and diagnosis of mental illness, and that such diagnoses are used to justify the use of violent and punitive action against those identified as mentally ill. Hill writes ascerbically

The diagnosis 'schizophrenia' is used to discharge people from society; people who are contributing nothing to the continuation of the official version of reality as determined by the dehumanizing values of our competitive society, who are unusable, not worth their economic salt.[21]

The process whereby mentally ill people are identified and treated by psychiatrists is summarised thus:

Having grouped certain unusual behaviors and called them 'symptoms', having exaggerated their unusualness with the concept of abnormality and by ignoring their social context, and having denied the responsibility of the individuals concerned by calling them 'sick', one is free to indulge in the fourth component of the process [of social control by psychiatry], the actual control of unwanted behaviors. In this particular version of the social control process, this final step is called 'treatment'.[22]

Having problematised and put in socio-political context the Welfare State and the medical model of mental illness, questioning the view that they are neutral and unequivocally benevolent, this analysis can be extended to ask who comes to be regarded as mentally ill in our society, and what happens to them as they pass through (or fail to pass through) the various services offered by the welfare state? I will continue to suggest that the factors affecting the diagnosis, care, and situation of mentally ill people within and outside the structures of the Welfare State are profoundly influenced and shaped by the socio-economic practices, values, and assumptions associated with the present capitalist social order.

---

[21] David Hill, *The Politics of Schizophrenia*. Lanham, MD: University Press of America, 1983, p. 226.
[22] Hill, *The Politics of Schizophrenia*, p. 134.

All social problems are products of a process of definition. Social policies are the product of legislation. An understanding of who does the defining, of what is defined, as well as who shapes legislation and in what ways is, clearly, crucial to the student of the welfare state.[23]

[23] George and Wilding, *Ideology and Social Welfare*, p. 2.

CHAPTER 6

Who becomes mentally ill?

Asking the question, 'Who becomes mentally ill?' in the present context begs a second question: 'What is mental illness?'

There are many ways of regarding the nature and causes of mental disorder. Radical libertarian critics believe that there is no such thing as mental illness, only problems of personal unhappiness and culpable deviant behaviour.[1] Laing suggested that the symptoms of mental disorder are a language of protest against intolerable familial pressures.[2] Psychoanalysts find the causes of mental affliction in conflicting emotions engendered during childhood, while some behaviourist psychologists suggest that the basis of what we regard as mental illness is learned dysfunctional behaviour. Meanwhile, sociologists have argued that mental illness is a function of social definition or labelling ('illness is in the eye of the beholder') and the medically trained psychiatrists who dominate the treatment services are content to see it as having basically physical origins and a somatic form like any other disease.[3]

I have discussed the nature and implications of some of these

---

[1] Thomas S. Szasz, *The Myth of Mental Illness*. St Albans: Granada, 1972.

[2] R. D. Laing and A. Esterson, *Sanity, Madness and the Family*. Harmondsworth: Penguin, 1964.

[3] For labelling theory see Thomas J. Scheff, *Being Mentally Ill*. Chicago: Aldine, 1972. For accounts of the medical model of mental disorder see R. E. Kendell, *The Role of Diagnosis in Psychiatry*. Oxford: Basil Blackwell, 1975; John K. Wing, *Reasoning About Madness*. Oxford: Oxford University Press, 1978. For critical reviews of basic models of mental disorder see Anthony Clare, *Psychiatry in Dissent*. London: Tavistock, second edn., 1980; Miriam Siegler and Humphrey Osmond, *Models of Madness, Models of Medicine*. New York: Macmillan, 1974; Peter Tyrer and Derek Steinberg, *Models for Mental Disorder*. Chichester: John Wiley, 1987. For a radical critique see Sedgwick, *PsychoPolitics*.

viewpoints (and others) elsewhere.[4] They all have important social and political implications, and I shall return to the sociological and medical models of mental disorder in particular at various points below. Controversy continues about the nature of what is called mental illness. Here I shall remain formally agnostic about the inner or 'real' nature and causes of this phenomenon (I accept Ingleby's assertion that, 'The most we can say about the condition itself ... is that it consists of experiences or behaviour deemed undesirable and incapable of being understood within the common-sense framework of accountability (that is, as the products of a responsible agent)').[5] This need not impede the analysis of the socio-political factors surrounding the incidence, prevalence, treatment procedures and outcomes of what is designated mental illness, which is the main purpose of this part of the analysis.

From an epidemiological point of view there is a very simple, clear answer to the question, 'Who becomes mentally ill in our society?' It is members of the lower social classes who are disproportionately likely to experience mental disorder of some kind or to be diagnosed as mentally ill. Although rates of mental disorder between men and women differ considerably, with women forming the majority of those diagnosed mentally ill and seeming to have higher rates of depression, eating disorders, anxiety, and phobias, a very large number of studies conducted from many theoretical orientations point to the inverse class distribution of mental disorder generally.[6] As with many other illnesses, the lower down society you are, it seems, the more likely you are to experience and/or to be diagnosed as mentally ill.[7]

---

[4] Stephen Pattison, *Alive and Kicking: Towards a Practical Theology of Illness and Healing*. London: SCM Press, 1989, ch. 5.

[5] David Ingleby, 'Mental health and social order' in Cohen and Scull, eds., *Social Control and the State*, p. 162.

[6] For a discussion of the difference between rates of mental disorder between men and women see Jane Ussher, *Women's Madness*. Hemel Hempstead: Harvester Wheatsheaf, 1991, pp. 162ff.

[7] For the inverse distribution of illness and social class see D. Black, J. Morris, C. Smith et al., *Inequalities in Health*. London: Penguin, 1988.

This unpalatable finding can be difficult for some people to accept:

The idea that stratification in our society has any bearing on the diagnosis and treatment of disease runs counter to our cherished beliefs about equality, especially when they are applied to the care of the sick.[8]

When I first started researching and giving talks in this area, people would invariably assume that it was mainly highly pressurised social leaders who had breakdowns or became mentally ill. They would also tell me of their own friends and relatives, middle class people, who had experienced mental illness. Surely, they said, anyone can get a mental illness. It is, of course, true that in theory anyone can get a mental illness. But in reality if you are poor or working class you are far more vulnerable than your upper- or middle class-counterpart. In the end, I took round two large envelopes full of research articles making this point, to refute the sceptics who insisted that there could be no class relationship to the incidence of mental disorder.

It is not just a question of luck, chance, or fate whether someone becomes mentally ill. There is good evidence to suggest that it is a condition in which social and class structure is heavily implicated. One writer has even suggested that 'depression is essentially a social phenomenon'.[9] I will now review briefly some of the evidence which links social class inversely to mental disorder, and examine some of the intervening mechanisms which have been advanced to explain this relationship.

'The most consistent demographic finding reported in the social psychiatric field studies is an inverse relationship between social class and psychological disorder.'[10] This judgement by Dohrenwend is representative of the many varied

---

[8]   August B. Hollingshead and Fredrick C. Redlich, *Social Class and Mental Illness*. New York: John Wiley, 1958, p. 6.

[9]   George W. Brown, 'Depression: a sociological view' in David Tuckett and Joseph M. Kaufert, eds., *Basic Readings in Medical Sociology*. London: Tavistock, 1978, p. 225.

[10] Bruce P, Dohrenwend, 'Social status and psychological disorder, *American Sociological Review* 31, 1966, 14–34.

studies using different methodologies undertaken throughout the industrialised world by psychiatrists, epidemiologists, and sociologists, few of whom would identify themselves as Marxists.[11] Typical of such studies is the finding that rates of hospital admission for schizophrenia amongst men were 100 per cent higher than they would be if distribution was equal through all classes.[12] While Kohn cautions that 'all together, the results of the studies of class and schizophrenia are hardly definitive', he goes on to assert that on aggregate they do 'probably point to something real'.[13]

Behind the bald fact that mental disorder appears to be negatively and inversely correlated with social class position lies a complex set of interlocking factors and intervening variables. In his study, *Recovery from Schizophrenia*, the psychiatrist Richard Warner makes connections between the socio-political order and the incidence of schizophrenia.[14] Warner believes that schizophrenia is an illness with a physiological basis, but that many social factors bear upon whether people experience the illness in their lives or not. He suggests that a variety of factors come together to produce a schizophrenic episode. So people may be *predisposed* to the illness by genetic factors. Early in their lives factors such as infections, maladaptive learning or family communication problems may lead them to become *vulnerable* to schizophrenia. Thereafter, precipitant factors, such as stressful life events like unemployment or a stressful environment, may lead to a *schizophrenic episode*. In this psychotic period similar and other factors, for example, drug use, stressful family environment, social isolation, labelling, and stigma, can help or hinder recovery from schizophrenia. Warner argues that, in wage-earning Western societies such as Britain and the USA, lower-class people are

[11] A *locus classicus* for this kind of research is Hollingshead and Redlich, *Social Class and Mental Illness*.

[12] E. M. Goldberg and S. L. Morrison, 'Schizophrenia and social class', *British Journal of Psychiatry* 109, 1963, 785–802.

[13] Melvin L. Kohn, 'Social class and schizophrenia: a critical review and reformulation', in P. M. Roman and H. M. Trice, *Explorations in Social Psychiatry*. Philadelphia: F. A. Davis, 1974, p. 121.

[14] Warner, *Recovery from Schizophrenia*.

exposed to enormous stress caused by for example, alienation at work, poor living conditions, vulnerability to unemployment, greater mortality amongst friends and relations. It is this exposure which is likely to form the network of intervening variables between social class position as such, and increased incidence of schizophrenia amongst working-class people.

Melvin Kohn argues that probably it is not so much stress in itself which is greater in lower class life situations, but rather that people in the lower social classes have fewer institutional and personal resources for dealing with it. Kohn emphasises the importance of personal resources, suggesting that the view of reality internalised in working-class culture tends to be rather rigid, limited, and conservative. It does not cope well with change and stress. Thus, lower-class people find it difficult to deal with the problems which confront them. Because such people are poorly educated, and work at jobs of little complexity under conditions of close supervision with little freedom to vary their routine and work pattern, their sense of social reality is limited and they may have little sense of personal efficacy and power. This minimises internal resources and personal flexibility.[15]

Turning from schizophrenia to depression, a similarly complex multi-factorial picture emerges in Brown and Harris' classic study of depression amongst London women.[16] This study which looked at the incidence of depression amongst a sample of randomly selected women showed that

Psychiatric disorder, and depression in particular, is much more common among working-class women: 23% were considered cases in the three months before interview compared with only 6% of middle-class women.[17]

---

[15] See Kohn, 'Social class and schizophrenia'. Light is cast on this theory by a study of attitudes towards health and illness amongst working-class people in London which showed that people's attitudes to health and problems are shaped by, and consonant with, their views of work. Thus, people with little power and autonomy at work, for example, working-class people, may be rather passive in their views and attitudes towards illness. See Jocelyn Cornwell, *Hard-Earned Lives*. London: Tavistock, 1984.

[16] George W. Brown and Tirril Harris, *Social Origins of Depression*. London: Tavistock, 1978.

[17] Brown and Harris, *Social Origins*, p. 151.

It was also found that prevalence of chronic cases of depression lasting for a year or longer is five times greater amongst working class than amongst middle class women.[18]

Like Warner and Kohn, Brown and Harris suggest that there is a strong element of social causation in depression amongst working-class women. Episodes of depression, they argue, are triggered by severe life events and difficulties, for example, the death of a near relative. However, the provoking or triggering agent is only one factor in the development of depression. Vulnerability factors such as lack of intimate relationship with a husband or boyfriend, three or more children under the age of 15 years at home, the loss of a mother in childhood, and unemployment greatly increase the chance of breakdown in the face of a triggering agent. It was found that there was a greater prevalence of all severe life events and of three out of the four vulnerability factors amongst working-class women. This, they believe, induces a loss of hope and sense of efficacy in these women, thus directly contributing to depression. Based on these findings, Brown and his associates state

Certain groups of women in our society have a significantly greater than average risk of suffering from depressive conditions. To the extent that the unequal distribution of such risk is the result of more widely recognised inequalities in our society ... we believe that it constitutes a major social injustice.[19]

So far, this review has suggested that factors involved in occupying a lower social class position directly contribute towards the incidence of mental disorder. It must be emphasised, however, that we still know very little about why lower-class people suffer from, and are diagnosed disproportionately as having, mental illnesses of various kinds. Some critics argue, against the social causation views advanced above, that more mentally ill people are found in the lower social classes because people from higher social classes drift down the social scale as a

[18] Ibid., p. 195.

[19] George W. Brown, Maire Ní Bhrolcháin and Tirril Harris, 'Social class and mental disturbance among women in an urban population', *Sociology* 9, 1975, 225–54, at p. 248.

result of their illness. Others have suggested that lower-class people delay seeking treatment until their disorders are of clinical severity, perhaps because they do not have easy access to early treatment facilities. Sociologists might argue that there is a social role of being a mentally ill person, and that lower-class people find it more difficult to avoid having their deviant behaviour labelled thus by higher class professionals.[20] (Historically, 'A wide range of nineteenth-century observers commented on how much laxer the standards were for judging a poor person to be insane, and how much readier both local poor-law authorities and lower-class families were to commit decrepit and troublesome people to the asylum, individuals who, had they come from the middle and upper classes, would never have been diagnosed as insane.'[21]) There is much scope for investigating this area further. However, I want now to draw out some of the implications of what has been said so far.

A proper evaluation of the situation of mentally ill people cannot be divorced from their position within the context of the wider socio-political order. There appear to be factors within our present capitalist social order which lead to a greater incidence and prevalence of identified mental illness amongst working-class people. These might include work practices, stresses, and the uneven distribution of vulnerability factors which both expose working-class people to greater risk, and deprive them of the attitudes and resources needed to deal with that risk. Higher-class people are not affected by mental disorder in the same way as their lower-class counterparts. Therefore, at the very least, it can be said that there exists a fundamental injustice and inequality in the distribution of circumstances which minimise mental disorder in society. It will, therefore, take changes in the wider social order if the gap in incidence between higher and lower-classes is to be reduced. It seems likely that only if lower-class people gain access to the kind of life style and circumstances that higher-class people presently enjoy will we see the gap closing.

[20] This evidence is reviewed in Agnes Miles, *The Mentally Ill in Contemporary Society.* Oxford: Martin Robertson, 1981, ch. 7.
[21] Andrew Scull, *Social Order/Mental Disorder.* London: Routledge, 1989, p. 245.

Two important points which underlie my whole argument here and below, are that the incidence and treatment of mental illness and the situation of mentally ill people must be seen as integrally linked to the wider socio-political order. Furthermore, it cannot be expected that these things will improve or change without changes in that order. Mental illness, mentally ill people, and the facilities from which they receive care are not isolated on a socio-political island, though they may appear to be so if viewed through the lense of individual pathology. It is this fundamental precept which will continue to illuminate the analysis of the care situations experienced by mentally ill people which follows.

The significance of social class for mentally ill people continues far beyond the circumstances and factors which appear to engender disorder. People from the lowest social classes 'enjoy' a higher rate of diagnosis of clinical mental disorder. They form a disproportionately high proportion of the population of treatment facilities. They are more likely to be treated in less good and less prestigious facilities than members of higher classes.[22] Their long-term prognosis is poorer and their recovery takes longer. Thus speed of recovery, quality and type of treatment facility, length of hospital stay, and long-term prospects are also inversely and negatively linked to social class position.[23] From an American study, Levinson and Gallagher sum up the position of lower-class psychiatric patients thus:

Lower-class patients are likely to delay entering a hospital until their outside social relationships have been severely damaged; they are likely to enter a public hospital which is ill-equipped and understaffed. Once in the hospital, they are more likely to receive organic treatment (such as electric shock) or minimum custodial care than psychotherapy. Further, their hospital stay may be prolonged, partly

---

22 Anne Cartwright and Maureen O'Brien, 'Social class variations in health care' in Magaret Stacey, ed., *The Sociology of the NHS*. Keele: University of Keele, 1976; Richard Mollica and Mladen Milic, 'Social class and psychiatric practice', *American Journal of Psychiatry* 143, 1, 1986, 12–17; Jeremy Holmes and Richard Lindley, *The Values of Psychotherapy*. Oxford, Oxford University Press, 1989, pp. 71ff.

23 See further Simon Dinitz, Mark Lefton, Shirley Angrist, and Benjamin Pasamanick, 'Psychiatric and social attributes as predictors of case outcome in mental hospitalization' in Thomas J. Scheff, ed., *Mental Illness and Social Processes*. New York, Harper and Row, 1967.

because of severe pathology at admission, partly because their families have limited physical and emotional resources for dealing with a member now defined as mentally ill.[24]

At this point it is worth pointing out that not only do working-class people have higher rates of mental disorder, but that women and black people are disproportionately represented here too, probably for very similar reasons. Black people and women form a 'super-oppressed' and 'super-exploited' group even within the lower-class.[25] Their conditions, the stresses they experience, and the ease with which they can be stereotyped and labelled as mentally ill in a racist and sexist society are compounded by their low social position. The result is high rates of diagnosis of mental disorder and, particularly in the case of black people, considerably more diagnosis of schizophrenia and use of restraint orders and radical physical treatments.[26]

This summary sets the scene for a socio-political analysis of the institution which has dominated care services for mentally ill people over the last 150 years, the psychiatric hospital or asylum. What socio-political forces and factors shape and structure this institution which deals with a client group which can already be seen as arguably 'one of the most truly powerless constituencies in our society'?[27]

[24] Daniel J. Levinson and Eugene B. Gallagher, *Patienthood in the Mental Hospital.* Boston: Houghton-Mifflin, 1964, p. 169.
[25] Miliband, *Divided Societies,* p. 40.
[26] See further Ussher, *Women's Madness,* pp. 162ff; Roland Littlewood and Maurice Lipsedge, *Aliens and Alienists.* London: Unwin Hyman, second edn., 1989, ch. 11; Suman Fernando, *Mental Health, Race and Culture.* London: Macmillan, 1991.
[27] J. A. Talbott, *The Death of the Asylum.* New York: Grune and Stratton, 1978, p.68.

CHAPTER 7

The historical and social context of the psychiatric hospital

Mentally ill people come disproportionately from the lower social classes. In Marxist terms they might be described as members of the proletariat or working class, as opposed to the ruling or bourgeois class. In so far as many mentally ill people (even those who originate in higher social classes) do not directly participate in the process of production at all, they might be assigned to the Marxist category of the *lumpen-proletariat* or 'under-class', that group of people who contribute little or nothing to the economy and the production of wealth.

From this kind of Marxist perspective, and in the light of earlier comments about the state's need to assist in the maximisation of exploitation and assure effective social control in capitalist society, one might expect that the provision of care for mentally ill people is unlikely to be over-generous, over-kindly or unambiguous. This chapter begins an examination of the treatment settings available to mentally ill people, with the purpose of further uncovering connections between socio-political context and pointing up issues of power, exploitation, inequality, injustice, and control. At all points, the care and treatment of mentally ill people is affected by wider political economic factors. There is a case to answer that most forms of treatment and care can easily be, and often are, niggardly, inadequate, unjust, controlling and heavy-handed (even violent). All this usually to the detriment, and at the expense, of those who are least powerful already, and to the advantage of the powerful and influential within the care services, in particular, and in the capitalist social order, in general. I will begin with the history of the psychiatric hospital.

LUNACY CONFINED: THE ORIGINS OF THE ASYLUM

As one drives round the country's motorways it is often easy to recognise what are, or have been, major psychiatric institutions. With their grandiose sprawling buildings, chapels, and distinctive water towers, these isolated complexes are often visible for miles around. They dominate the surrounding countryside, just as they have dominated mental illness services for many decades. At their peak, just after the last war, the 170 or so mental hospitals in England and Wales accommodated no less than 151,000 in-patient beds.[1] It is hard to think of a world without large institutions for mentally ill people. Yet 200 years ago such places hardly existed; there were a few small subscription hospitals founded at the end of the eighteenth century, a scattering of private madhouses, and most 'lunatics' lived outside institutions in the community. What happened to bring these places into existence in such profusion?

Conventional, Whig accounts of the history of mental illness services have it that the advent of mass asylum care which gathered impetus throughout the early part of the last century represents a step in a fairly simple and straightforward progress towards more humane care for the mentally disordered:

> The basic motivations in the growth of the mental hospital were to make a refuge from the degradation and anti-therapy of the poorhouse, a place of safety from the cruelty and inhumanity of both the public gaze and the private madhouse, and a hospital where hope and the possibility of treatment were not altogether lacking.[2]

Those who promoted the growth of institutional care, culminating in 1853 with legislation for the mandatory setting up of asylums in every county and borough, undoubtedly believed that these institutions promised cure and a more humane environment, modelled as they were on the moral management pioneered by the Quaker William Tuke at The Retreat in York

---

[1] Kathleen Jones, *A History of the Mental Health Services*. London: Routledge and Kegan Paul, 1972, p. 358.
[2] J. A. Baldwin, *The Mental Hospital in the Psychiatric Service*. London: Oxford University Press, 1971, p. 5.

from 1792 onwards.[3] From the beginning of their existence, however, asylums showed their limitations: cure rates were poor, they quickly became over-crowded, they were short staffed and from the earliest times there was evidence of plenty of scope for cruelty, neglect, and scandal. The cycle of public scandal, temporary improvement of conditions, public apathy, deterioration of conditions, then scandal once again, which has dogged asylums throughout their history, was established early on.[4] This contradiction at the heart of what was a very expensive, innovative, ambitious project of public provision for a 'great confinement' of a previously non-institutionalised social group prompts us to look beyond the conscious, rational arguments of the reformers to identify relevant underlying social and economic factors.[5] For, as Rothman writes, 'institutions, whether social, political or economic, cannot be understood apart from the society in which they flourished'.[6]

Adopting a historical materialist approach, the sociologist Andrew Scull has constructed a critical account of approaches to mental disorder and the advent of the asylum, which is informed by the belief that these things are linked with, and refract, albeit in an indirect or distorted way, the nature of the socio-economic conditions and interests of the time in which they are situated.[7] A materialist critique of the emergence and persistence of the asylum must start with consideration of the socio-economic conditions and context which produced this institution almost *ex nihilo* in the early nineteenth century. Vast social and economic changes were taking place at that time.

[3] See Andrew Scull, 'Humanitarianism or control?' in Cohen and Scull, eds., *Social Control and the State*, 1985, p. 132. On The Retreat and moral management see Anne Digby, *Madness, Morality and Medicine*. Cambridge, Cambridge University Press, 1985; Joan Busfield, *Managing Madness*. London: Hutchinson, 1986, chs. 6 and 7.

[4] See Ivan Belknap, *Human Problems of a State Mental Hospital*. New York: McGraw-Hill, 1956, pp. vii–viii. For conditions and scandals in the nineteenth-century asylum see Jones, *A History of the Mental Health Services*.

[5] The term, 'great confinement' is from Michel Foucault, *Madness and Civilization*. London: Tavistock, 1971.

[6] David Rothman, *The Discovery of the Asylum*. Boston: Little, Brown and Co., 1971, p. xx.

[7] Andrew Scull, *Museums of Madness*. London: Allen Lane, 1979. Scull states that the definitions, boundaries, and meanings of madness 'are but a distorted mirror image of the shifting social order' (Andrew Scull, *Social Order/Mental Disorder*, p. 8).

The growth of the capitalist market economy was changing the social order and organisation. Feudal bonds between rich and poor were disintegrating, allowing a large, cheap workforce to come into existence. Poor people were very vulnerable in this situation, and could not afford to maintain idle or non-productive dependents, such as the insane.

At the beginning of the last century, the ruling classes rejected the idea of giving people outdoor relief, i.e. social security support, as they believed this would encourage idleness and indolence amongst people who should be working. Thus, the only public support to be made available was in enclosed, extra-familial settings such as workhouses. In these institutions it was thought that the poor would learn industrious habits, and enjoy a sufficiently rigorous life style to encourage them not to want to remain at the mercy of public charity. This social moulding of the poor was hampered by disruption caused by the inclusion of insane people. It therefore became desirable to provide differential treatment for different groups amongst the poorer and working classes. Those who might possibly be assimilated into the workforce were retained in the workhouses, while the economically useless and obstructive, criminals and the insane for example, would be dealt with in special institutions. These would be cheaper than outdoor relief, allowing targeting of public funds on the genuinely impotent, as well as better control and deterrence for potential 'scroungers'. This solution to the new 'problem' of the insane was only feasible because central government and bureaucracy had become strong enough to respond to problems of deviance on a national level and was committed to saving money on outdoor relief.

The identification and segregation of deviant groups within the working class into special institutions was to a large extent a product of the needs of the capitalist economy. While the reformers, who included many prominent utilitarians and evangelicals from the upper social classes such as the Earl of Shaftesbury, were sincere in their humanitarian concern for the insane, Scull argues that the asylum solution was deeply consonant with the interests of the ruling classes in British society: 'Only the asylum offered the advantage of allowing scope for the exercise of humanitarian impulses, without requiring any fundamental changes in society.'[8] The reformers could not act fundamentally against their own class interests. They had a very limited range of options to choose from to ameliorate the condition of the insane and encourage them to become wage-earning members of society (unlimited outdoor relief was not ideologically or practically possible, for example). The asylum solution was compatible with, and serviceable within, the capitalist economy as a whole. It was accompanied by a view of mental disorder which emphasised the inner psychological control and behaviour modification necessary to become a full working member of society.[9] Thus, to put it crudely, an ideological 'package' was formed which was complete, coherent, and practicable within the socio-economic order of the time.

Scull has extended his critique to show that, just as a particular constellation of socio-economic factors brought the asylum into existence, so changes in the material infrastructure were necessary before alternatives to the mental hospital could be envisaged in the form of community care.[10] I will now locate this institution in its more recent history and functioning within the National Health Service.

THE PSYCHIATRIC HOSPITAL AND THE NATIONAL HEALTH SERVICE

Social institutions reflect and refract the socio-economic order, conditions, and values of their time. This is true of the psychiatric hospital as a discrete organisation, as we shall see later. It is also true of the National Health Service (NHS) within which the psychiatric hospital is situated. Here I want to look briefly at the NHS context of the psychiatric hospital, highlighting issues of power, influence, injustice, and inequality again to

[8] Scull, *Museums of Madness*, p. 101
[9] On views of mental disorder and implicit social moulding which suggested that mental health was the same thing as being a good, responsible, wage-earning worker see Digby, *Madness, Morality and Medicine*.
[10] Andrew Scull, *Decarceration*. Englewood Cliffs, NJ: Prentice-Hall, 1977.

provide another vantage point for analysing the situation of mentally ill people and the services they receive. Essentially, there are two main points to be made. The first is that patterns of power and influence in the NHS are congruent with those in society generally, to the detriment of working-class people generally, and of mentally ill people and those who work in services for them. The second is that financial and other resources are unequally distributed in the NHS, again to the disadvantage of the psychiatric services.

A slightly naïve view of the NHS might have it that this service was created by a welfare consensus amongst the vast majority of people in Britain after the last war, and that it is run by the people for the people, so everyone can have access to the health care they need when they need it. If this idealistic view still survives, it needs to be demolished in the present context. Even non-Marxists can see the NHS as an arena of conflict and competing political interests in which the rationing of scarce resources is probably more important than the meeting of needs.[11]

A Marxist view of welfare and health provision suggests that any state-run system is likely to reflect the conflicting interests of capital and labour, with the former dominant. Historical materialist views of the history of the NHS reveal considerable class conflict implicated in its origins.[12] It is not clear that members of the working class have been the chief beneficiaries of socialised health care, dominated as it has been by the professional-interest groups whose goodwill had to be obtained to bring the service into existence in the first place. In fact, the NHS has acted in many ways as a rationing system for health care, firmly dominated by, and perhaps principally benefitting, the interests of capital and members of the ruling classes. Arguably, a centralised state health service has served the interests of the upper classes by offering them facilities for which they could not afford to pay and creating markets for

---

[11] See, for example, Rudolf Klein, *The Politics of the NHS*. London: Longman, second edn., 1989.
[12] See, for example, Vicente Navarro, *Class Struggle, the State and Medicine*. London: Martin Robertson, 1978.

private industry in drugs and equipment.[13] It has certainly not done much to eradicate inequalities in health between the upper and lower classes, which are actually continuing to grow.[14]

At a political level, the service has had little accountability to local people, particularly to members of the lower classes. In 1973, Tudor Hart found that of the 281 health authority members nominated by the secretary of state

78 are bankers, company directors, business executives, property developers and brokers, 39 are doctors; and there are 19 solicitors, 6 accountants, 5 retired army officers, 3 ex-colonial governors and 24 other professionals. Representing the sons of toil, we have 6 farmers (1 lord and 1 knight), 11 shopkeepers, 10 supervisory staff, 18 full-time trade union officials, 3 railwaymen, 1 coalminer and 1 engineer. There are 4 of unstated occupation, and as most of the 53 women are listed as housewives, they are difficult to classify ...[15]

With reforms subsequent to 1973, health authorities have been reduced in size, union and local authority membership has been abolished, and all members are now appointed from above by the secretary of state for health or his representatives. So, over the past two decades the NHS has become even less representative of working-class interests in general.[16]

Within this fundamentally upper-class dominated polity, doctors (themselves members of the higher social classes who form only 7 per cent of the NHS workforce) have had a disproportionate influence on policy and expenditure patterns.[17] Doctors from the prestigious and expensive acute hospital sector of general medicine (i.e. surgeons and physicians)

13 See Vivienne Walters, *Class Inequality and Health Care*. London: Croom Helm, 1980.
14 G. Davey Smith, M. Bartley and D. Blane, 'The Black report on socioeconomic inequalities in health 10 years on', *British Medical Journal* 301, 1990, 373–7.
15 Julian Tudor Hart, 'Industry and the health service', *Lancet* 2, 1973, 15 September.
16 Navarro (1978) wrote: 'Strengthening the central power of the NHS has determined a further deepening of, primarily, the class dominance and, secondarily, the professional dominance of the system' (Navarro, *Class Struggle*, p. 58).
17 See Stephen Harrison, *Managing the National Health Service*. London: Chapman and Hall, 1988. See John Robson, 'The NHS Co. Inc.?', *International Journal of Health Services* 3, 1973, 413–25, for doctors' social origins.

have been particularly influential.[18] This is in many ways consonant with the dominant interests of the capitalist socio-economic order. Industry can make enormous profits from the sales of drugs and highly sophisticated technology to the NHS. Doctors can command high salaries on the basis of their technical skills. Higher-class people in general can opt in to the state health services when private health care would be prohibitively expensive.[19] Psychiatrists have been a rather insignificant minority in the policy arena, representing a stigmatised group of chronically, rather than acutely, ill people, and being members of a fairly small specialty which has not been perceived as prestigious or influential within medicine.[20]

This has helped contribute to historic under-resourcing of mental illness services in the NHS.[21] In 1976 43 per cent of all patients in English hospitals were in psychiatric beds. At the same time only 11 per cent of all consultants were psychiatrists, and only 20 per cent of all nurses worked in psychiatry. Psychiatric consultants had to look after an average of 154 in-patients, as compared to the 30 which was the average for their counterparts in acute specialities. In hospitals for the mentally ill there were 36 nurses for every 100 patients, while in non-psychiatric hospitals there were 121 nurses for every 100 patients. The average cost of maintaining a patient for one week in an acute general hospital ward was just under £90, while only £30 was spent on patients in psychiatric facilities.[22] Even allowing that acutely medically ill patients might need a greater investment of resources, these comparative figures demonstrate why the mental health and mental handicap sectors of the NHS have been dubbed the 'Cinderella services'.

In addition to inequality of funding between different

[18] See Doyal, *The Political Economy of Health*, ch. 5; Stuart Heywood and Andy Alaszewski, *Crisis in the National Health Service*. London: Croom Helm, 1980; Tom Heller, *Restructuring the National Health Service*. London: Croom Helm, 1977.
[19] See further Heller, *Restructuring the National Health Service*, p. 35f; Doyal, *The Political Economy of Health*, ch. 5; David Widgery, *Health in Danger*. London: Macmillan, 1979, ch. 6.
[20] Cf. Christopher Ham, *Health Policy in Britain*. London: Macmillan, third edn., 1992, p. 24
[21] Cf. Ham, *Health Policy*, p. 23f, ch. 3.
[22] Clare, *Psychiatry in Dissent*, second edn., p. 400.

service sectors of the NHS, there are important geographical and class related inequalities of financial and service provision which probably adversely affect the psychiatric sector. In the north of England, where morbidity and mortality are generally higher, NHS funds and resources are less generous than in the south.[23] The implication of this is that the more likely you are to need psychiatric services, the less likely you are to receive them. Brown and his colleagues came to much the same conclusion on a local level in their survey of depression amongst women, finding that 'the same social factors that increase the risk of psychiatric disorder greatly reduce the chances of reaching psychiatric services'.[24] All of which appears to vindicate Tudor Hart's 'Inverse Care Law' which maintains that the lower down the class system you are in British society (and thus the more you need care), the less likely you are to receive the care you need.[25]

This brief sketch of the place of the psychiatric services within the context of the NHS as a whole in terms of influence, power, and inequality confirms the generally bleak picture of the situation of mentally ill people which is gradually emerging. Mentally ill people disproportionately come from the lower social classes, and within the capitalist social order they have little influence and power. They have poor representation and the services provided for them are marginalised and underfunded within the NHS. The more they need services, the less likely they are to get them. One cannot feel sanguine or optimistic as one turns more specifically to analyse the nature and functioning of the psychiatric hospital itself within the context of the present social order.

CONFLICTING ROLES FOR THE PSYCHIATRIC HOSPITAL IN SOCIETY

Although often physically isolated, the psychiatric hospital is not detached from the social order as a whole. Within it is

---

[23] Davey Smith, Bartley and Blane, 'The Black report'.
[24] Brown, Ní Bhrolcháin and Harris, 'Social class and psychiatric disturbance among women'.
[25] J. T. Hart, 'The Inverse Care Law', *Lancet* 1971; i:405–503.

found, yet again, a replication of the socio-economic patterns and assumptions which are beginning to be so familiar, accompanied by all the issues of class, injustice, inequality, power, powerlessness, care and control which have begun to emerge as leitmotifs in this analysis. Psychiatric services perform a publicly legitimated role on behalf of the particular society which funds and supports them. It would be surprising if we were not to find a close affinity between the social order, nature, and values of the psychiatric hospital and that of society as a whole. Similarly, one might expect to find the sorts of tensions and conflicts present in society as a whole mirrored and acted out within the hospital.

Psychiatric hospitals serve a number of officially sanctioned purposes or aims.[26] Predictably, the first of these is the *therapeutic–rehabilitative* aim, caring for mentally ill people while they are judged to be unable to fulfil their roles as independent citizens, and restoring them to health. A second main aim is that of *custody and control* of people judged to be a danger to themselves or to the community:

mental hospitals are still constrained to perform the task which they have always carried out for society, which is temporarily or permanently to remove from their place in society people who are socially defined as mentally ill.[27]

A third main aim of the hospital must be *maintenance* and the fulfilment of organisational and institutional needs.[28] Beyond this there may be subsidiary aims such as training care personnel and researching into mental disorder and its treatment.

There can be considerable practical tension and conflict between these official, socially sanctioned goals. The goal of meeting a particular patient's therapeutic needs, for example, for freedom to leave the hospital under supervision, may conflict with society's need to feel that mentally ill people are safely confined, or the hospital's maintenance need to ensure that

---

[26] Levinson and Gallagher, *Patienthood in the Mental Hospital*, p. 14f.

[27] Elizabeth Bott, 'Hospital and Society', *British Journal of Medical Psychology* 49, 1976, 97–140, at p. 97.

[28] See A. H. Stanton and M. S. Schwartz, *The Mental Hospital*. New York: Basic Books, 1954, p. 27.

there are enough staff on the wards at all times to maintain standards of surveillance and care.

This picture of potential conflict of interests and aims can be further developed and complexified. There may be unstated or informal goals which may conflict with formal aims and with each other. Officially, a hospital may want its patients to maintain or regain a normal life style, such as that which they enjoyed in the community; unofficially, it may encourage patients to adopt a passive, institutionalised role which makes life easier for the staff. (Goffman notes that 'this contradiction between what the institution does and what officials say it does, forms the basic context of the staff's daily life'.[29]) Different groups in the hospital, with varying amounts of status and power, may themselves have conflicting interests and goals. So, for example, doctors may wish to see their patients very actively engaged in rehabilitative therapy, while managers in the hospital may wish to balance their books, and nurses on the ward may just want a quiet time. The physical environment may affect the goals or aims which can be pursued; a ward built for the custodial care of a large number of people at the end of the last century may adapt very badly to use by a therapy group, for example.[30] Underlying these issues often lies the question of resources. If desirable 'official' goals such as active rehabilitation are not properly funded (and usually active forms of therapy are person-intensive, therefore expensive), then it may be that subordinate or unofficial goals are pursued in their stead. Thus custodial and pharmaceutical treatment can supplant more patient-centred care when resources are in short supply.

Underlying these conflicts is the view that society at large has of the psychiatric hospital. On the one hand, society seems to expect psychiatric hospitals to be benevolent, curative institutions in which the sick are healed. Thus when it is discovered that, for example, staff have been abusing or imprisoning

---

[29] Erving Goffman, *Asylums*. Harmondsworth: Penguin, 1968, p. 73.
[30] For historical and physical constraints on aims and goals see Kathleen Jones and Roy Sidebotham, *Mental Hospitals at Work*. London: Routledge and Kegan Paul, 1962, p. 118.

patients there is great public outrage. At the same time, many people in society set a high premium by the containing and custodial functions of the hospital. Not many weeks pass, even now, when some psychiatrist or hospital manager is not arraigned in public for releasing a 'dangerous' patient into the community. In the public view, perhaps the control, rather than the care, functions of the hospital are uppermost. Ordinary members of society are largely indifferent to the internal workings of the hospital or to the welfare of patients on a day-to-day basis. They are, however, often afraid of 'dangerous mentally ill people on the loose'. This means that they are prepared to exert pressure on government for funding for custodial care, but such pressure may be lacking for adequate funding to guarantee the more positive curative and rehabilitative aims of the psychiatric hospitals. Perhaps it is not surprising that many hospitals and other psychiatric settings still seem more like the prisons which historically came into being at the same time as the asylums.

Social dynamics and factors, both internal and external, have enormous influence on the settings in which mentally ill people are treated. Wider social attitudes and their implications for policy are crucial to understanding the day-to-day functioning of the hospital, and conflicts of aims and views amongst different groups within and outside the hospital are endemic. As we will see, there are enormous disparities of class, status, and power within psychiatric hospitals which have a real impact on the situation of patients treated or contained within them.

CHAPTER 8

The socio-political order of the psychiatric hospital: the staff

General social attitudes and perceptions affect the goals of psychiatric hospitals, as well as the amount and type of prominence and resource they receive. This is one way in which the hospitals are linked to wider social structure. A further dimension of social connection is the way in which the hospitals replicate the order of class, status, power, and gender found in patriarchal capitalist society generally.

HIERARCHY, POWER AND THE PATIENT-STAFF DIVIDE

Navarro writes about NHS hospitals generally that

within the health team, we find a well-defined hierarchical order with the physician, most often a man of upper-middle class extraction at the top; below him, the supportive nurses, most often women with lower-middle class backgrounds; and at the bottom, under both of them, we find the attendants and auxiliaries, the service workers, who most frequently are of working class backgrounds.[1]

Navarro comments elsewhere, 'Within the health sector, the state replicates the class hierarchy that characterizes capitalist societies.'[2] Had he written specifically about psychiatric hospitals, he might have added that at the bottom of this hierarchy come the patients who tend to come from the poorest parts of society, to be women, and to have lower class position, lower

---

[1] Navarro, *Class Struggle*, p. 87. Women occupy the lowest levels of employment disproportionately in the NHS as in society generally – about 75 per cent of the NHS workforce is female but only 20 per cent of doctors are female. See Doyal, *The Political Economy of Health*, p. 202.

[2] Vicente Navarro, *Medicine Under Capitalism*. New York: Prodist, 1976, p. 206.

status, and less power than any other group in the hospital. I want to suggest that, while there is a graduated hierarchy of power and influence in the hospital, there is a huge gap in potency between patients as a group and members of staff taken together as a group.[3] I call this gap the 'patient–staff divide'.

I will now consider briefly the main groups within the psychiatric hospital hierarchy. I will start with the doctors–psychiatrists.

MEDICAL DOMINANCE AND POWER

Doctors are only a small minority of the NHS workforce, but they form the single most powerful and influential group in it.[4] Although psychiatry is not a high-status medical speciality, all psychiatrists have a medical training and entrants to medicine come almost exclusively from the upper classes with a bias towards white upper class men.[5] One survey found that three quarters of all medical students came from social classes 1 and 2, while only a quarter came from classes 3, 4, and 5 put together.[6] Similarly, women and ethnic minorities are historically under-represented within the medical profession with only 23 per cent of medical practitioners being women in 1985.[7] Because of psychiatry's low-status as a medical speciality (probably partly to do with its close association with a stigmatised, low status clientele), it has tended to attract disproportionately more women and doctors from overseas into its ranks.[8] However, psychiatrists in general, especially those who

---

[3] For patients as a separate class or group see Waitzkin and Waterman, *The Exploitation of Illness*, p. 69.

[4] There are about six times as many nurses as there are hospital doctors in the NHS – 397,000 of the latter as compared with 40,000 of the former in 1983. See Ruth Levitt and Andrew Wall, *The Reorganized National Health Service*. London: Croom Helm, third edn., 1984, p. 206.

[5] For the relatively low status of psychiatry see Littlewood and Lipsedge, *Aliens and Alienists*, pp. 9ff.

[6] Robson, 'The NHS Co. Inc.?'.

[7] Margaret Stacey, *The Sociology of Health and Healing*. London: Unwin Hyman, 1988, p. 190.

[8] Elaine Murphy, *After the Asylums*. London: Faber, 1991, p. 80; Littlewood and Lipsedge, *Aliens and Alienists*, pp. 9ff.

reach the top of their profession, come from the highest social and economic classes. They receive relatively high salaries compared with other groups within the hospital (a top-grade consultant in the NHS with the highest additional merit awards could earn £56,000 p.a., as against the £6,225 paid to a staff nurse and the £3,880 payable to a nursing cadet in 1986.[9]) Stacey points out that as a part of an economically powerful elite in both the NHS and society in general, some doctors 'not only reflect but also help to reproduce the values of a class-divided capitalist society. Their high level of remuneration permits them to invest, to become property owners or share-holders.'[10]

The high social class position of doctors in the hospital which gives them transferred social authority is buttressed with charismatic authority (derived probably from a sense that doctors as a group are intimately in contact with, and can influence, the course of illness and death) and expert authority which derives from perceived knowledge and skill.[11] Doctors also belong to a very powerful self-regulating profession, sanctioned and legitimated by society through legislation, which has much scope to control its own work and that of other occupational groups, for example, nurses and psychologists.[12] This increases doctors' autonomy and decision-making power over against others. Doctors as individuals can legitimately see themselves as having technically complete clinical freedom to do what they think is in the best interests of their individual patients. This can bring them into conflict with other groups, such as psychologists and managers, who would often wish to curb or influence absolute medical autonomy.[13]

The medical profession has not always dominated the treatment of mental disorder as it does today. Scull describes

---

[9] See Stacey, *Sociology of Health*, p. 189.   [10] Ibid., pp. 189–90.
[11] Cf. M. W. Susser and W. Watson, *Sociology in Medicine*. Oxford: Oxford University Press, second edn., 1971, pp. 241ff.
[12] See further, for example, Eliot Freidson, *Profession of Medicine*. New York: Dodd, Mead and Co., 1975.
[13] See Nigel Goldie, 'Psychology and the medical mandate' in Michael Wadsworth and David Robinson, eds., *Studies in Everyday Medical Life*. London: Martin Robertson, 1976.

the early medical specialists in mental disorder as 'moral entre-preneurs'.[14] Although doctors did not have any effective medical methods for dealing with mental disorder in the last century, in the interests of increasing their influence in an important sector of care and control, they took over and medicalised the moral treatment methods introduced by lay people such as William Tuke. This entrepreneurial activity culminated in the various Acts of Parliament in the present century which have firmly situated mental disorder within the medical realm as mental illness. In dealing with mental 'illness' doctors have a decisive, not to say exclusive role in defining, treating, and ordering mental disorder, as well as ordering the work of other professions within the psychiatric hospital today.

Most psychiatrists in Britain today would probably describe themselves as eclectic in their approach to mental disorder.[15] Not surprisingly, given their basic training as doctors, they see mental disorder basically in terms of its being an illness, and so look primarily to physiological means of intervention to treat it, while supplementing powerful drugs and other physical interventions, for example, Electro Convulsive Treatment, psychosurgery, with group therapy, behaviour therapy or psychotherapy in appropriate cases.[16] This medical or mechanistic approach to mental disorder tends to fit in well to the wider capitalist social order, as it raises few questions about the social origins, implications, or consequences of this phenomenon. Interestingly, one survey found that the more organically oriented psychiatrists are, the more likely they are to be socially conservative also.[17] However, there is no reason to suppose that psychiatrists, like most other doctors, are not

[14] Scull, *Museums of Madness*, chs. 4 and 5. See also Andy Treacher and Geoff Baruch, 'Towards a critical history of the psychiatric profession' in David Ingleby, ed., *Critical Psychiatry*. Harmondsworth: Penguin, 1981.

[15] D. J. Pallis and B. E. Stoffelmayer, 'Social attitudes and treatment orientation among psychiatrists', *British Journal of Medical Psychology* 46, 1973, 75–81.

[16] For more on different treatment methods see, for example, Clare, *Psychiatry in Dissent*; Peter Hill, Robin Murray and Anthony Thorley, eds., *Essentials of Postgraduate Psychiatry*. London: Academic Press, 1979.

[17] Pallis and Stoffelmayer, 'Social attitudes and treatment orientation among psychiatrists'. See also Goldie, 'Psychology and the medical mandate' for psychiatrists' orientation to treatment.

fairly conservative anyway, having a large investment in the present social order which rewards them well.[18] The findings of recent studies of non-organically inclined psychiatrists, i.e., those who are psychodynamically oriented, leave little room for the illusion that this professional group as a whole is truly socially radical, either within or outside the hospital. Jeffrey Masson and David Hill, for example, document the voluntary collusion of psychoanalysts, amongst others, with the Nazi regime and the euthanasia of 275,000 mentally ill people, while Claire Baron shows how a psychodynamic psychiatrist managed to engineer a miniature totalitarian regime within a psychiatric day unit using the power and charisma of his office.[19]

In more concrete terms, the dominance or hegemony of the doctors in the psychiatric hospital means several very important things. Psychiatrists reserve to themselves the diagnosis of mental illness. They alone have authority to admit and keep people in mental illness treatment facilities. In some circumstances this can be done against a person's will under a section of the Mental Health Act. All patients receiving treatment for mental disorder 'belong' to a particular psychiatrist who is legally responsible for them. All such treatment must be directly or at least indirectly authorised by a psychiatrist. Psychiatrists direct the treatment of patients, prescribe drug, physical, and other therapies, and orchestrate the activity of the therapeutic team as a whole. They are in a position to ignore the advice of other members of their teams if they so wish.

Being few in number, psychiatrists do not have much time to see patients. Patients suffering from acute episodes of mental illness are likely to receive more medical time than old or chronically ill patients and even they may only receive 30

---

18 Littlewood and Lipsedge (*Aliens and Alienists*, p. 11) suggest that psychiatrists are probably less socially conservative than other doctors, with half of those who are politically active being Labour Party supporters, but this probably does not indicate anything like mass radicalism.

19 Jeffrey Masson, *Against Therapy*. London: Fontana, 1989, ch. 4; David Hill, *The Politics of Schizophrenia*, ch. 1; Claire Baron, *Asylum to Anarchy*. London: Free Association Books, 1987.

minutes or so in a week.[20] Given the large gap in relative power, status, and class between psychiatrists and many members of their clientele, there is much scope for patients to be misunderstood or to have their own wishes and perceptions ignored. It may seem ironical that doctors in general spend less time than other staff with patients – and more ironical still that consultant psychiatrists, who have ultimate responsibility and power for the care and treatment of patients, should have almost no contact with their charges at all.

THE NURSING STAFF

Nurses are the single largest component of the NHS workforce and are the largest staff group within the psychiatric hospital also. In terms of class analysis, the majority of qualified nurses have tended to come from the middle- and lower-middle classes, i.e., from strata lower than those from which doctors have been drawn. The majority of nurses in the NHS as a whole are female, and their relatively poor pay probably reflects this female dominance and the low value accorded to women's work in society at large.[21]

This general picture of nursing can be modified in the case of mental nursing. Just as NHS psychiatrists are descendants of the low-status nineteenth-century asylum keepers rather than the higher status psychoanalysts, and their speciality enjoys low esteem in medicine, so mental nurses are the descendants of the old asylum attendants, chosen from the working classes for their physical stamina and strength to contain patients, rather than for their therapeutic skills. This means that there are more men in psychiatric nursing than in general nursing, they are probably less well educated and come from a lower class background than general nurses, but they do receive slightly better pay and have a greater tradition of militancy and assertion than their counterparts in general nursing.[22]

---

[20] Clare, *Psychiatry in Dissent*, first edn., pp. 399–400.

[21] See Stacey, *Sociology of Health*, especially chs. 6 and 8.

[22] For more on the background to asylum nursing see, for example, Mick Carpenter, 'Asylum nursing before 1914' in Celia Davies, ed., *Re-writing Nursing History*. London: Croom Helm, 1980.

General nursing has served as a model for psychiatric nursing to upgrade itself away from its stigmatised origins of asylum attendance which consisted largely of unskilled manual labour. This means that qualified psychiatric nurses have been encouraged to adopt some of the general features of nursing such as uniforms, hierarchical organisation, a subordinate position to doctors, and a broadly somatic view of mental disorder.[23] Although the general approach of nurses to their tasks and to psychiatric disorder may have changed over the years as this group has sought to professionalise itself, Rubenstein and Lasswell's description of the traditional nurse in the psychiatric hospital in the 1960s still looks broadly accurate for the medically dominated contemporary British psychiatric hospital. These researchers found that psychiatric nurses were quite conservative in their approach, concentrating on a practical, common-sense, non-intellectual approach to their task. They were content to see mental disorder as fundamentally a medical problem. They were not interested in changing the nature or routine of their tasks and saw themselves as part of a rigid hierarchy over which they had little control. These nurses were happy to implement hospital rules and policy, content with rigid hierarchy, respected hierarchical relationships and were clearly differentiated from patients by their uniforms.[24]

Qualified nurses in the psychiatric hospital function as first level managers. They have considerable formal power at hospital level, representing a large part of the workforce and being directly involved in the main management structures at the highest levels. At ward level they can have considerable influence over the lives of patients, setting the tone of wards, administering medically prescribed treatments, and determining to a large extent the amount of freedom and privileges

---

[23] For the broad features of general nursing see Una Maclean, *Nursing in Contemporary Society*. London: Routledge and Kegan Paul, 1974. For the subordination of nurses to doctors see Leonard Stein, 'The doctor nurse game' in Rober Dingwall and Jean McIntosh, eds., *Readings in the Sociology of Nursing*. Edinburgh: Churchill Livingstone, 1978.

[24] Robert Rubenstein and Howard D. Lasswell, *The Sharing of Power in a Psychiatric Hospital*. New Haven: Yale University Press, 1966, ch. 4.

which a patient may enjoy. However, like the doctors, qualified nurses may be in short supply, and they may have to give much of their time to administrative tasks leaving time for patient contact at a minimum. This can mean that the staff group who have most to do with patients on a day-to-day basis are the unqualified or auxiliary nursing staff.

AUXILIARY NURSING STAFF

A fundamental split has been identified in the evolution of nursing between qualified nursing staff and unqualified or auxiliary staff. This latter group come from the lowest social classes, often they are women, and frequently they come from ethnic minority groups. As one might expect, their pay levels are minimal. Auxiliary nurses are numerous in psychiatric hospitals, particularly where it is difficult to recruit qualified staff or too expensive to pay them. They are particularly prevalent in parts of the hospital where elderly or chronically ill patients predominate, those who need physical care and are unpromising material for 'cure'.[25]

Traditionally, little research has been conducted into the place, attitudes, and nature of this group which, theoretically, has no real power in the structure of the hospital. However, there is some evidence that auxiliaries or nursing assistants, like other working-class people, tend to see mental illness in organic terms. Psychological or psychotherapeutic approaches are not accepted.[26] Auxiliaries may often prefer to adhere to a cus- todial–medical model of mental illness and to concentrate on the physical and custodial tasks to do with patients and their illnesses, believing that patients are in some sense suffering from a physical complaint, but also that they need a strong hand:

the custodial aide handles the functions of authority and control that must be met in his role *vis à vis* the patient by showing that he is 'the boss' and by threatening the patient. He reacts personally to the

[25] See David Towell, *Understanding Psychiatric Nursing*. London: Royal College of Nursing, 1975, p. 34, Table 1.

[26] For more on these points see Anselm Strauss, Leonard Schatzman, Rue Bucher, Danuta Ehrlich, and Melvin Sabshin, *Psychiatric Ideologies and Institutions*. London: Transaction Books, 1981, pp. 244ff; Talbott, *The Death of the Asylum*, p. 48f.

patients who are assaultive and unco-operative and is likely to get back at these patients. His primary function is to keep the ward quiet ... In general he avoids all contacts with and leaves all therapy to the doctors. He is relatively insensitive to the individual problems of patients ... He often talks in an angry or condescending way to patients. With supervisors he resents being given orders and when criticized, he justifies himself by blaming the patients.[27]

These attitudes may be very different from those of other staff members. However, they have real influence on patients. Although nursing assistants have little formal power and little chance of attaining it through promotion in the hospital, they are the people who have most to do with patients and can have a crucial influence on them, for good or ill. Often, it is the nursing assistants who really know the patients. They can represent the patients' interests to the staff who administer treatment. Unfortunately, often they use this informal knowledge and power 'not in terms of the individual patient's psychiatric needs but rather in terms of the requirements of their own social system'.[28] Where few good quality qualified staff are available, unqualified assistants can run the wards according to their own lights, medicalising the undesirable behaviour of patients and manipulating treatments, for example, in an informal system of rewards and punishments.[29] Although assistants often share a common class background with their patients, there is some evidence that this can lead to a desire to distance themselves from them and to emphasise the gap in authority and power between them. One researcher records that new attendants were taught by older colleagues to relate to their charges as superiors to inferiors.[30]

STAFF ATTITUDES IN GENERAL

The foregoing analysis of staff groups in the psychiatric hospital has pointed up some of the differences in terms of class,

[27] Doris C. Gilbert and Daniel J. Levinson, 'Role performance, ideology and personality in mental hospital aides' in Milton Greenblatt, Daniel J. Levinson and Richard H. Williams, eds., *The Patient and the Mental Hospital*. Glencoe: Free Press, 1957, p. 197f.
[28] Ivan Belknap, *Human Problems*, p. 67.   [29] Ibid., pp. 164, 170.
[30] Ibid., p. 182.

status, formal and informal power and influence within the hierarchy of the hospital organisation. Broadly speaking, the group with most status and highest-class membership, i.e., doctors, has the most official and legal power, while qualified nurses have somewhat less. The group drawn from the lowest social class, i.e., nursing assistants, has little formal or legal power, but much informal power, especially over the patients.

The groups discussed are just some of the largest and most influential ones working in the hospital. In principle, it would be possible to analyse the place, function, and attitudes of other groups such as managers (a small group drawn on the whole from the middle classes with a crucial influence on patterns of resource distribution in the hospital), psychologists (a highly qualified professional group drawn from the higher social classes with increasing influence, but relatively few numbers in the hospital), or of support staff such as catering workers. Enough has been said about some of the main group actors, however, to show that there are considerable disparities of influence and attitude amongst the various social groups in the hospital, and many nascent areas of conflict and dispute which have an influence on the working of the institution and on patient care.

There are some common features of relevance to more than one, or all, of the groups described. First, many nurses and nursing assistants share a fairly negative custodial–bureaucratic view of their own task and that of the psychiatric hospital, rather than taking a more positive caring–therapeutic attitude.[31] Talbott has anatomised some of the negative attitudes to be found amongst staff in psychiatric hospitals. There is the factory mentality in which staff see themselves as being like factory workers, simply doing a job. The bureaucratic mentality is evident when organisational needs and procedures dominate at the expense of individuals. The police mentality is present where 'policing replaces caring, monitoring replaces evaluating and personal surveillance replaces treatment supervision.'[32] Then there is the survival mentality when people act

---

[31] See Talbott, *The Death of the Asylum*, pp. 74ff.   [32] Ibid., p. 75.

conservatively and cautiously to avoid drawing adverse attention to themselves. Staff with the property mentality give more priority and attention to buildings and physical structures than to programmes, people, and services. This is closely related to the quantification mentality in which quantity, numbers, and appearance are prioritised over intangible features of quality, substance, and inner workings. Lastly, there is the nihilistic mentality which holds that to do nothing is better than to do something, as almost any action might produce negative results. This springs from, and feeds into, stagnation and the discouragement of innovative ideas and practices.[33]

Secondly, many staff, even those who start out with high humanitarian ideals, come to see the people in their care not as individuals, but as depersonalised stereotyped mental patients whose entire behaviour is to be understood in terms of their disease condition.[34] It is within the last 2 years that I heard a senior psychiatrist in the NHS describe his patients universally as 'wasters', and not so very long ago that I heard the following advice offered by a senior to a junior member of staff in a psychiatric hospital: 'Just treat them as planks and you'll be alright.'

Thirdly, the hegemony of the medical model amongst almost all groups discourages an imaginative or socio-politically aware approach to mental disorder. Staff in psychiatric hospitals may see their role as nothing more than dealing with episodes of physical illness which can be controlled and contained, but not cured. The wider social conditions which influence illness and may make it recur are often of little concern to them. This helps to make recurrence inevitable.

Lastly, within the hierarchical structure of the hospital those with most formal power and training spend least time with the patients. Working with mentally ill people confers on workers a kind of 'courtesy stigma'.[35] The further one is away from close association with the stigmatised, the easier it is to keep one's status untainted. Thus Belknap notes that the level of staff

---

[33] Ibid., ch. 7.   [34] Goffman, *Asylums*, p. 18.
[35] Erving Goffman, *Stigma*, Harmondsworth: Penguin, 1968, p. 43f.

with the most authority, training, and prestige are the furthest removed from the patient population in terms of daily individual contact, and administrative work is most heavily concentrated on those positions in the system which also carry the greatest medical and psychiatric responsibility for treating the patient.[36]

It is time now to look at the other side of the patient–staff divide at the patients, the other large significant group in the hospital. It must be asked what the implications of this analysis are for them. What kinds of status, power, and influence do they have, and what is their view of the world and of their situation?

[36] Belknap, *Human Problems*, p. 68.

CHAPTER 9

The socio-political order of the psychiatric hospital: the patients

Patients are, of course, one of the biggest groups in any psychiatric hospital. It is ostensibly for their benefit that the hospitals exist in the first place; their care, treatment, cure and rehabilitation provides the official *raison d'être* of the institution.

There are many types of mental disorder, and different patients have different needs. Many people diagnosed as having a mental illness are not hospitalised in large psychiatric hospitals, being treated either in district general hospital psychiatric units as day patients or in-patients. Higher-class patients, particularly those with mild mental disorders, often avoid treatment in a psychiatric hospital altogether.[1] This means that the clientele of the traditional psychiatric hospital tends to consist of (i) some, often younger, people who are very acutely ill; (ii) quite a large number of people who are chronically ill and who have either been in hospital for a long time or who have been in on many separate occasions; and (iii) some elderly mentally ill people who are suffering from senile dementia and need intensive physical nursing care. There is a disproportionate number of people who are lower class in origin, and there are considerably more women than men. It is chronically and elderly mentally ill people who principally suffer the depredations of institutional structures and power over a long period.

---

[1] See references in ch. 6 n. 2.

PATIENTS' PERSPECTIVES

Research findings reveal that lower-class people often view mental illness and its treatment as an organic matter to be sorted out by doctors using physical means.[2] They therefore see themselves as occupants of the passive patient role in the hands of a medical expert, rather than as active participants in their own treatment and care.[3] Lower class and older patients tend to be more authoritarian in personality and have a more custodial attitude to treatment.

> The more authoritarian, custodial-minded patient tends to see himself as a passive object in the hands of the physician; he expects to 'receive treatment' rather than to participate actively in a therapeutic relationship.[4]

This fits in well with the somatic–custodial ethos of many hospitals and their staff.

It might, therefore, be expected that patients would have a very positive view of the hospital, given that in one survey many of them appear to welcome the staff's authoritarian role of 'keeping the patients in line' and not to regard it as oppressive.[5] However, it appears that patients are often hostile to the institution and its staff. Goffman reported that the latter are often seen as captors with psychiatrists in particular being regarded as arbitrary tyrants imposing their will on patients. Later researchers found that lower-class patients regard the hospital as exploitative and demanding.[6] One study showed that lower-class patients regarded their psychiatrists as a

[2] Hollingshead and Redlich, *Social Class and Mental Illness*, ch. 11.

[3] Szasz and Hollender identify three types of patient–doctor interaction: doctor activity – patient passivity; doctor guidance – patient co-operation; and mutual participation. The first type of interaction is most common within most settings in the NHS even today. See David Tuckett, 'Doctors and patients' in David Tuckett, ed., *An Introduction to Medical Sociology*. London: Tavistock, 1976, pp. 200ff.

[4] Eugene B. Gallagher, Daniel J. Levinson and Iza Ehrlich, 'Some socio-psychological characteristics of patients and the relevance for psychiatric treatment' in Milton Greenblatt, Daniel J. Levinson, and Richard H. Williams, eds., *The Patient and the Mental Hospital*. Glencoe: Free Press, 1957.

[5] Madeline Karmel, 'The internalization of social roles in institutionalized chronic mental patients', *Journal of Health and Social Behaviour* 11, 1970, 231–5.

[6] Goffman, *Asylums*, p. 321; Daniel J. Levinson and Eugene B. Gallagher, *Patienthood in the Mental Hospital*. Boston: Houghton-Mifflin, 1964, p. 176.

mixture of law enforcer and moral authority as well as being regular doctors. Another found that nurses were seen as 'the opposition' by patients in a private hospital, and that patients regarded doctors as omnipotent, omniscient, and inaccessible.[7] Bott suggests that patients and staff collude in a reciprocal relationship which locates all power and goodness amongst the staff, and all badness and impotence amongst the patients.[8]

A few survey-based studies have been published which seem, *prima facie*, to demonstrate a more positive view of the hospital.[9] However, it should be remembered that patients get used to the situation they are in, their expectations may be low, and they may want to please people who are perceived to be in authority, such as researchers, so they retail an 'official' view of the hospital. Plant and his colleagues note that in some circumstances

not only will the existing structure of power prevent felt needs from being articulated within the political arena, but also, the power structure that is both legitimated by and reflected in all kinds of meaning systems – moral norms in institutions, social rituals etc. – may so mould individuals that they are in some sense unaware of their real needs or the depths of the poverty and deprivation.[10]

In reality, I have spoken to patients who are well aware that they have been very miserable in hospital and may even have been maltreated, but who continue to say that the hospital and its staff are wonderful when asked about it in general terms. This may reflect the consciousness of the oppressed person in a highly controlled and regressive environment. Even so, 46 per cent of patients in one survey were brave enough to admit that

---

[7] Hollingshead and Redlich, *Social Class and Mental Illness*, p. 345; Rubenstein and Lasswell, *The Sharing of Power*, p. 55.

[8] Elizabeth Bott, 'Hospital and society', *British Journal of Medical Psychology* 49, 1976, 97–140.

[9] L. S. Linn, 'The mental hospital from the patient perspective', *Psychiatry* 3, 1968, 213–23; Winifred Raphael, *Psychiatric Hospitals Viewed by their Patients*. London: King's Fund, second edn., 1977.

[10] Raymond Plant, Harry Lesser and Peter Taylor-Gooby, *Political Philosophy and Social Welfare*. London: Routledge and Kegan Paul, 1980, p. 107. For more on false consciousness, the problem implicit here, see 'false consciousness' in G. Duncan Mitchell, ed, *A New Dictionary of Sociology*. London: Routledge and Kegan Paul, 1979.

they did not like being in psychiatric hospital, as opposed to 96 per cent of patients in acute general hospitals who did like being there.[11] It is probably fair to conclude that patients have a fairly negative view of the psychiatric hospitals in which they are treated.

LEGAL ASPECTS

Many patients in psychiatric hospitals are admitted, and remain there, voluntarily, at least in theory. However, some are admitted or detained for assessment or treatment under the provisions of the Mental Health Act in the interests of their own health and safety or that of others.[12] Although the revised Act of 1983 makes substantial provision for the preservation of patients' rights and freedoms, this legislation makes it possible for people to be removed to a hospital without consent, to be detained on psychiatric advice against their will for periods of time ranging from 6 hours to 6 months (or longer for an indefinite period if a section application is renewed), to be treated against their will with any kind of method which seems appropriate to their psychiatrist (this might include using powerful chemicals or ECT), and to have their mail intercepted in some circumstances. All this threatens personal autonomy and decision-making. Furthermore, the threat of using the provisions of the Mental Health Act can be used as a powerful coercive tool to gain compliance from uncooperative patients. Those who administer the Mental Health Act are specifically exempted by it from civil or criminal prosecution, so it is difficult to obtain redress against wrongful detention or treatment. In any case, this would be likely to follow some time after the provisions of the Mental Health Act were used. The concept of mental illness is not closely defined in the Act and so particular medical practitioners are left to implement it as they see fit. Altogether this legislation is far-reaching, and all

[11] Raphael, *Psychiatric Hospitals.*
[12] In 1986 there were 15,932 admissions to hospital under specific sections of the Mental Health Act. See MIND, 'Mental Health Statistics', London: MIND, 1990.

patients or potential patients in psychiatric hospitals live under the shadow of its provisions.

THE PATIENT–STAFF RELATIONSHIP

When a patient consults with her psychiatrist, a meeting which may happen only very occasionally, she is encountering a person who has enormous potential power under the provisions of the Mental Health Act, and who is likely to outrank her considerably in terms of class and authority. Patient and doctor have probably had very different social backgrounds and experiences, and may view the patient's problem in completely different ways. The doctor–patient interview or encounter can be seen as a time of negotiation and potential conflict over problem definition and treatment solution in which both the parties have to try and reach an accommodation satisfactory to each. Freidson suggests that 'the separate worlds of experience and reference of the layman and the professional worker are always in potential conflict with each other'.[13] There is much room for failures of communication and disagreement, particularly when these are exacerbated by class inequality.

A number of researchers have examined the conflictual nature of the doctor–patient relationship, drawing attention to differences in power in which doctors are dominant, and class-related communication difficulties which may work to the disadvantage of the patient.[14] In the state psychiatric hospital, these problems may be multiplied. Patients mostly cannot choose which doctor to consult. They cannot withdraw themselves from consultations with their psychiatrists or refuse to pay their bills thus terminating the relationship. Their

[13] Eliot Freidson, 'Dilemmas in the doctor–patient relationship' in Caroline Cox and Adrienne Mead, eds., *Sociology in Medical Practice*. London: Collier Macmillan, 1975, p. 286.

[14] See, for example, Freda Fitton and H. W. K. Acheson, *The Doctor–Patient Relationship*. London: HMSO, 1979; G. Stimpson and B. Webb, *Going to See the Doctor*. London: Routledge and Kegan Paul, 1975. For the differential use of linguistic codes in different social classes see David Tuckett, 'Work, life chances and lifestyles' in Tuckett, ed., *An Introduction to Medical Sociology*, pp. 145ff.

compliance with particular treatment regimes is monitored all the time by nurses obeying the doctor's instructions.

A further feature which diminishes a patient's power and influence with professional staff of all kinds is the fact that staff tend to see the whole of a patient's behaviour as symptomatic of mental illness; they therefore tend not to take patients' perceptions and views seriously. Patients are stripped of their outside identity as citizens and then treated as if their illness comprised the totality of their being.[15] In a famous study, Rosenham and colleagues infiltrated ordinary people into a psychiatric hospital. Once admitted, these researchers behaved as they normally did, yet their behaviour, which included things like reading books or taking notes, was taken as being evidence of insanity and they were kept in the hospital for quite a long time. At no point were the researchers detected as pseudo-patients.[16]

The medicalisation of the whole of a patient's behaviour can have serious consequences. For example, a young patient in a British hospital broke his leg, but did not receive any treatment for it for 19 days because the medical and nursing staff did not believe him when he complained that he had difficulty in walking and was in pain. His mother was the person who insisted that he have treatment after witnessing his crawling about, supporting himself with the walls and having to slide down stairs on his bottom.[17] One professor of experimental psychology, who was clearly very capable and occupied a high social position outside hospital before being hospitalised for manic-depressive illness, protests that, 'many of us felt oppressed because we could not deal on equal terms with doctors or nurses, we were mad, they did not need to take us seriously'.[18]

The younger doctors and nurses tended to treat patients as though they were insane, and this could be infuriating and upsetting ... The point is that none of the patients was totally out of touch with reality

[15] Goffman, *Asylums*, pp. 23ff.

[16] David L. Rosenham,'On being sane in insane places' in Alfred Dean, Alan M. Kraft and Bert Pepper, eds., *The Social Setting of Mental Health*. New York: Basic Books, 1976.

[17] David Leigh, 'Hospital named after X-Ray row', *The Guardian* 2 12 1980.

[18] Stuart Sutherland, *Breakdown*. London: Granada, 1977, p. 41.

and their illness only affected part of their lives ... Because doctors and nurses could always shelter behind the belief that patients were mad, they were in an impregnable position, and it was easy for patients to feel completely in the power of the hospital authorities .[19]

An important implication of this total medicalisation of patients' behaviour is that health can become equated with good behaviour, and treatment can come to be used as a punishment. Jordan notes

Treatment is clearly an attempt to influence behaviour and thus a form of control; but equally clearly it is not necessarily a punishment. However ... psychiatrists do overtly or covertly use the threat of compulsory detention to ensure voluntary admission, and of locked wards to procure co-operation in treatment methods.[20]

In this situation, it not surprising that patients feel that what they most want to do is to behave well in conformity with staff and institutional expectations, whether legitimate or not, so they can escape from the total regime imposed by ward life in a psychiatric hospital.

TREATMENTS

In general, the actual treatment methods used in the average psychiatric hospital do not enhance patients' power and autonomy. The medical means of treating people predominates with the use of drugs and other physical treatments. This controls symptoms rather than curing any putative disease, and does not require the active participation of patients. Their main contribution is to take medicines as ordered and to assume a classic 'sick role' passivity while doctors and nurses act ostensibly in their interests.[21] It should be noted that medical treatments are cheap, easy to administer, impersonal, economic on staff time, and profitable for drug companies.

---

[19] Sutherland, *Breakdown*, p. 30.
[20] Bill Jordan, *Freedom and the Welfare State*. London: Routledge and Kegan Paul, 1976, p. 153.
[21] For the 'sick role' see, for example, David Mechanic, *Medical Sociology*. New York: Free Press, second edn., 1978, pp. 84ff.

However, the use of powerful psychoactive drugs and techniques such as ECT and psychosurgery has been questioned and condemned in some quarters as very harmful to patients' long-term health and well-being. Hill, for example, condemns many physical treatments as 'psychiatric violence' which is abusive, physically damaging and punitive because of its severe physical side-effects.[22]

Over the years mentally ill people have been subject to some uniquely cruel and therapeutically barren methods of treatment. In the eighteenth century they were chained up and beaten like the irrational beasts they were supposed to have become. In the nineteenth century, they were placed in asylums which quickly became warehouses of mass confinement. Once effective moral treatment, itself a mode of change imposition, became an impossibility, they were purged, bled, and vomited by their medical attendants as a matter of course. Other popular physical treatments included various kinds of shock treatment such as swing-chairs and dousing with cold water. In our own century, new kinds of radical physical 'cure' such as malaria treatment, insulin coma therapy, and psychosurgery have been hailed as the great panacea for mental illness only to be recognised later as being of limited or no use, or even as positively harmful. Within this kind of historical perspective perhaps one should look with some suspicion upon medical claims that ECT and psychoactive drugs are beneficial, and be prepared to take more seriously the claims of patients and others that the treatments cause considerable harm and distress in many cases.[23]

Behaviour modification, based on the tenets of the kind of behavioural psychology associated with writers like B. F. Skinner, is becoming more popular as a form of treatment, especially in relation to anti-social or dysfunctional aspects of

[22] Hill, *The Politics of Schizophrenia*. Further discussions of the damaging effects of psychiatric treatments can be found in Johnstone, *Users and Abusers of Psychiatry*, ch. 9. Clare, *Psychiatry in Dissent*, gives a rationale for these treatments.

[23] For more on the various kinds of treatment methods mentioned and patients' responses to them see Porter, *The Faber Book of Madness*, ch. 12.

patients' behaviour.[24] While this is less physically invasive than direct medical intervention and, ideally, it enlists the consent and participation of the patient, behavioural regimes with their token economies and sanctions of reward and punishment can be very oppressive indeed, especially in an institutional setting:

In order to set up a system of rewards, it is often necessary to deprive patients of other methods of gaining whatever is used as a reward. Hence, although staff may see patients as working for a system of rewards, the patients themselves may feel that they are working to escape from a punishment they have done nothing to deserve ... Furthermore, the system can never be any better than those administering it, and the power to give rewards can always be misused to persuade patients to do things which are patently for the good of staff members but not so obviously for the patient's good.[25]

There are strong similarities between the principles underlying behaviour therapy and the practice of milieu and administrative therapeutic regimes and therapeutic communities.[26] Although practitioners of these latter modes of treatment would not necessarily want to see their descent as being from behaviourism (therapeutic communities, for example, have been more influenced by psychotherapeutic ideas), the basic principle on which they work is that of using group and structural engineering of the therapeutic environment to effect desired change in patients who can then be rehabilitated into society. Therapeutic communities can simply be places where considerable group pressure is exerted on individuals to change: 'We need ... have no qualms of guilt about saying that our therapeutic community is going to teach its members certain kinds of behaviour and discourage undesirable behaviour.'[27]

24 See Paul Bebbington, 'Behaviour Therapy' in Peter Hill, Robin Murray and Anthony Thorley, *Essentials of Postgraduate Psychiatry*. London: Academic Press, 1979.

25 Sutherland, *Breakdown*, p. 177.

26 See further, for example, David Clark, *Administrative Therapy*. London: Tavistock, 1964; Maxwell Jones, *Social Psychiatry in Practice*. Harmondsworth: Penguin, 1968.

27 Clark, *Administrative Therapy*, p. 68. For the political dimensions of therapeutic communities and milieu therapies see Brian Haddon, 'Political implications of therapeutic communities' in R. D. Hinshelwood and Nick Manning, eds., *Therapeutic Communities*. London: Routledge and Kegan Paul, 1979.

Custodialism is not an 'official' system of thought and therapy in relation to mental disorder. It is one which has been particularly operant in psychiatric institutions in the absence of other treatment ideologies, funds, staff, and morale. The aggregate of miscellaneous views and practices which comprise the 'ideal type' of custodialism has been characterised thus:

> The model of the custodial orientation is the traditional prison and the 'chronic' mental hospital which provide a highly controlled setting concerned mainly with ... detention and safekeeping ... Patients are conceived in stereotyped terms as categorically different from 'normal' people, as totally irrational, insensitive to others, unpredictable and dangerous. Mental illness is attributed primarily to poor heredity, organic lesion and the like. In consequence, the staff cannot expect to understand the patients, to engage in meaningful relationships with them, nor in most cases to do them any good. Custodialism is saturated with pessimism, impersonalness, and watchful distrust. The custodial conception of the hospital is auto-cratic, involving as it does a rigid status hierarchy, a unilateral downward flow of power, and a minimizing of communication within and across status lines.[28]

Of the 'treatment methods' outlined here, this is clearly the most oppressive. Custodialism leads to the institutionalisation and demoralisation of patients and staff alike.[29] It has no potential for curing people or enhancing their individuality and autonomy. Although it seems eminently undesirable, elements of custodialism are not uncommon in institutions which care for mentally ill people from psychiatric hospitals through to community care hostels. Custodialism flourishes where resources are scarce, staff are poor, and morale is low. It is a cheap option for disposing of groups of people whose social and personal needs are not given a high financial priority by society. It is highly compatible with the use of behavioural and medical treatments outlined above.

There are treatment options available for working with

---

[28] Doris C. Gilbert and Daniel J. Levinson, '"Custodialism" and "humanism" in mental hospital structure and in staff ideology' in Milton Greenblatt, Daniel J. Levinson and Richard H. Williams, eds., *The Patient and the Mental Hospital*, p. 22.

[29] See further, for example, J. K. Wing and G. W. Brown, *Institutionalism and Schizophrenia*. Cambridge: Cambridge University Press, 1970.

mentally disordered people which do, at least in theory, enhance the sense of autonomy and responsibility of the patient. Psychotherapy and group therapy based on talking about problems are perhaps the best known of these methods.[30] However, psychotherapy is not a popular mode of treatment in British hospitals. This is partly because of its lengthiness and, therefore, its expense. It also has to do with the fact that it is believed that it simply does not work effectively with many mentally ill people. It is more an indulgence which can be paid for by the mildly neurotic affluent on a private basis, rather than a treatment which should be available to all at public expense.[31]

Significantly, it is individual psychotherapy which gives the mentally ill person most time with a skilled professional, requires her own co-operation, and maximises her personal autonomy and freedom to express herself. The therapist is dependent on the patient to effect her own cure and administers no drug. Although psychotherapists can influence their patients significantly in different directions, particularly if they are perceived to be superior in knowledge, wisdom, or status, in general, psychotherapy implies an unusual equality of relationship in the treatment of mental disorder. It does not do to idealise any treatment mode, however. Any process designed to intervene in the lives of needy others conducted by professionals can have an oppressive effect. In *Asylum to Anarchy*, Baron demonstrates how a psychodynamically inclined treatment regime became oppressive to patients in a psychiatric day hospital, while Masson points out that psychotherapists can dominate, abuse and assault their clients like any other kind of doctor.[32]

---

[30] See further, for example, Anthony Storr, *The Art of Psychotherapy*. London: Secker and Warburg and Heinemann, 1979; Hinshelwood and Manning, eds., *Therapeutic Communities*; David H. Clark, *Social Therapy in Psychiatry*. Harmondsworth: Penguin, 1981.

[31] For a defence of psychotherapy being efficacious and relevant to all sectors of society see Holmes and Lindley, *The Values of Psychotherapy*.

[32] Baron, *Asylum to Anarchy*; Masson, *Against Therapy*; Jeffrey Masson, *Final Analysis*. London: Harper Collins, 1992.

PATIENTS AND POWER

So far, a picture has been created which suggests that patients are almost entirely powerless and bereft of decision-making power in relation to the psychiatric hospital and its staff. This is, I think, a fair impression. Patients are often actively, if implicitly, encouraged to conform to institutional norms and to behave passively:

> Someone who sits miserably but quietly in a corner, taking their medication regularly, is easier to deal with than someone who is prepared to disagree, protest and complain . . . Patients are likely to acquire labels like 'aggressive' and 'paranoid' if their behaviour becomes too challenging.[33]

For the women who comprise the majority of the patient population, this is but an extension of the sort of passive role which they are expected to play in society outside generally.[34] The hospital is a highly regressive and controlling institution in which obedience and conformity to staff norms are rewarded while deviance is punished.

It seems likely, however, that individual patients do have some limited informal power in the institution and in encounters with staff. The first of these is called 'impression management', whereby a patient can modify her behaviour or symptoms in order to achieve desired ends, for example, transfer to another ward or discharge.[35] The second is what Goffman calls 'living between the rules', whereby patients manage informally to achieve some of their own ends while outwardly conforming to institutional rules and practices.[36]

Unlike prisoners, however, there is little social solidarity to attain common goals. Patients seldom band together in hospitals to protest at, or change, their conditions. It seems that very

---

[33] Johnstone, *Users and Abusers of Psychiatry*, p. 18.

[34] For the reinforcement of outside passive social roles see Johnstone, *Users and Abusers in Psychiatry*.

[35] See Benjamin J. Braginsky, Martin Grosse and Kenneth Ring, 'Controlling outcomes through impression management', *Journal of Consulting and Clinical Psychology* 30, 1966, 295–300.

[36] Goffman, *Asylums*, pp. 187ff.

little sense of corporate interest or identity builds up in patients, due perhaps to their illness:[37]

Mental patients are among the most private of citizens. To the extent that their condition is severe and stressful, it is liable to remove them from the possibilities of common association and organisation.[38]

They are thus largely at the mercy of the more powerful, higher-status staff groups who order the institution in conformity to society's wider expectations and the resources it provides.

THE PATIENT–STAFF DIVIDE

In *Asylums*, Goffman characterised psychiatric hospitals as total institutions. A total institution is one characterised by a mixture of bureaucracy and community in which many human needs are handled by the bureaucratic organisation of whole blocks of people. It has the following attributes: (i) All aspects of life are conducted in the same place and under a single authority; (ii) each phase of members' daily activity is carried out in the company of other people all of whom are treated alike and required to do the same thing together; (iii) all phases of the day's activities are tightly scheduled, with the whole sequence of activities being imposed from above by a system of explicit formal rulings and a body of officials; iv) the various enforced activities are brought together into a single rational plan which fulfils the official aims of the institution.[39] Although psychiatric hospitals have changed over the years, for example, people do not stay in them for so long and they may be more flexible in their routines, they still have many of these features (as do other psychiatric facilities outwith the hospital setting). One of the most prominent features of the total institution which continues to pertain to psychiatric hospitals today is a fundamental patient–staff divide.

The basic split between the inmates of an institution and those who have responsibility for managing and supervising

---

[37] See R. Sommer and H. Osmond, 'The schizophrenic no-society', *Psychiatry* 25, 1962, 244–55.
[38] Sedgwick, *PsychoPolitics*, p. 222.   [39] Goffman, *Asylums*, p. 17f.

them is an essential aspect of a custodial bureaucratic organisation. There is a great divide which is almost absolute in terms of communication, information, status, and power: 'Two different social and cultural worlds develop, jogging alongside each other with points of official contact but little mutual penetration.'[40] Furthermore,

Each grouping tends to conceive of the other in terms of narrow hostile stereotypes ... Staff tend to feel superior and righteous; inmates tend, in some ways at least, to feel inferior, weak, blameworthy and guilty.[41]

In a psychiatric hospital the staff have considerably more power than the patients. They can impose sanctions on patients, including rewards such as cigarettes, money, and trips out of the hospital, or punishments like unpleasant forms of treatment, confinement, deprivation, or threats. (It is not for nothing that the mental hospital has been called 'a place where ordinary civil liberties are called privileges'.[42]) They also often have more knowledge about a patient's destiny and treatment than she does herself. Patients, in turn, have few sanctions which they can exercise against the staff, and are often not consulted either about their own treatment and future, or about the running of the institution. The hospital is perceived to belong to the staff rather than to its users, even if the latter have been there longer than the former:

Significantly, the institutional plant and name come to be identified by both staff and inmates as somehow belonging to the staff, so that when either grouping refers to the views or interests of 'the institution' by implication they are referring to the view and concerns of the staff.[43]

Attempts to break down the staff–patient divide to try and equalise power and decision making between clientele and professional workers, for example, in therapeutic communities

---

[40] Ibid., p. 20. [41] Ibid., p. 18.
[42] A. G. Stanton and M. S. Schwartz, *The Mental Hospital*. New York: Basic Books, 1954, p. 244. See further Arlene Kaplan Daniels, 'Advisory and coercive functions in the hospital' in Gary L. Albrecht and Paul C. Higgins, eds., *Health, Illness and Medicine*. Chicago: Rand McNally, 1979.
[43] Goffman, *Asylums*, p. 20.

and social therapy experiments have often been subverted by the staff's continuing desire to hang on to ultimate power and influence.[44] As long as psychiatric services are required by society to provide custody and control for a despised deviant group with very limited resources, it is likely that the divide will continue to gape.

A parable of the staff–patient divide and the difficulties in crossing it is to be found in a recent account of patients being resettled in a community setting. At first, patients and staff shared the same facilities and utensils. However, after a while staff started to bring in their own mugs – an important distinction of staff from patients in the old hospital setting.[45] Old habits and the attitudes underlying them will die very hard, and the dynamics lying behind the staff–patient divide in the hospitals continue to function today within the hospitals as well as in the newer community settings.

THE APOTHEOSIS OF ABUSE AND NEGLECT

Psychiatric patients

have been defeated in long, protracted, at times subtle, at times violent, power struggles within the families, and by friends and colleagues in school, work and the other communities in which they have unsuccessfully sought to participate.[46]

When people are diagnosed as mentally ill and are hospitalised they may be treated in a large, isolated, decrepit building, dating back to the turn of the century or beyond, and designed for the mass warehousing of the mentally ill. It is likely that the hospital will be short of financial and human resources due to the low priority given historically to care for the mentally ill. The treatment regime is therefore a mixture of custodial, medical, and behavioural methods, none of which do much to

---

[44] See Rubenstein and Lasswell, *The Sharing of Power*, p. 257.

[45] Dylan Tomlinson, *Utopia, Community Care and the Retreat from the Asylums*. Milton Keynes: Open University Press, 1991, p. 150. A friend of mine tells me that when he was a new hospital chaplain a nurse was horrified to see him drinking out of one of the patients' cups and offered him a staff cup instead. I myself have had the curious experience of being abjectly apologised to by a doctor who was very sorry that he had mistaken me for a patient!.

[46] Rubenstein and Lasswell, *The Sharing of Power*, p. 4.

enhance a sense of power, autonomy, or efficacy amongst patients, particularly long-term, chronically ill or elderly patients. Resources in the hospital are likely to be unequally distributed with acute services for younger people gaining more financial and medical support. Patients will find that there is a hierarchy of power and influence, both formal and informal, amongst the staff group. This broadly reflects the social and class structure of society outside the hospital. The position of patients is at the bottom of this hierarchy. They have little influence over their own lives or that of the institution as a whole, and will find themselves subject to the active control of the staff. If they are particularly unfortunate, they may find themselves the victims of abuse and neglect.

The potential of the psychiatric hospital to damage its vulnerable clientele has been apparent since this institution was first conceived. Since the last war, the voices pointing this out have become louder and better informed. A psychiatrist, Russell Barton, coined the term 'institutional neurosis' to describe the effect that psychiatric hospitals have on young and middle-aged long-stay psychotic patients. He suggests that there is a socially caused syndrome which afflicts these patients independently of their disease after they have been in hospital for a while. Institutional neurosis is

a disease characterised by apathy, lack of initiative, loss of interest, especially in things of a personal nature, submissiveness, apparent inability to make plans for the future, lack of individuality, and sometimes a characteristic posture and gait.[47]

The factors which contribute to this are loss of contact with the outside world, enforced idleness and loss of responsibility, brutality, browbeating and teasing, bossiness of the professional staff, loss of personal friends, possessions and personal events, drugs, ward atmosphere and loss of prospects outside the institution.[48]

These findings are echoed by Wing and Brown who found that the negative symptoms of schizophrenia were much more

---

[47] Russell Barton, *Institutional Neurosis*. Bristol: Wright, third edn., 1976, p. 76.
[48] Ibid., p. 77f.

likely to occur in an impoverished social environment where there is little outside contact, nursing attitudes are unfavourable, and where patients have few possessions, little to occupy their time, and live in restricted conditions. Wing and Brown concluded that, 'a substantial proportion, though by no means all of the morbidity shown by long-stay schizophrenic patients is the product of their environment'.[49]

The apotheosis of the negative effects of psychiatric hospitals is best revealed, however, by the reports on scandalous conditions of abuse and neglect which became public during the 1970s. During this decade about one tenth of all the psychiatric hospitals then in operation enjoyed the dubious distinction of having a public enquiry into allegations of abuse and neglect, mostly of elderly and chronically ill patients on 'back wards'.[50]

At one hospital, for example, the following allegations were found proven by a commission of inquiry. Patients were sworn at and hit around the head, as well as being threatened by one nurse. One patient was slapped for not urinating. Electroconvulsive therapy (ECT) was given to an unwilling voluntary patient (i.e., a patient who was not compulsorily detained under the provisions of the Mental Health Act) who had to be manhandled to be made to comply. Another patient was kept locked in a bare, smelly side room for a month.

Psychogeriatric patients on some wards received baths only very infrequently. Patients' property and presents brought for them were denied them. They were deprived of their spectacles and had little opportunity to engage in any kind of stimulating activity. Patients did not receive the pocket-money to which they were entitled. On one ward, patients were deprived of liquid if they were incontinent. Sometimes patients were made to 'perform' in front of groups of students by a charge nurse. Clothing supplies were inadequate (a very serious problem when dealing with repeatedly incontinent patients). One charge nurse deprived a patient of food for several weeks. Some

[49] J. K. Wing and G. W. Brown, *Institutionalism and Schizophrenia.* Cambridge: Cambridge University Press, 1970, p. 77f.
[50] For a list of these enquiries and analysis of the lessons to be learned from them see J. P. Martin, *Hospitals in Trouble.* Oxford: Blackwell, 1984, pp. 256–7.

patients were verbally abused and openly called 'dumbos' by nurses. A patient was kept in his pyjamas and dressing gown for 9 months. Some patients almost never saw their doctors and a patient was given ECT without first being physically examined by a doctor. It became apparent subsequently that she was not fit enough to have this treatment.[51] Whenever mostly junior staff tried to draw the attention of managers and health authorities to conditions like these as 'whistleblowers', they were ignored, intimidated, or fired.[52] In general, nursing unions were as keen to avoid taking the situations seriously as were the management.

The extreme conditions described above are an extreme symptom, the 'tip of an iceberg' of the structural problems facing the psychiatric hospitals in general. Underlying incidents like those described are a raft of interlinked problems. These have been identified as lack of resources, low staff morale, lack of clear understanding by staff of their responsibilities, and lack of contact and co-operation between different disciplines and departments.[53] Lack of financial and physical resources leads to a poor working environment as well as making it impossible to hire the right number of qualified staff of sufficient calibre. Shortages of staff mean that only very basic nursing care can be given to patients, and sometimes their most fundamental needs may be neglected. It also means that there is inadequate supervision of junior and unqualified staff. Lack of leadership emanates from confusion about roles and parallel hierarchies of responsibility which mean that patients are sometimes ignored. Often nurses assumed a subordinate role, expecting doctors to take a lead and main responsibility when the latter were not really available and were concentrating their efforts on acute, younger patients, rather than on the areas of the hospital filled with elderly and chronically ill people who are, in all respects, the most vulnerable and deprived. Doctors in their turn were unwilling to give

[51] South East Thames Regional Health Authority, *Report of a Committee of Enquiry, St Augustine's Hospital, Chartham, Canterbury*. London: South East Thames RHA, 1976.
[52] Virginia Beardshaw, *Conscientious Objectors at Work*. London: Social Audit, 1981.
[53] DHSS, *Report of a Working Group on Organisational and Management Problems of Mental Illness Hospitals*. London: DHSS, 1980.

up their power and delegate their functions effectively. All this was exacerbated by poor communications between staff groups, and an attitude on the part of rather distant senior managers that there could not really be anything seriously amiss in their hospitals. As we have seen, in this situation it is the powerless and relatively inarticulate patients who suffer and fall through the net of care.

CONCLUSION

Mostly, the patients in hospitals have to endure shabby conditions and boredom, rather than active abuse and neglect. The picture I have painted of the psychiatric hospital has emphasised the potentially negative, oppressive, and unjust aspects of that institution without giving weight to its more positive features. There are positive features, too, of course. For some patients these might include getting away from difficult home circumstances (i.e., receiving asylum) and even an enhancement of life in that there are other people in the hospital with whom to have a social life, and there is a certain amount of employment and organised leisure activity. Patients in hospitals might benefit, for example, from the large, spacious grounds. One critic has suggested that, far from stripping patients of their liberties, 'for some patients hospitalization provides a means of reclaiming rights and privileges lost in the outside world'.[54] There are better hospitals as well as worse ones. There are high-morale units with good calibre staff, as well as demoralised and depressed ones where staff do not or cannot care.[55]

Looking at the recent and not so recent shortcomings and actual harm done by so many psychiatric hospitals to their

---

[54] L. S. Linn, 'The mental hospital from the patient perspective'.
[55] See, for example, David Towell and Clive Harries, *Innovation in Nursing Care*. London: Croom Helm, 1979. For defence of the institutions and a critique of the critics see Jones and Sidebotham, *Mental Hospitals at Work*; Kathleen Jones, 'Re-inventing the wheel' in MIND, *The Future of the Mental Hospitals*. London: MIND, 1981; Kathleen Jones and A. J. Fowles, *Ideas on Institutions*. London: Routledge and Kegan Paul, 1984.

patients, however, it is difficult not to agree strongly with some of the judgements made on American state psychiatric hospitals which seem to share many of the defects and limitations of their British counterparts. Belknap, for example, writes,

Against continual deficits of staff and material, and against occasional instances of indifference and neglect, or outright abuse, progress has been made from time to time; but the uneasy feeling exists that reform and regression in mental hospital affairs are inseparable processes. The cycle has repeated itself too often to be fortuitous. The sequence of expose, reform, progress, indifference, apathy and decline has been repeated with variations in a dozen states of the Union in the past twenty years.[56]

He goes on:

The indictment that can reasonably be levelled at the state hospital is not so much that it lacks treatment effectiveness, but rather, first that it has persistently developed conditions which are cruel and inhuman both for patients and employees, and, second, that it tends regularly to degenerate into the kind of social organisation that does not permit the application of the little that is actually known about the treatment of mental disease.[57]

This kind of judgement is echoed at a distance of nearly 20 years later by Talbott:

It should be obvious by now that state hospitals, as they are currently constituted, do not work, seem designed not to work, and have never worked. Critics ... continue to point out the problems, decade after decade, without any perceivable effect.[58]

I would not want to deny for one moment that there have been positive features to some hospitals some of the time. The point I want to make is that the psychiatric hospital can be seen as a microcosm of capitalist society and reflects its attitudes, priorities, structures, injustices and inequalities. In many ways, it is required by that society to control an unwanted, powerless, economically unproductive, stigmatised group and it is funded accordingly. It is therefore under-

---

[56] Belknap, *Human Problems of a State Mental Hospital*, pp. vii–viii.
[57] Ibid., p. 13.
[58] Talbott, *The Death of the Asylum*, p. 125.

funded. A corollary of this is that mentally disordered patients, who come at the bottom of the social hierarchy both within and outside the hospital are often exposed to poor conditions, low-calibre staff, and custodial structures which do little to maximise their well-being. They may be positively harmful, as the account of abuse and neglect above indicates.

That this can be the case buttresses my overall contention that there are substantial social and political factors bearing on the incidence and treatment of mental disorder in our society. As we have seen, there are broad social and political factors, such as class position, which affect the incidence of mental illness. Other, similar factors also bear significantly upon the treatment of mentally ill people in hospital in regard, for example, to the hierarchical order of the institution and the attitudes and resources available within it. Much of the discomfort and misery suffered by mentally disordered people is owed not to disease, but to the circumstances in which they are treated and in which they find their powerlessness reinforced. Mentally ill people in hospital must be regarded as a group of poor and potentially or actually oppressed people whose sufferings are compounded by the structures within which they are situated. And those structures must be seen as centrally related to wider social order – it is not an accident of blind fate that mentally ill people are in the situation they are; it is, at least partly, a problem of social organisation, attitudes, and priorities. The question is, will the advent of community care for mentally ill people solve the problem of the potential marginalisation and oppression of this group in the future?

CHAPTER 10

The 'brave new world' of community care

This century has seen mentally ill people returned to the community. In 1961, Enoch Powell, then minister of health, unexpectedly proclaimed the demise of the psychiatric hospitals and the advent of community care outside institutions as government policy for mentally disordered people.[1] This policy, formalised and systematised in a White Paper, *Better Services for the Mentally Ill*, in 1975, and given new impetus by a further White Paper, *Caring for People*, in 1989, now shapes service provision for mentally ill people, people with learning disabilities and elderly people in British society.[2]

Powell's initiative was unexpected because, at the time, the psychiatric hospitals were full and flourishing. Historians holding a progressive view of psychiatry suggest the following factors for the timing. First, powerful psychoactive drugs like the chlorpromazines were becoming available, permitting more control of symptoms and thus obviating the need for patients to be controlled within a restrictive environment. Secondly, administrative and social therapies were demonstrating that more could be done to rehabilitate patients than had been supposed. Lastly, the public were becoming intolerant of the inhumane conditions exposed in psychiatric hospitals and reported in books like Goffman's *Asylums* and Barton's *Institutional Neurosis*; it wanted to see an end to hospital care for idealistic reasons.[3]

---

[1] Jones, *History of the Mental Health Services*, p. 321.
[2] *Better Services for the Mentally Ill*. (cm 6233) London: HMSO, 1975; *Caring for People*. (cm 849) London: HMSO, 1989.
[3] See Jones, *History of the Mental Health Services*, ch. 13.

This interpretation has been questioned from a historical materialist perspective by Scull. He situates the policy change amidst wider interests in the socio-economic order rather than in the realm of scientific or ethical progress.[4] Scull points out that patient numbers in the hospitals had started to decline before chlorpromazine use became widespread; that the inhumane conditions in the hospitals had been known about for decades with no action being taken to improve them; that there is no evidence to suggest that the public were particularly concerned to ameliorate the condition of mentally ill people or to have them living in their midst, and that books like Goffman's were, in any case, published after the policy shift was announced (*Asylums* was published in 1962). Most significantly, the deinstitutionalisation of mentally ill people was paralleled by an exactly contemporaneous move to run down the populations of prisons where most of the factors which ostensibly explain the move in psychiatry should not apply. Scull argues that the motivator for the changes was not enlightened humanitarian and therapeutic concern (nobody knew whether community settings would be more therapeutic for mentally ill people because no research had been undertaken), but socio-economic change making it no longer expedient for government and the ruling classes to deal with the problem of mental disorder in an institutional way.

The main benefit to government and taxpayers of community care is that it appears cheaper than institutional care.[5] Hospitals are expensive to run, and it costs a good deal to keep a person in one (£17,000 per annum in 1986–7[6]). In 1960, many of the hospitals were worn-out and a substantial outlay in building work was required to make them good. The

---

[4] See Scull, *Decarceration*.

[5] The cheapness of community care and the fiscal benefit of this has been a leitmotif in most governmental publications in the last three decades. A 1981 document asserts that, 'although the cost to the community health and social services of providing care for people transferred from hospital is difficult to assess, there are good reasons for believing that in many cases it would be lower and better value' (DHSS, *Care in the Community*. London: DHSS, 1981, 3.7). Economy was also a central feature in Audit Commission, *Making a Reality of Community Care*. London: HMSO, 1986. For further detailed discussion of costs see Murphy, *After the Asylums*, pp. 234ff.

[6] Murphy, *After the Asylums*, p. 235.

alternative of running down and closing them was conceivable because, by the middle of the twentieth century, outdoor relief in the form of supplementary and other welfare benefits was not proscribed as it had been under the old Poor Law. Thus, the poor and needy could be relieved in the community, not in an expensive institution. Welfare capitalism favours outdoor relief because it saves on public expenditure, and places some of the burden of care and expenditure on the friends and relatives of those who have hitherto been institutionalised.

Scull might have gone on to note the decline of corporate welfarist solutions to social problems, and the rise of the ideology of sturdy individualism and personal and family responsibility which has burgeoned over the past few decades, culminating in the rolling back of the Welfare State by the Conservative government in the 1980s. This movement, into which community care fits well, has left many needy groups and individuals to provide for their own welfare needs while restoring money to the pockets of the tax-paying ruling class.[7]

In addition to taxpayers and central government benefiting from economies through deinstitutionalisation of mentally ill people, a key group, the medical profession, also gains.[8] The medical asylum superintendents vigorously resisted the idea of care outside an asylum in the nineteenth century on the grounds that patients might be neglected and abused.[9] Modern psychiatrists, however, mostly have not resisted the move out of the large stigmatising psychiatric hospitals whose wards were clogged with chronically ill people, into new short-stay mental illness units in district general hospitals. There they can be identified more clearly with their higher-status medical colleagues, and concentrate on administering physical and drug-based therapies to acutely ill patients who are more

[7] See further Mishra, *The Welfare State in Capitalist Society*; Gillian Dalley, *Ideologies of Caring*. London: Macmillan, 1988, ch. 2.

[8] 'The latent function of the shift in policy was to provide for the desegregation of the psychiatric profession' (Geoff Baruch and Andrew Treacher, *Psychiatry Observed*. London: Routledge and Kegan Paul, 1978, p. vii).

[9] William Ll Parry-Jones, 'The model of the Geel Lunatic Colony and its influence on the nineteenth century asylum system in Britain' in Andrew Scull, ed., *Madhouses, Mad-doctors and Madmen*. London: Athlone, 1981.

likely to 'get better'.[10] They may also have gained financially from the new system, as home visits to patients command additional fees on top of basic salary.

The advent and dominance of community care policies for mentally ill people can be explained in historical and material terms, rather than simply as 'humane progress'. This is a valuable prelude to a closer look at what community care means, some of the problems it faces, and the implications of this for the client group which it concerns.

WHAT IS COMMUNITY CARE?

It is easier to describe some of the constituent features and practices involved in community care than to state exactly what it is.[11] Broadly speaking, a mentally ill person experiencing community care will expect not to have to become a patient in a large old psychiatric hospital. She will live within an area in which health and social services provide a range of care and treatment facilities which should, theoretically, suit her needs. For example, she may relate to a locality-based community care team composed of psychiatrists, nurses, and others who may administer medication to her either at home or in some kind of local treatment facility or clinic. If she needs to have a period of hospitalisation for an acute episode of disorder, she may go for a relatively brief stay into a psychiatric ward or unit at a local general hospital.

Chronically mentally ill people, or those recovering from episodes of illness, may find a range of facilities in their area. These might include day hospitals or day centres, small work or therapy units and drop-in centres in which a mixture of treatment, rehabilitative work, companionship, and leisure activities could be available. A person might attend these intensively or occasionally, according to availability and need.

---

10 See further, Baruch and Treacher, *Psychiatry Observed*.
11 For general discussion of the history, definition, and nature of community care see Richmond Fellowship, *Mental Health and the Community*. London: Richmond Fellowship, 1983; Alexander H. Leighton, *Caring for Mentally Ill People*. Cambridge: Cambridge University Press, 1982; Shulamit Ramon, ed., *Beyond Community Care*. London: Macmillan, 1991.

Many people who are experiencing, or have experienced, episodes of mental disorder now often continue to live at home with their families. When this is not possible or desirable, there are residential facilities ranging from 'half-way' houses for people coming out of hospital, through to supervised hostels with some nursing care, and hotels or houses where they can live with other ex-patients. Such facilities, and many of the other services mentioned, are not run by the NHS, but by local authorities or by voluntary organisations such as local branches of MIND (The National Association for Mental Health) or the local church. Some people prefer to live on their own and, of course, many people who have been mentally ill in the past are perfectly integrated into the community and make no use of specialised personnel, facilities, or accommodation at all. This is as it should be in the philosophy of community care, for the ideal is that people should live a normal life in normal circumstances, and not be unnecessarily distinguished as mentally ill.[12]

PROBLEMS WITH COMMUNITY CARE

It is one thing to describe the facilities and services which might, theoretically, be available to persons in receipt of community care in respect of long- or short-term episodes of mental illness. However, community care is surrounded by many unresolved issues making its actual implementation problematic.

An important difficulty has been a lack of clear understanding as to how 'community care' is to be defined. This affects the expectations surrounding community care. The term is vague and non-specific, with resonances of local goodwill and concern for mentally ill people which may lack any cutting edge or basis in reality. 'Community', for example, can designate a geographically or adminstreatively defined area, a well-integrated district or neighbourhood where people know each other well, a group of people who have a definite common

---

[12] For the general features and 'normalisation' philosophy of community care see Murphy, *After the Asylums*, chs. 7 and 8.

interest, or, in the present context, anywhere outside a large institution:

To the politician, 'community care' is a useful piece of rhetoric; to the sociologist, it is a stick to beat institutional care with; to the civil servant it is a cheap alternative to institutional care which can be passed to the local authorities for action – or inaction; to the visionary, it is a dream of the new society in which people really do care; to the social services departments it is a nightmare of heightened public expectations and inadequate resources to meet them. We are only just beginning to find out what it means to the old, the chronically sick and the handicapped.[13]

There has been vagueness and confusion about what community care means. The term has been accepted as a blank prescription for a progressive humane alternative to institutional care without having publicly to justify itself ideologically, rationally, practically, or ethically. Even the latest definition which guides government action is not specific: community care 'means providing the right level of intervention and support to enable people to achieve maximum independence and control over their own lives'.[14]

Lack of resources has also been a problem for community care. No attempt has been made to measure and cost the actual needs of mentally ill people, and little money has ever been made available specifically to provide community care. Health and local authorities have made available resources according to their own lights, but this has been variable. For example, in 1986 the city of Newcastle upon Tyne spent £7.43 per head of population on mental health services, while Redbridge near London spent only £0.49. In the same year in the NHS, Oxford Region spent proportionately half what the Mersey Regional Health Authority spent.[15] Relatively few local or health authorities have made expenditure on care of mentally ill people a top priority because of the lack of political visibility of this group as compared to, for example, children.

Much of the money that might be available for community

---

[13] Kathleen Jones, John Brown, and Jonathan Bradshaw, *Issues in Social Policy*. London: Routledge and Kegan Paul, p. 114.
[14] *Caring for People.*   [15] Murphy, *After the Asylums*, p. 115.

care is still tied up in keeping the old psychiatric hospitals running. While the NHS spends 16 per cent of its total budget on mental illness services, 90 per cent of this continues to be spent on traditional hospital based services even though 90 per cent of mentally disturbed people receive their treatment in the community.[16] The hospitals are difficult to shut down; while they remain open they consume vast amounts of resource, human and financial. Money has not followed patients out of the hospitals into the community. Government and health authorities have been unable or unwilling to provide bridging finance so that new facilities and services can be built up in the community in advance of the hospitals closing.

The consequence of lack of resource is that there is a very serious shortfall of community based mental health facilities. The Audit Commission noted that in 1984 there were only 6,800 residential places in local authority, private and voluntary sector facilities as against the 11,500 needed, only 17,000 day hospital places against 45,800 needed and 9,000 day centre places against 28,200 required.[17] There is a similar shortfall in the need for suitable housing and accommodation.

The problems identified so far have been compounded by organisational difficulties leading to diffused responsibility and considerable confusion. Both Local Authorities and Health Authorities have responsibilities towards mentally ill people, together with other interested organisations such as MIND which provides some facilities. However, local and health authority boundaries are not coterminous, budgets are separate and compartmentalised, and these organisations have very different ways of operating, different priorities and different views of how care should be shaped. Often, it has proved difficult to transfer money from the health sector into the social services sector to follow patients. All this has been exacerbated by frequent organisational and boundary changes which make effective liaison difficult even where the desire to pursue it is present. Joint planning, of which there has been some using earmarked money, has proved a trying, cumbersome, and

[16] MIND, *Mental Health Statistics*, p. 5.
[17] Audit Commission, *Making a Reality of Community Care*, p. 17.

complex matter at all levels, even when there has been good will and political consensus between health and local authorities.[18]

The problems cited here are underlain by a lack of clear vision and political will on the part of central government. Having enunciated the advent of community care in 1961 on the basis of very little research or knowledge of what it meant, the government has steadfastly refused to do very much about it, choosing to muddle along in the general direction of closing hospitals without clarity or commitment to positive alternatives. In 1975, the secretary of state for health and social security welcomed the White Paper, *Better Services for the Mentally Ill*, but categorically stated in her introduction to it that, due to the necessity for financial restraint 'Very little material progress in the shape of new physical development is to be expected in the next few years.'[19] This kind of attitude has pervaded the 'progress' of community care since its inception. It is a matter of speculation whether recent government proposals, outlined and encodified in the National Health Service and Community Care Act (1990), represent a real renewal of political determination and will.

THE PLACE OF MENTALLY ILL PEOPLE

There has been little consultation with mentally ill people and their families about what mental health services they want. The policy of community care was sprung upon this client group without prior consultation and without pressure from patients to have the hospitals closed. There is a lack of knowledge as to whether community care is good for patients in the long term (there is still very little research to demonstrate whether or not community care is better than institutional care). Furthermore, there has been a lack of consideration about what should happen to very needy chronically mentally ill people who continue to accrete gradually in the community

[18] For an exploration of what these difficulties mean in practice see Dylan Tomlinson, *Utopia*.
[19] DHSS, *Better Services*, p. iv.

care system and who would formerly have been accommodated in long-stay hospitals. Finally, there has been a lack of thought about what will happen as needy mentally ill people get older and need more resources and care which presently do not exist.[20]

It is important to ask what the implication of all this is for mentally ill people and their relatives, for whom community care is supposed to provide the liberation, emancipation and opportunity which was denied during the asylum years. In concrete terms a number of problems confront mentally ill people within the ambit of community care.

For patients who were formerly hospitalised, initial research suggests that there is satisfaction about being freed from an institutional setting.[21] However, mostly patients are not asked whether, or when, they would like to move out of hospitals where they may have been for many years and which they may regard as a home where they have friends and familiar circumstances. Patients are often moved back to areas from which they may have come years ago and with which they no longer have any connections, away from people whose lives they have shared in the institution for a long time.

When former hospital patients are deinstitutionalised, they begin to share in some of the problems which confront all mentally ill people in the community. They may have a limited choice of accommodation and housing, or no housing at all. Ex-patients are often resettled in 'ghetto' areas of poor housing which are isolated and neglected (one vicar told me that he saw no prospect of his parishioners visiting ex-psychiatric hospital patients in the parish because the depressing flats in which most of them were accommodated were known to be a haunt of criminals and there had been a recent shooting incident in them).[22] Some mentally disordered people end up on the 'long-stay wards' of the streets, actually homeless because of current housing shortages. One study found that in an Edinburgh common lodging house 14 per cent of the residents had previously been in psychiatric hospitals while 26 per cent were

---

[20] See further Tomlinson, *Utopia*.   [21] Ibid., p. 137.
[22] See further, Scull, *Decarceration*, p. 153.

diagnosable as actively schizophrenic.[23] Many people can find themselves living in poor residential accommodation in public or private ownership which replicates the negative, custodial, and authoritarian atmosphere pervading the old hospitals in miniature, while being effectively cut off from the surrounding community.[24]

There is no evidence to show that the public in general have become more tolerant of mentally ill people; they still suffer from a negative, stigmatised image. This means that they find it hard to gain employment, especially at a time of recession when jobs are in short supply.[25] It is difficult for mentally ill people to obtain enough money from the state benefit system to meet their basic physical needs and to exercise choice in the market place.[26] There is a shortfall in day accommodation, local mental health facilities and activities organised to include them, so they may face considerable isolation and boredom in the community.

Because many of the old hospitals have reduced their bed numbers quite considerably and treatment is now focussed on more local, basically non-residential facilities, mentally disordered people face a limited choice of treatment which revolves around the administration of symptom controlling drugs. There is little scope for residential 'asylum' when the going in the community gets tough, and there is beginning to be some evidence that more mentally ill people are finding their way into prisons rather than hospitals, perhaps because there are inadequate residential beds and treatment facilities in the latter:

---

23 See John Leach, 'Providing for the destitute' in J. K. Wing and Rolf Olsen, eds., *Community Care for the Mentally Disabled*. Oxford: Oxford University Press, 1979, pp. 92–3. These results have been replicated many times more recently. See, for examaple, MIND, *Mental Health, Housing and Homelessness*. London: MIND, nd.

24 See Peter Ryan, 'Residential care for the mentally disabled' in Wing and Olsen, eds., *Community Care for the Mentally Disabled*; Bernardette Holmes and Andrew Johnson, *Cold Comfort*. London: Souvenir Press, 1988.

25 See MIND, *Putting People First in Employment*. London: MIND, 1991; N. Wansborough and P. Cooper, *Open Employment After Mental Illness*. London: Tavistock, 1980.

26 Murphy, *After the Asylums*, pp. 150ff.

A study by Professor John Gunn ... found that 20 per cent of prisoners serving six months or more needed psychiatric help for disorders ranging from delusions and depression to alcoholism. Three per cent required hospital treatment. The figures for remand prisoners are thought to be even higher.[27]

Mentally ill people's relatives may also find themselves in a poor position. They have to bear the expense and inconvenience of having their needy relatives around, often at cost to themselves. Women particularly are often exploited as carers and may be required to give up working to look after them, diminishing their own autonomy and reducing household incomes which are often not large in the first place. The government has never costed the price of community care, including the financial and human costs to those who 'voluntarily' pick up the burden of care. If this cost was included, it might well be the case that community care is financially more expensive than institutional care. Lack of residential and community facilities may mean that relatives have to look after very needy people, when they actually need a respite from them. They may experience intense psychological pressure and curtailment of their own freedom.[28]

Meanwhile, back in the old psychiatric hospitals, most of which are still running in a diminished way, the buildings continue to deteriorate, the patients are a 'rump' of the most chronically needy who cannot easily be resettled in the community, and staff morale continues to drop as a result of 'planning blight'. I first worked in a psychiatric hospital in 1973. For some 10 years the hospital had been under the shadow of closure and so nothing was being done to improve the poor physical conditions there. As far as I know, it is still standing and functioning. There are still about 50,000 people in the old hospitals; only a handful have actually closed so far. In 1961 Powell talked of the psychiatric hospitals as 'doomed

---

[27] John Carvel, 'Disturbed prisoners "in limbo of neglect"', *The Guardian*. 21 March 91, p. 4. Cf. Clare Dyer, 'Mentally ill "sent to prison for treatment"', *The Guardian*. 17 June 92, p. 4.

[28] See further, Dalley, *Ideologies of Caring*; Andrew Walker, 'The meaning and social division of community care' in Andrew Walker, ed., *Community Care*. Oxford: Basil Blackwell, 1982.

institutions'.[29] Almost certainly, many of them will now celebrate their two hundredth anniversaries.

LOOKING FORWARD

With the report of the Audit Commission, *Making a Reality of Community Care* and the enactment of the 1990 National Health Service and Community Care Act (1990) the move to community care has received new impetus.[30] The so-called ' disaster years' of inertia and prevarication from 1962 to 1990 may now be at an end.[31] It might be possible to look forward to a properly funded future for mentally ill people in the community which will help to realise the goals of autonomy, independence, choice and self-determination which are part of the current ideology of consumer choice and power in health care.

However, it is difficult to be optimistic. Although the government has now released some money for bridging funding (£30 million) and is making a further small amount available for the resettlement of severely mentally ill people, this is a drop in the ocean compared to the £0.75 billion new

[29] Jones, *A History of the Mental Health Services*, p. 322.
[30] The main proposals of the White Paper, *Caring for People*, which sought to address long-standing confusions and problems in the organisation of community care for groups such as elderly people and people with mental illnesses or learning difficulties, hastily embodied in the 1990 legislation, are as follows: Local Authorities are to become responsible (in collaboration with medical, nursing, and other interests) for assessing individual need and designing care arrangements; they will have to produce and publish clear plans for community care services which will be open to public inspection, and comment upon which reports to government will be made; they will be required to make full use of the independent sector and will have to convince government that they are doing this; a new funding structure will be created whereby local authorities will take responsibility for the financial support of people seeking public support in private and voluntary residential care; levels of income support and housing benefit will be the same for individuals whether they are living in their own homes or independent residential or nursing homes; local authorities will establish 'arm's length' inspection and registration units separate from routine management structures to inspect publicly run and independent residential care homes; there will be a new specific grant payable to local authorities to promote the development of social care for seriously mentally ill people. There is to be a separation between the provider and purchaser functions in a market-like arrangement whereby contracts will be exchanged between service providers such as owners of old people's homes and the purchasing agents who will be local authorities.
[31] Murphy, *After the Asylums*, ch. 4.

money which local authorities reckon they will need to provide adequate services, and the £2 billion which the National Schizophrenia Fellowship, a relatives' organisation, thinks will be needed. The government proposes to give only £539 million to local authorities for the implementation of the 1990 legislation in 1993. This means there will be a substantial community care gap. It has also declined to appoint a special cabinet minister for community care to give the whole area a high continuing political profile.

There will still be problems of organisational liaison between health and local authorities, though at least the latter have now been given clear primary responsibility for purchasing services. There will be complex demarcation disputes over who should care for mentally ill people and when they are to be deemed ill enough to fall within the purview of the NHS rather than the local authority (illness is not defined in the legislation, but seems to mean being in a condition where you are being actively treated under the supervision of a doctor). There is no guarantee that mentally disordered people will get what they want or need. Their 'care packages' will be determined by a third party appointed by the local authority. If funds for purchasing care run out, they could be assessed for a care package which contains absolutely nothing.[32]

Experience in the USA suggests that there is much to be concerned about in relation to the defects of community care:

We have learned what we should have known but missed in our enthusiasm for change. Community life is no panacea unless the patient's suffering is alleviated and social functioning improved. We have learned that community life, without adequate services and supports could be as dehumanising and debilitating as the poor mental hospital. We have learned that if the patient is sufficiently disturbed and disoriented ... residence in the home or community can cause innumerable difficulties for family and others and may result in a general outcome inferior to good institutional care.[33]

---

[32] There is an outline of these and other problems in Joyce Rowbottom, *Seamless Service – A Stitch in Time*. London: Institute of Health Services Management, 1992.

[33] David Mechanic, *Mental Health and Social Policy*. Englewood Cliffs: Prentice Hall, 1980, p. 20. For critical studies of US experience see Murray Levine, *The History and Politics of Community Mental Health*. New York: Oxford University Press, 1981;

Failure to provide good facilities in the community, to co-ordinate community responses, and to educate the general public about mental illness so that it welcomes mentally ill people rather than rejecting them, leads one to suspect that community care might be a euphemism for universal neglect. For government, it is a cheap way of dealing with mentally ill people who can be maintained in a twilight world of night-shelters, sub-standard hostels, isolated housing in the ghetto areas of towns and cities, even on the long-stay wards of the streets themselves, at much less expense than in hospital. Mentally ill people receiving community care are free from many restraints, but they lack positive freedom to participate fully in society. They may experience greater deprivation, inequality, and injustice than they did in the psychiatric hospitals. Political and financial expediency dressed up as humanitarian concern appears to have carried the day.

Despite the rhetoric, history suggests that there can be little ground for optimism that mentally ill people will be empowered and enabled by the 'new' community care. In the end, as ever, they will get what they are given, what other parties deem to be appropriate or affordable. It is an interesting metaphysical question to ask whether there are different kinds of nothing which can be offered to, and appreciated by, the very needy. There is little to protect mentally disordered people as a group from experiencing the same powerlessness and neglect which was so much part of their experience in the psychiatric hospitals. *Plus ça change, plus c'est la même chose?*

Cohen, *Forgotten Millions*, ch. 4 (entitled 'America: pamper the neurotics and neglect the sick').

CHAPTER 11

The plight of mentally ill people

About two hundred years ago, mentally disordered people were swept into large lunatic asylums where they experienced a good deal of neglect and powerlessness, out of sight and out of mind of the general population.

The public in general, having achieved a comfortable disposition of its local responsibility by sending its mentally ill citizens to a large, centralized, and somewhat isolated institution, found it easy to forget them and settled into an indifference which has persisted well into the twentieth century.[1]

Ironically, dispersing mentally disordered people into the community seems to promise little increase in their social or political visibility. 'Normalising' their situation may have the effect of making their needs and problems disappear. An unproblematic group of people is not perceived as having needs; it can be invisible. People, and in particular governments, seem literally not to see mentally disordered people and their needs. This is politically and economically convenient in capitalist society, for it means that scarce resources need not be committed to those perceived to be indigent and socially non-contributive.

The analysis undertaken above has made a case for seeing mentally ill people as prominent among the poor and oppressed in society generally, as well as in the treatment and care settings in which they find themselves. At all points, their situation is affected by social and political factors which stem from, and reflect, traits and values in the wider capitalist social

---

[1] Belknap, *Human Problems*, p. 18.

order. Mentally ill people come disproportionately from the lower social classes. Within and outside the welfare services they come at the bottom of the heap in terms of resources, class, status, power, and decision making. At best, they are discriminated against and deprived of the human and financial resources which would enable them to lead fuller, more autonomous lives. At worst, they are neglected and even abused. In hospital and community settings there must be concern that a group of people who are disadvantaged in the first place have their sufferings deepened by social and political factors which could be altered.

At the beginning of the analysis it was acknowledged that looking at the situation of mentally disordered people with the lenses of Marxist explanatory tools emphasising class, status, power, socio-material context, injustice, and inequality is only one way of taking a section through reality. There have been moments when I have felt that this way of seeing badly distorts reality. Surely, I have continued to say to myself, things cannot be that bad for mentally ill people. There must be many people who have gained valuable things from mental health services; there must be some very good and adequate services; not all people who experience mental disorder are socially disabled for life by it; many people have valued being released from hospital into community settings. Have I therefore erred in the direction of creating a conspiracy theory in which some real, but relatively minor, concerns have been inflated to a point of rhetorical exaggeration?

I wish I could give more weight to these doubts, but when I look around me I find my pessimistic analysis of the situation of mentally ill people deepened, not dispelled. During June 1992 I noted articles in my national daily paper which said that mentally ill people who commit minor offences are deliberately admitted to prison for treatment because there is no room for them in mental health facilities, that at one hospital for the criminally insane nine nurses had been arrested on suspicion of murdering a patient, and that an official enquiry was about to report on conditions of abuse and neglect of patients by nurses in another special hospital. A feature warns of impending chaos in the community care services because government is not giving adequate resources and has not given enough thought to organisation. The losers will be the most vulnerable members of society. Another article suggests that people who live in isolated conditions in the community are no better off than people living in institutions, because they can in no sense participate in normal social life, and live a shapeless, boring existence which is dependent on the whims and resources of others. It is only a few months since a report on irregularities and abuses was published about a district general hospital psychiatric unit.[2] The radio today reported from a MIND conference that black people are three times more likely to be diagnosed as mentally ill than white people, and are ten times more likely to be diagnosed and treated as schizophrenic.

Meanwhile, if I look out of my window I can see an eccentrically dressed middle-aged man sunbathing on the drive of the hostel for mentally ill people which is next door. He is nearly always there when the sun is shining and seems happy enough – but he does not seem to have anything to do all day. Perhaps at the foot of the tree at the back of my flat a solitary elderly man from the nearby hotel for homeless people will be standing. He is often there for long hours, winter and summer. His clothing is shabby. Mostly he stands completely still looking depressed. Sometimes, however, he shouts at the cars or the mothers pushing their prams, and wanders into the road. People are alarmed, amused or indifferent by turns. Maybe this is how he wants to spend his life; maybe not. He does not tell us.

This brings me to another critical point about the analysis. I have almost exclusively used literary resources authored by professional academics to construct my critique of the socio-political situation of mentally ill people. This may convey the impression that mentally ill people themselves have nothing to say about their situation, or that I am deaf to their voices.

---

[2] SW Hertfordshire District Health Authority, *Report of the Investigation into Serious Incidents Occurring at The Shrodells Psychiatric Unit October 1989–November 1990*. Watford: SW Herts. DHA, 1992.

There is a danger of falling into the professional trap of psychiatrists and others

The pontifications of psychiatry have all too often excommunicated the mad from human society, even when their own cries and complaints have been human, all too human.[3]

People who have experienced mental disorder are often articulate critics of the particular structures and practices to which they are subject. In general, those who take the trouble to express their opinions are disillusioned with mental health services and facilities, and are more radical in their criticisms of their own treatment and experience than I have been. I have yet to read an account of conventional psychiatric treatment by a patient or ex-patient which is basically positive. (A flavour of the negative, often harrowing experiences of mentally ill people down the ages in their own words can be gained from reading *The Faber Book of Madness.*[4]) The limitation of this kind of testimony, which tends to confirm and amplify my analysis anyway, is that it is subjective, anecdotal, individualistic, and mostly unconcerned about the wider socio-political context of the individual's suffering and situation. It is relatively easy to establish from individuals' own accounts that they perceive themselves to be in an oppressed, exploited, unhappy position. It is more difficult to suggest convincingly, using academic evidence that there is a certain objectivity, socially and politically, to the subjective impressions of injustice and oppression to which mentally ill people bear witness in their own utterances and writings.

The implication of discovering that wider social and political factors impinge substantially and often negatively on the situation of mentally ill people is that those who wish to ameliorate this situation must be prepared to think and act at a social and political level. Marxist analysis suggests that the

[3] Roy Porter, *A Social History of Madness*, p. 233.
[4] Porter, ed., *The Faber Book of Madness*. More sources include, for example, Porter, *A Social History of Madness*; Kate Millett, *The Loony Bin Trip*. London: Virago, 1991; Jimmy Laing and Dermot McQuarrie, *Fifty Years in the System*. Edinburgh: Mainstream Publishing, 1989; Sue Read, *Only for a Fortnight: My Life in a Locked Ward*. London: Bloomsbury, 1989.

fundamental nature of capitalist society, which tends to favour the ruling class need to make money over the needs of the working class, contributes not only to the causation of mental disorder, but also, in its values and the resources it provides, to the overall shape, structure, and nature of the mental health services. The implication is that fundamental social change is required if mentally disordered people are to acquire greater justice, equality, and power with adequate services suited to their needs. Talbott writes of the psychiatric hospitals:

Society's creation and maintance [sic] of custodial mental hospitals is dependent on powerful forces, forces that do not individually or collectively lend themselves to easy alteration. This factor is one reason why, while internal and external changes may affect them it is probably not until there are systems or societal changes that the total functioning of the state hospitals can be improved.[5]

This insight can be equally applied to the entire situation of mentally ill people and the facilities which are allotted to them outside and within the hospitals.

Within this awareness of the need for a fundamental change in the social order so that it values economically marginal and lower-class people more, areas of incremental change which might benefit mentally ill people can be discerned. Steps can be taken to move public attitudes away from stigmatising rejection. Within the NHS and local authority services it would be possible to try and gain greater priority, attention and resources for mental health. At the level of actual service delivery more could be done to alert workers and service users alike to inequalities, biases, and unjust structures, so that mentally disordered people and their families were less likely to be oppressed and victimised. There is an urgent need for socio-politically aware and committed action at all levels to change the situation of a historically oppressed group of very vulnerable people.

It is difficult to think of a more powerless and neglected group than mentally ill people in Britain today (though other groups like elderly people and people with learning disabilities

---

[5] Talbott, *The Death of the Asylum*, p. 88.

also share many of the same disadvantages). Mentally ill people as a group, whatever their individual social backgrounds, are severely disadvantaged in terms of social influence and power. Society has little interest in them. They have little purchase on the the main political and economic structures ordering society. Economically, they produce little and have no money to spend; strikes and boycotts are therefore not means which they can use to attract attention to their grievances and needs. Politically, mentally ill people are mostly not sufficiently well organised to lobby policy makers effectively. Although advocacy groups like MIND exist, and there are signs that mentally ill people are becoming more organised and articulate through self-managed campaigning groups like Patients Speak Out, there is a long way to go before they will be a really significant political force for change.[6] Mentally ill people have substantially reduced rights and opportunities. Their protests can be interpreted as symptoms of their disorder, and dealt with by threats of compulsory detention and treatment, or by being ignored. The social and political impotence of mentally ill people and their associates is summarised by an American writer:

Mental patients do not write letters to their state representatives or to newspapers; they do not picket or demonstrate in front of state capitols ... As opposed to labor, business and the professions ... they are almost completely powerless to affect the political process. Even compared to other have-not groups – alcoholics, prisoners, or welfare mothers – they have no clout ... The mentally ill do not have ... a body of mentally intact relatives, due to the complex socio-environmental and genetic etiology of serious mental illness ... As a result *they constitute one of the truly powerless constituencies in our society.*[7]

This has been a lengthy analysis of the situation of mentally ill people because the socio-political reality surrounding mental illness and mentally ill people is complex. Approaching mental disorder from this angle is unusual for people used to

---

6 Anne Rogers and David Pilgrim, '"Pulling down churches": accounting for the British Mental Health Users' Movement', *Sociology of Health and Illness* 13, 1991, 129–47.
7 Talbott, *The Death of the Asylum*, p. 68. Emphasis added.

thinking in individualistic terms about mental illness. I hope I have shown that this approach is illuminating and that there is a serious case for taking the reality of social and political factors impinging on the situation of mentally ill people seriously. Additionally, I hope I have demonstrated that there is a case for seeing mentally ill people as an oppressed and powerless group, the roots of whose problems lie to a large extent in the wider social order which must therefore be acted upon if their suffering is to be minimised and their well-being to be maximised.

I now go on to analyse the situation of pastoral care in relation to mentally ill people. Have pastoral carers shown any knowledge and awareness of the social and political factors which impinge on the situation of mentally disordered people? In what ways have they exercised pastoral care, and has this challenged or confirmed the socio-political *status quo* inside and outside the hospital? Have pastoral carers been committed to social change which might benefit mentally ill people, or have they implicitly supported the powerful over against the powerless? These are the issues which can now be addressed.

PART III

The politics of pastoral care

CHAPTER 12

Pastoral care with mentally ill people

I will now examine the theory and practice of the main group of pastoral carers whose focus is overtly upon mentally ill people in hospital and community settings, i.e. paid professional psychiatric or mental health chaplains.

Among the most significant recent developments in the theory and practice of pastoral care has been the recognition that pastoral care is not just the work of the clergy.[1] All kinds of people are implicitly or explicitly involved in this activity. In the present context, this means that NHS staff, as well as 'ordinary' members of local churches and others who have an active concern for mentally disordered people might be seen as exercising pastoral care. While welcoming this broadening of pastoral care, the next few chapters will be chiefly concerned with the pastoral activity of chaplains and explicitly designated pastoral workers. There are two main reasons for this regrettably narrow focus. First, these workers consciously acknowledge themselves to be involved in pastoral care. Secondly, there is enough written and other material available about what they do and what they think they do for meaningful analysis to be feasible.

In this chapter, I will describe the actual role of the chaplains in hospital and community, drawing upon relevant literary resources, informal interviews with chaplains, and my own personal experience. Subsequently, I will try to expose elements of socio-political awareness before going on to suggest how a Marxist-informed analysis might question the function

---

[1] Frank Wright, *Pastoral Care for Lay People*. London: SCM Press, 1982.

of pastoral carers within the mental health sphere. Finally, I will discuss the appropriateness of this function with a view to asking whether and in what ways this might need to change.

The analysis which follows is conducted at a high level of generalisation. I do not try to describe in detail the work of particular chaplains, nor to laud or criticise individual practitioners. This would be inappropriate in a socio-political analytic framework, as well as invidious for the individuals concerned. Where any individual's work or writing is cited, it is to illustrate typical general attitudes and stances. The personal sincerity, commitment, motivation, and goodwill of individual pastors is not in question here. The socio-political position and implications of pastoral theories and practices, apparently held and practiced by a corporate group within the NHS, are at issue here. The aim is to gain a broad critical perspective on the practice of pastoral care to ask whether it can or should be reoriented.

CHAPLAINS' ROLES IN MENTAL HEALTH SETTINGS: THE HOSPITAL

Under the provisions of the Lunacy Act of 1890, each asylum was required to appoint a minister of the Church of England to be its chaplain (before this, it had been a matter of local preference). With the advent of the NHS in 1948, all hospital managers and boards were required to 'Give special attention to provide for the spiritual needs of both patients and staff', and each hospital was required to appoint chaplains of the major different denominations (Church of England or Scotland, Roman Catholic, and Free Church) to meet these spiritual needs.[2] This was seen as an important step as now

the chaplain was paid for his [sic] work, and was paid by money provided by Parliament. His position in the hospital was recognised and the importance of that position emphasised.[3]

[2] Hospital Chaplaincies Council, *A Handbook on Hospital Chaplaincy*. London: Hospital Chaplaincies Council, 1987, p. 7.
[3] Church Information Office, *The Hospital Chaplain – Report of the Working Party Appointed by the Joint Committee*. London: Church Information Office, 1973, p. 5.

Most of the chaplains were and are appointed part time, according to the number of beds occupied by members of a particular denomination. Of the approximately 5,000 chaplains working in all types of hospital in the NHS in 1987, about 300 are full time.[4] There are about 60 full-time psychiatric hospital or mental health chaplains, all, with a couple of exceptions, ministers of the established Church of England.[5] The role of part-time chaplains is generally a more limited one than that of full-time chaplains, concentrated on 'essential duties' such as organising services or visiting very ill patients.[6] It is not surprising, therefore, that the dominant articulate voice in the theory and practice of pastoral care in psychiatric and other hospitals is that of the Anglicans (in Scotland chaplaincy reflects a similar bias to the established Church of Scotland). All chaplains have a dual loyalty to the NHS which appoints and pays them, and to their own denominational authorities who must agree to their appointment and license their work.

The official job description or 'charter role' for chaplains in all types of hospital agreed between the church authorities and the NHS authorities lays out the minimum duties and responsibilities for chaplains. They are to

make provision for the spiritual needs of patients and staff

conduct services of worship regularly

visit patients and staff in wards and departments

meet and welcome new members of staff

co-operate with medical, nursing and administrative staff in departmental meetings

be available to relatives and patients

be available for consultation to parish priests and ministers

---

[4] See further, HCC, *A Handbook on Hospital Chaplaincy*, p. 9.

[5] See John Browning, *Chaplaincy Modes in Mental Health*. Nottingham: Trent Regional Health Authority, 1986, p. 8.

[6] But see Ronald Messenger, 'The church in the hospital' in Elizabeth Schoenberg, ed., *A Hospital Looks at Itself*. London: Cassirer, 1972, for the wide scope that some part-time chaplaincy can have.

make public information about services of worship

keep records of all services and write reports as required by the health authority

co-operate with others to ensure that chapels, places of worship, and mortuary facilities are suitably furnished.[7]

This skeletonic outline is not very illuminating in relation to what chaplains actually have done, particularly in the psychiatric sector where there are few medical emergencies of the kind experienced in general hospitals. It is, therefore, helpful to turn to what chaplains themselves have said about the various role models they use to rationalise and account for their activity.

The most obvious, though not necessarily the most popular, ideal role is that of the priest who utilises his own distinctive spiritual and sacramental techniques to mediate between humanity and God. A priestly ministry emphasises the importance of worship and the administration of sacraments, rather than administrative or directly therapeutic activities. The priest may see himself as the independent representative of God and of the wider church within the hospital. Historically, the best statement of this position is to be found in Autton's influential work, *Pastoral Care of the Mentally Ill*:

The priest is not just another therapist . . . His [*sic*] ministry often does have therapeutic effects, but these are quite secondary . . . to his prime ministry as a priest. First and foremost he is leading (his people) to God and only secondarily to mental health. His sphere is spiritual care . . . As well as his own 'instruments', the priest also has his traditional language, and this should not be put apart for psychiatric jargon or medical terminology.[8]

Autton's version of this role suggests a good measure of independence and detachment for the pastor. He warns against clergy attempting to imitate other disciplines within the hospital, maintaining that 'the more [the priest] tries to imitate these other disciplines, the less of a priest he will

[7] HCC, *A Handbook on Hospital Chaplaincy*, pp. 11–12.
[8] Norman Autton, *Pastoral Care of the Mentally Ill*. London: SPCK, second edn., 1969, pp. 142–3.

become'.[9] While the ideal type of priesthood which Autton presented 25 years ago may seldom have been found in its pure form in hospitals, the distinctively priestly role of chaplains has found echoes in more recent writing. Roger Grainger, for example, lays great importance on the facilitation of worship in psychiatric hospitals.[10]

The role of pastor or 'shepherd' is an important ideal type in chaplaincy. Although this tends to be left rather vague in terms of content, it seems to imply the listening, visiting, caring, and counselling aspect of chaplains' personal work with patients and staff, whether believers or not. Autton includes a whole chapter on the priest as pastoral counsellor in his book, while Longbottom states that 'the listening, visiting aspect of our work is part of the role of the chaplain as pastor'.[11] Many psychiatric chaplains have seen their role as mainly a pastoral one based on pastoral conversation. I will discuss this later.[12]

A role closely associated with that of priest and pastor in Christian theology and ministry is that of prophet. Classically, a prophet is one who forthtells the action of God to a community in the present events of history. The prophet uncovers God's action and purpose to elicit a response of faith and obedience from his audience. There are also elements of proclaiming judgement and moral, social, and political protest within the role.[13] In an early work, Autton confidently proclaims

The chaplain comes to his people with the grace and authority of God, and so exercises the ministry of a prophet ... He will see himself as someone who has been called to fulfil a very special task in the

9 Autton, *Pastoral Care of the Mentally Ill.*, p. 155.
10 See, for example, Roger Grainger, *Watching for Wings*. London: Darton, Longman and Todd, 1979; *A Place Like This*. London: Regency Press, 1983; Frank Longbottom, 'Paper on chaplaincy in psychiatry and mental handicap' in HCC, *A Handbook on Hospital Chaplaincy*.
11 Longbottom, 'Paper on chaplaincy', p. 89. Cf. Autton, *Pastoral Care of the Mentally Ill*, ch 2.
12 For more on this aspect of the chaplain's role see Heije Faber, *Pastoral Care in the Modern Hospital*. London: SCM Press, 1971; John Foskett, *Meaning in Madness*. London: SPCK, 1984.
13 See further, for example, Robin Gill, *Prophecy and Praxis*. London: Gill and Macmillan, 1981.

whole work of healing, not only for individuals but for the spiritual life of the community which is the hospital.[14]

More modestly and more specifically, Longbottom suggests that

it is part of the chaplain's prophetic role to ask questions of the institution. He alone is the non-hierarchical member of the team and part of his role as patients' advocate should be to ask such questions as 'Is this a healthy place to be?'[15]

The prophetic role seems to be widely accepted amongst chaplains as a description for any activity, however mild, which questions the way in which an institution or service is run.

Turning from these more conventional ideal role types for chaplaincy, some newer ones have been coined. Roger Grainger, author of much of the very sparse literature on psychiatric chaplaincy, approaches the role from the perspective of a kind of functionalist sociology, and suggests that the chaplain functions as a licensed anarchist or jester within the hospital's structure. Emphasising the difference between chaplains and other professional groups and their relative independence, being in the hospital but not of it, Grainger suggests of the jester's role that

the chaplain is well-equipped for the role simply because he is in the hospital, but not of it. As a clergyman, he is accustomed to represent alternatives to social norms. This is, and always has been his prophetic role in society. And when the normative force of society approaches totalitarian pitch, his critical presence is most necessary. So the chaplain is at hand to play the part in the hospital that the clergy should be prepared to play in wider society.[16]

Grainger believes that the chaplain provides a 'focus for a measure of individual non-conformity'.

Thus chaplain-as-jester manages, indirectly, to appear as chaplain-as-prophet. He creeps under the institutional guard, giving support to the individual staff member, challenging the individual patient, standing by at times of personal reappraisal ... introducing the

[14] Norman Autton, *Pastoral Care in Hospitals*. London: SPCK, 1968, p. 32.
[15] Longbottom, 'Paper on chaplaincy', p. 91.
[16] Grainger, *Watching for Wings*, p. 7.

notion of distance into the monochrome landscape of institutional expectations and attitudes.[17]

The chaplain is a clown with authority given by membership of the staff of the hospital. He is an ally of the dominant social ethos, but not a subscriber to it.[18] He functions to ensure social stability which changes the face and form of the institution through creating space for himself, other people and the spirit.[19]

To the jester and clown roles, Grainger adds two others: that of reconciler and that of apologist/advocate for the hospital. He writes that the chaplain's ministry 'is above all work of reconciliation', and suggests that, 'From the point of view of the hospital, the chaplain justifies his place within the institution as its advocate and interpreter, explaining the ways of authority to the patient.'[20]

For the sake of comprehensiveness, it is worth mentioning the human ontological role described by Michael Wilson. Wilson suggests that the primary role of the chaplain is to attempt to be fully human in order to help others in the institution also to be so:

A chaplain, like all other men [*sic*], has a vocation by birth to be human and to be human means a consistent attempt to be yourself and no other person ... The man who makes a consistent attempt to be himself in these different roles, to be truthful in his role relationships, will make truth possible for others.[21]

For Wilson, being precedes performing particular roles.

Having dwelt on what chaplains and others write about the roles which they believe themselves to perform, it is important to amplify this with practical information about what chaplains actually do. There is great scope for individuals to do different things in psychiatric hospitals, and little of what is done has been made public in published form. However, one

---

[17] Grainger, *Watching for Wings*, pp. 8–9.
[18] Cf. Grainger, *Watching for Wings*, p. 121.
[19] Cf. Grainger, *Watching for Wings*, pp. 123–4.
[20] Grainger, *Watching for Wings*, pp. 41, 57.
[21] Michael Wilson, *The Hospital – A Place of Truth*. Birmingham: Institute for the Study of Worship and Religious Architecture, 1971, pp. 54–5.

hospital chaplain in the late 1970s, who did publish his list of activities, included in it taking Sunday services in the chapel and on the wards, attending ward community and staff meetings, holding a Christian discussion group for staff, attending art therapy and music sessions, going to committee meetings, teaching theological students, working with occupational therapists, going to relatives' group meetings, attending staff sensitivity groups, and holding a discussion group for local clergy.[22]

Beyond a core of liturgical duties which tends to take up a fair amount of time for most chaplains practice is very diverse. When I interviewed chaplains in hospitals in 1980, I found them involved in their institutions in many different ways.

Many of them involved themselves fairly directly in therapeutic activities. These included counselling and psychotherapy for patients or staff, as well as family therapy, staff group supervision, involvement in therapeutic community work, and attendance at ward rounds or ward meetings.[23]

It was common for chaplains to be engaged in teaching and training roles both within the hospital (for example, helping in the training of nurses) and outside it (helping to train local clergy and theological students to improve their knowledge and practical skills). Community liaison work, in connection with moving patients out of the hospital, was an important part of the work of most.

Although they usually belonged to the hospital heads of department meeting at that time, chaplains were mostly not much involved in committees or policy-making bodies. For some, administration and planning took up quite a lot of time, for example in relation to planning training courses. Very few full-time chaplains seemed to have a policy of leaving their time unstructured and simply wandering aound the hospital seeing what would happen and 'loitering with intent'.[24] Contact with people was usually through deliberate action, for

---

[22] Michael Law, Douglas Hill and Clive Harries, 'Exploring the work of a hospital chaplain in a psychiatric hospital', *Nursing Times 74*, 1978, 1478–82.

[23] This direct interest in becoming therapists is reflected in Foskett, *Meaning in Madness*, a book principally about counselling in psychiatric hospitals.

[24] Cf. Longbottom, 'Paper on chaplaincy', p. 90.

example, attending ward meetings, receiving definite referrals from other members of staff.

Beyond the activities mentioned which were to be found generally among chaplains, individuals were severally to be found editing hospital newspapers, conducting relaxation sessions for patients, befriending patients, and participating in drama groups, discussion groups, hospital Leagues of Friends, and district joint staff committees.

One important common denominator amongst chaplains, which is implicit in the citations above from Grainger, was an emphasis on the perceived independence and non-hierarchical position of the chaplain. Most of the chaplains I interviewed were keen to emphasise their availability, and the fact that they did not have their activities rigidly set out and structured so they could respond to the needs of individuals or groups *ad hoc*. This finds voice in Longbottom's assertion, made as recently as 1987, that

we can see that chaplains are acceptable to staff because they are free from hierarchical intervention and accountability and are thus deemed to be 'safe'. This enables chaplains to be used as sounding boards on all sort of ethical issues ... Much of this ministry is exercised informally as the chaplain goes about his daily business of being available.[25]

Paradoxically, however, this independence and freedom can leave chaplains feeling rather marginalised and irrelevant. Hence a complementary, if almost opposite, view that chaplains should be effectively involved in the work of the 'therapeutic team', i.e., the work of other professional members of staff who work actively to treat and rehabilitate patients. There must be a nexus of contact with other staff members if chaplains are to be known and seen as relevant. The trouble is that this kind of involvement and identification represents a surrender of freedom, independence, and availability. While all chaplains spoke to me of the importance of not being identified with any particular group in the hospital, each being, therefore, a kind of universal figure in the midst of

[25] Longbottom, 'Paper on chaplaincy', p. 88.

hierarchy, there are problems about maintaining a completely neutral stance.[26] The implications of this wished-for universalism must be of concern given the socio-political analysis undertaken above, and will be explored further below.

CHAPLAINS' ROLES IN MENTAL HEALTH SETTINGS: THE COMMUNITY

As the movement to community care has accelerated, chaplains, along with other staff groups, have seen their role change and widen. Many chaplains spend as much, if not more, time outside their hospital base as within it. Many of them are designated 'mental health chaplains', rather than hospital chaplains, in recognition of this change. Again, literature on what chaplains are now doing is in short supply. However, recent guidelines from the Hospital Chaplaincies Council offer an extension and change to those proposed for hospital chaplains in general which were outlined above.

In *Chaplaincy in Mental Illness and Mental Handicap*, it is proposed that the chaplains' task is fourfold. First, they need to continue to offer pastoral and spiritual care to individual patients and staff members, both in the hospitals and in the community. Secondly, they are to become involved in consultancy in hospital and community, providing information, advice, and liaison to patients, their families, and local churches, as well as continuing to highlight the spiritual dimension. Thirdly, chaplains should provide education and advocacy in relation to mental illness to local clergy, congregations, the institutional churches, and the NHS, seeking to promote 'wholeness'. Lastly, they are to be involved in the co-ordination of activities between churches and other professions and voluntary groups.[27] The emphasis throughout the document is upon smoothing the transition from hospital to

---

[26] For chaplains' involvement with therapeutic teams see Faber, *Pastoral Care in the Modern Hospital*, pp. 69ff; Leonard Stein and John R Thomas, 'The chaplain as a member of the psychiatric team', *Hospital and Community Psychiatry 18*, 1967, 197–200.

[27] Hospital Chaplaincies Council, *Chaplaincy in Mental Illness and Mental Handicap*. London: Hospital Chaplaincies Council, 1989.

community care, enabling, and participating in, co-operation and liaison with different groups and ministering to mentally ill people and their services wherever they may be.

In this connection, chaplains are now taking part in a number of different activities reflecting the diversity of their interests and contexts and the very fluid environment of change in community care. Amongst these activities are

trying to educate local churches about the nature and needs of mentally ill people through preaching and teaching

initiating and taking part in the life of day centres and group homes through visiting, counselling, and working with staff

initiating and helping to develop local church-based day centres and drop-in centres

getting housing projects for ex-hospital patients going, and participating in group work in these houses

training chaplains, church members, and members of staff for work with mentally ill people

developing Clinical Pastoral Education for theological students in hospital and community settings

facilitating churches in developing their own local responses to, and resources for, mentally ill people

providing support for staff and patients in the changing and traumatic environment of hospital closure

belonging to, and contributing directly to, locality or sector mental health teams

being engaged in interest and therapeutic groups of staff and patients

liaising between hospitals and day centres

visiting patients and relatives in their homes, and working with them in support groups

liaising with clergy inside and outside the hospital over particular cases involvement in local voluntary groups which lobby for mentally ill people and also provide housing and services, for example, MIND

advocacy and speaking up for patients on occasion

conducting worship and providing overtly religious services.

Doubtless there are many other roles and activities which particular chaplains adopt, but enough has been said to give a general picture of what is going on. From the perspective of the analysis of socio-political awareness which follows, it is worth pointing out that counselling, group work, and traditional religious and personal pastoral care activities still seem to provide a core of time-consuming activities for most chaplains in addition to the other more innovative activities mentioned.[28] It should also be noted that many chaplains are still anxious to be associated with the work of the psychiatric team in their activity.

[28] I am indebted to John Foskett for most of this list of activities.

CHAPTER 13

Socio-political awareness and commitment

The situation of mentally ill people must be seen in the context of the whole socio-political order. The mental health services form a microcosm of society, reflecting dominant interests and values. Mental illness and its treatment are profoundly affected by socio-political factors like social class. Psychiatric services are also thus affected. So psychiatric hospitals, for example, can be seen as part of the mechanism of social control; within these institutions there are conflicts and inequalities of power between groups which broadly reflect conflicts and class differences in society as a whole. Those with least power in society in general, i.e., members of the lower classes, have least power, influence and facilities in the mental health services also.

Having described the roles that chaplains perform in the mental health sector, it can now be asked how far they have displayed awareness of this kind of socio-political context, and how far this may have informed their practice. It will be argued that, in general, chaplains have shown little awareness in theory of these factors. This theoretical vacuum mirrors and encourages a lack of socio-political commitment in practice.

SOCIO-POLITICAL AWARENESS AND COMMITMENT IN THEORY

To begin with the theoretical aspect. The official duties and responsibilities of chaplains in all kinds of hospitals described in the last chapter have a very individualistic focus, centred on meeting the personal religious needs of patients and staff.[1] It is

[1] See above p. 175f.

true that they leave plenty of scope for particular chaplains to develop a more broadly based role. Meeting the rather un-defined 'spiritual' needs of individuals also theoretically allows space for wider socio-political awareness and action.[2] However, no kind of socio-political awareness or action is mentioned or required. The general guidelines for hospital chaplains do not even allude to a prophetic role for chaplains which would encourage them to question the nature of the institutions in which they work. There is no incentive to take this dimension seriously or to make it central in chaplaincy from the perspective of the NHS or the Hospital Chaplaincies Council.

This impression might be modified by the more recent and more specific guidelines, *Chaplaincy in Mental Illness and Mental Handicap*. Here there is mention of chaplains undertaking a prophetic role within pastoral care. This is understood as chaplains encouraging the hospital 'to consider its effect on both staff and residents, and how it can influence them posi-tively and negatively'.[3] An advocacy role for chaplains is also suggested whereby chaplains represent the needs of service users to churches and managers 'at the highest level' and try to ensure, by educational and other means, that churches and communities recognise and receive the contributions which mentally ill and mentally handicapped people have to give.[4] There is awareness of the structure of caring services, the changes taking place within them, and a need to think and act organisationally. However, this represents at most an organi-sational and structural consciousness and activity, rather than socio-political awareness and commitment. There is, for example, no mention of inequality, injustice, class, status, power, or conflict in the guidelines. Chaplains are not encour-aged to take up a political stance or develop a bias towards any particular group. The caring services are regarded as consen-sual and benevolent. There is then no reason for chaplains not

[2] For a discussion of possible ways of regarding the spiritual needs of patients in a broader sense than that of immaterial transcendence relating to the 'souls' of religious believers see Janet Mayer, 'Wholly responsible for a part, or partly responsible for a whole?', *Second Opinion* 17, 3, 1992, 26–55.
[3] HCC, *Chaplaincy in Mental Illness*, p. 5.   [4] Cf. ibid., pp. 9, 12.

to play a role which helps other members of professional staff to execute their plans. The document is facilitative rather than questioning in its approach to the policy and practice of transition to community care.

Turning to the less formal literature on chaplaincy, there is relatively little evidence that chaplains have taken a critical socio-political approach at all seriously. There are occasional mentions of sociological factors, for example, labelling of mental illness and the corporate nature of the Judaeo-Christian tradition in some works on chaplaincy in general.[5] However, although Norman Autton's training programme for clinical training for theological students and ministers and Peter Speck's work on hospital chaplaincy take some social and cultural factors into account, for example, the sick role, these are situated within a functionalist view of the NHS, hospitals, and health care which ignores issues of power, conflict, and injustice and accepts the parameters of present organisation as given and essentially unproblematic.[6]

For an approach which transcends a fairly narrow focus on individuals and their needs for counselling, one has to turn to a non-chaplain, Michael Wilson. Wilson, a medical doctor turned priest–academic, highlights the social and corporate aspects of health, healing, and illness. *The Hospital – A Place of Truth* draws attention to the importance of having regard to the nature and function of the hospital as a social institution:

The pattern of hospital chaplaincy work is directed at present for the most part to the service of the individual patient in need ... The individualism of hospital medicine and the clinical approach to illness create a milieu into which ... ministry fits comfortably. This means that hospital work may proceed faithfully and effectively (by present criteria) without influencing the institution. The essential power structures are untouched by the chaplain. Indeed he may feel impotent in the hospital ... and not see how the structure itself denies what he wants to say.[7]

[5] See, for example, Ian Ainsworth-Smith and John Perryman, 'Hospital chaplains' in A. S. Duncan, G. R. Dunstan and R. B. Welbourn, eds., *A Dictionary of Medical Ethics*. London: Darton, Longman and Todd, revised edn., 1981.

[6] See further Norman Autton, *A Handbook of Sick Visiting*. Oxford: Mowbray, 1981; Peter Speck, *Being There*. London: SPCK, 1988.

[7] Wilson, *The Hospital – A Place of Truth*, p. 107.

Unfortunately, Wilson fails to develop a full socio-political analysis of the pastoral situation in the hospital, leaving his critique at a level of generality. Ultimately, he, too, takes a consensual rather than a conflictual view of this organisation, a perspective embodied in his vision of the chaplain as 'universal man [sic]' rather than as one who might take sides. 'The chaplain is universal: he belongs to all men. In this regard he is like a naval chaplain, without rank.'[8]

Homing in specifically on the writings of mental health chaplains themselves, Grainger's *Watching for Wings* must be considered as one of the most extended and considered statements of the nature of pastoral care in psychiatric hospitals. Grainger overtly adopts a sociological perspective on the institution, seeing the hospital as a microcosm of the world outside which can teach much about the nature of the life of the world in general.[9] He draws on writers like Goffman and is aware of the ambiguities of the hospital as an institution

The institutional structure of the hospital has preserved its own tradition. The machinery of repression still exists. And it is used. After all, it is much easier to use force than persuasion if force is always readily available.[10]

However, far from developing perceptions like this into a full-blown critique of socio-political issues of, for example, deviance and social control, Grainger retreats into an individualist, functionalist view of the role of the chaplain. The chaplain is a licensed clown, who ultimately affirms the social structures of the hospital by his basically harmless deviant acts (much as the appointment of boy bishops and occasional reversals of social order and expectations actually relieved social pressure for change and affirmed the feudal hierarchical social order in medieval times).[11] Grainger emphasises that the anarchic and subversive acts initiated by the chaplain do not, in fact, constitute a social protest

---

[8] Ibid., p. 53.   [9] Grainger, *Watching for Wings*, pp. ix–x.   [10] Ibid., p. 63.
[11] Compare Kai Erikson, 'Notes on the sociology of deviance' in Scheff, ed., *Mental Illness and Social Processes*, for the conservative function of individual deviants.

This corporate celebration [e.g., of the Eucharist]; is not, basically, an organised statement, a social protest . . . Fundamentally it remains the sum total of any number of individual communications, all of which are different.[12]

'Liberation' in Grainger's usage refers principally to deliverance by the spirit from psycho-spiritual alienation, reflecting an individualist, existentialist view of pastoral care based on individual consciousness and small-scale interpersonal relationships.[13] It is no accident, then, that the chaplain is described as a clown or jester, one who basically acts on his own. Notions of justice, social class, political inequality, etc. make almost no appearance in Grainger's thinking, while they would seem to be at the centre of the issues facing mental health services.

The most recent book on pastoral care with mentally ill people is Foskett's *Meaning in Madness*. Written by the chaplain of a well-endowed teaching hospital in the middle of London, it is perhaps not surprising that this work continues the customary silence on the socio-political dimensions of pastoral care with mentally ill people. The book concentrates on counselling with individual patients and small groups in relation to specifically religious meanings surrounding mental disorder. A chapter promisingly entitled, 'Counselling with groups and institutions' never gets beyond thinking about psychodynamics in small groups, while the revolutionary perspective which Christian theology brings to mental illness is to do with changing peoples' attitudes to their suffering to more positive ones, rather than helping to change the world that may bring that suffering into being in the first place.[14] Though an excellent book on pastoral counselling, *Meaning in Madness* confirms the general impression that pastoral care is an asocial, apolitical, individually focussed activity which takes and leaves society and health care institutions uncritically as it finds them.

This impression is amplified in Longbottom's recent authoritative statement of the role of chaplains in mental illness and mental handicap included in *A Handbook on Hospital Chaplaincy*.

[12] Grainger, *Watching for Wings*, p. 104.   [13] Cf. ibid., pp. 70–1.
[14] Foskett, *Meaning in Madness*, p. 166.

Longbottom, a senior mental health chaplain, sees this role basically as one of counselling and individual care. While he recognises that chaplains may expect to listen to people's 'grumbles, troubles, hopes and fears', there is no sense in which the chaplain is supposed to act upon these or to attempt to change the structures in which they might occur.[15] Chaplains use their independent, non-hierarchical position to ask questions of the institution in the role of prophet, but there is no sense they should have a socio-political analysis of that institution or its context, nor that they should take action in that realm to change it.

In fact, the prophetic role espoused by chaplains seems, from the literature considered, to be at best emaciated and at worst non-existent if the classical biblical tradition of prophecy is considered. The urgent, angry pleas of the Old Testament prophets for social justice are absent from the role of chaplains who regard sitting on committees as a part of the prophetic job.[16] It would probably be less confusing if chaplains were to abandon their rather inadequate understanding of themselves as prophets to recognise that they actually occupy a sort of rabbinic role which finds it very difficult to question the social and political structures of which they are a part. Don Browning writes:

On the whole the chaplain should resist seeing his or her moral concern in analogy with the prophet. Because of the high degree of autonomy which most secondary institutions have from the direct power of the church, the model of the ancient scribe and rabbi will serve the chaplain better. The moral concern and counselling of the chaplain should take the form of a midrash (a 'search' or 'enquiry') which can elicit the collaborative efforts of other professionals.[17]

Chaplains have effectively failed to develop a prophetic socio-political critique of their own role and the situation of mentally ill people and the mental health services. The theoretical literature almost totally ignores issues such as class, status, power, race, gender, justice, inequality. It prescinds for

---

[15] Longbottom, 'Paper on chaplaincy', p. 89.   [16] Cf. ibid., p. 91.
[17] Don Browning, 'Pastoral care and models of training in counselling', *Contact* 57, 1977, 12–19, at 17–18.

socio-political awareness and action. This failure to recognise the importance of social and political factors in theory reflects and contributes to a failure to promote justice and equality in practice.

SOCIO-POLITICAL AWARENESS AND COMMITMENT IN PRACTICE

Chaplains have not, on the whole, become noticeably involved in social or political activities within or outside the hospital which might help to bring pressure on wider society to pay more attention and give more money to services for mentally disordered people (though clearly the crossing of a picket line when low-paid workers are on strike, as reported by Longbottom, is an act of (unwitting?) political solidarity of one kind[18]). They have not mobilised the interest and power of the churches in this direction either. In 1980 few chaplains were fighting for changes in the Mental Health Act, then under consideration, and very few belonged to lobbying groups for mentally ill people such as MIND. Chaplains have not attempted to amplify the voice of the unheard patients and junior staff in hospitals, and few chaplains have attempted, until recently, to become involved in policy making in the mental health services. Written material suggests that chaplains, like other members of staff, have had a bias towards young and acutely ill people in institutions, away from the 'back wards' where the worst conditions often prevail and where chronically ill and old patients may need someone to give them priority. Chaplains seem naturally to gravitate to the place where they can exercise an active therapeutic or counselling role, rather than being in other kinds of supportive care.

In choosing to adopt therapeutic methods based on counselling and psychotherapy, chaplains may be building a bias against lower-class people in their work. Such methods originated among the articulate middle classes, and can depend

---

[18] See Longbottom, 'Paper on chaplaincy', p. 91.

heavily on the ability to verbalise, be personally introspective, and to gain insight.[19] A bias towards these methods may indicate a bias against those who appear not to be able to make ready use of them, such as inarticulate members of the lower classes.[20] Certainly, counselling techniques are difficult to use with the old and demented and reinforce the propensity of chaplains to concentrate their main efforts in the acute sector with younger people.

Perhaps the most devastating historical example of chaplains failing to act in ways which promote justice and challenge inequality is to be found in their responses to demoralised and potentially abusive situations in hospitals. Abuse and demoralisation are particularly likely to occur when a vulnerable client group is cared for institutionally where resources are short. As we have seen, a number of psychiatric hospitals had enquiries which demonstrated that abuse had occurred in the 1970s. Despite the endemic nature of the circumstances which produce abuse in many institutions, chaplains appear to have remained almost totally passive in regard to them. In no case, as far as I have been able to discern from written and other evidence, has a chaplain played a prominent part in exposing or protesting against abuse, demoralisation, or inadequate facilities. In only one of the official enquiries did a chaplain give evidence to the panel. Worst of all, there is no evidence that chaplains gave support or credibility to junior members of staff who risked their livelihoods and careers to expose inhuman conditions. They were left to run the gauntlet of the displeasure of their colleagues and superiors almost alone. It was my impression, from the informal interviews I conducted with chaplains in 1980, that most of them really did not know what was going on or expect there to be anything wrong in the neglected wards of their hospitals. A few weeks after my visits to two hospitals where the chaplains had assured me that all was well, the national newspapers reported that at one of the hospitals long-stay patients were being over-medicated due to

[19] See further Don Browning, 'Pastoral care and the poor' in Howard J. Clinebell, ed., *Community Mental Health*. Nashville: Abingdon, 1970.
[20] But see further Holmes and Lindley, *The Values of Psychotherapy*, ch. 4.

staff shortages, and at the other a nursing officer had committed suicide due to a ruinous management structure.

Turning to more recent developments in community care, there is no evidence to suggest that chaplains are any more socio-politically sensitive and aware than they were in the hospitals. Chaplains appear to have made no attempt to critique the philosophy of community care or to question the justice and feasibility of its implementation. Instead, they have done their best to fit in and make themselves useful in bringing the policy to pass. In a recent article Arthur Hawes, a chaplain who has himself publicly exposed poor conditions in a hospital (in his role as a Mental Health Act Commissioner, not in that of chaplain to his own hospital) notes that there are gaps in provision in community care and talks of the importance of ecclesiastical advocacy for mentally ill people as a powerless, vulnerable group. However, he does not go on to question the community care policy and its costs fundamentally, nor does he suggest ways in which chaplains and others could work to remedy shortages and the problems of under-provision, essentially practical social and political problems.[21]

Given that facilities are in fact inadequate and underfunded, and that there are conditions of squalor and despair in some parts of the community, one is left wondering what has to happen before chaplains in any setting actually protest about what is going on in such a way as to mobilise concern and resources. What price independence and freedom from hierarchy if all it means is that you co-operate willingly and blindly with those in power, joining the 'therapeutic' team, regardless of the consequences for the powerless?

PROSPECTS FOR SOCIO-POLITICAL AWARENESS AND COMMITMENT

One cannot be sanguine about the prospects for critical, socio-politically aware and committed chaplaincy. Managerial developments in the NHS mean that chaplains, in common

---

[21] Arthur Hawes, 'Mental health in society', *Crucible* July–September 1990, 116–21.

with all other NHS workers, are now in a managerial hierarchy where they are directly responsible to NHS authorities.[22] Such independence as they have may be threatened by the instruments of centralised managerial control such as individual performance review and short-term contracts.[23] In this situation, one would expect to see chaplains becoming more conservative and conformist to the *status quo* of the NHS rather than less so. It may become even more important for them to testify to the goodness and adequacy of the organisation for them to keep their jobs.

This potentially conservative drift is likely to be amplified by the desire of chaplains themselves to become more professionalised, and so like other groups within the NHS such as doctors and nurses. They have now formed a college of health care chaplains which will serve the same functions of training, accreditation, and licensing that the royal colleges of medicine and nursing do. Professions are often rather conservative self-serving bodies which tend to ignore power and political relationships except in so far as they promote and protect the good of the profession itself.[24] With the professional emphasis on the one-to-one client relationship, one cannot realistically hope that chaplains will become more socio-politically concerned and committed. The prospects of a more socio-politically aware and committed pastoral care biassed towards the poor and oppressed seem severely limited under present arrangements and assumptions.

---

[22] For more on the rise of managerialism in the NHS see Harrison, *Managing the National Health Service*; Philip Strong and Jane Robinson, *The NHS Under New Management*. Milton Keynes: Open University Press, 1990.

[23] For a critique of this see Stephen Pattison, 'A decade of managerialism?', *Crucible* July-September 1991, 143–6.

[24] See further, Paul Wilding, *Professional Power and Social Welfare*. London: Routledge and Kegan Paul, 1982. Cf. Alastair V. Campbell, *Moderated Love*. London: SPCK, 1984; *Paid to Care?* London: SPCK, 1985.

CHAPTER 14

Unction in the function: pastoral care in socio-political perspective

The fundamentally apolitical, asocial, individualistic and functionalist position which fails to challenge the socio-political *status quo* adopted by chaplains in mental health would probably not surprise liberation theologians. One of the distinctive features of their theology is the realisation that all institutions and ideologies (including ecclesiastical ones) have a particular social and temporal context which determines their shape. All religious ideas, institutions, and personnel serve socio-political functions, explicitly or implicitly, wittingly or unwittingly. In Latin America many religious ideas and institutions have served the interests of the ruling dominant classes. It looks as if a similar judgement of implicit unwitting collusion with the powerful against the powerless based on lack of socio-political awareness, might fairly be made about chaplains in mental health services in this country. In this chapter I shall explore some of the reasons why this may be so.

CHURCH AND PASTORS IN SOCIO-POLITICAL CONTEXT

The starting-point for analysis, here as elsewhere, must be the broad context of the church and religion in society as a whole. Although Karl Marx devoted comparatively little of his analysis to the place of religion in capitalist society, he saw it basically as a sign of alienation which would pass away with the end of capitalism. Religious institutions, while they could certainly express some working-class discontent and interests to an extent, were regarded by Marx as allied to the interests of the ruling classes; they were part of the capitalist super-structure which would eventually be overthrown.[1]

Subsequent Marxist criticism has maintained the same line. Miliband, for example, sees the church in British society as one of the organs whereby the ideological sway of the ruling class is maintained and legitimated over against the lower classes:

In their political competition with the parties of the Left, the conservative parties have always derived a very notable amount of direct or indirect support and strength from the Churches.[2]

While churches themselves maintain that they are politically neutral and non-partisan, they implicitly and strongly support the interests of the ruling class:

Organised religion, in most of its major manifestations, *has* played a profoundly 'functional' and 'integrative' role in regard to the prevailing economic and social system, and ... to the state which has defended the social order.[3]

In the specific case of the Church of England, which provides most of the full-time chaplains in hospitals and many of the part-time chaplains, the links between church and state in the establishment are formalised to a high degree. The head of the state is the governor of the church, a majority of diocesan bishops sit in the House of Lords, and all ordained clergy take an oath of allegiance to the sovereign just as army officers and other public officials do. Scott writes of this kind of elite social establishment,

The establishment is not simply a group of people; it is a group of people allied around certain social institutions. These institutions are the Conservative Party, the Church of England, the public schools and ancient universities, the legal profession and the Guards regiments.[4]

---

[1] For more on Marx's attitudes towards religion see Lochman, *Encountering Marx*; K. Marx and F. Engels, *On Religion*. Moscow: Progress, 1957; D. W. D. Shaw, *The Dissuaders*. London: SCM Press, 1978; Peter Hebblethwaite, *The Christian–Marxist Dialogue and Beyond*. London: Darton, Longman and Todd, 1977.

[2] Miliband, *The State in Capitalist Society*, p. 178.

[3] Ibid., p. 181. Emphasis original.

[4] John Scott, *The Upper Classes: Property and Privilege in Britain*. London: Macmillan, 1982, p. 159.

Matheson, a church historian, argues that the most common relationship between the church and the state has been one of assimilation, so that Christianity in its official forms is used to legitimise the political establishment. While this relationship may now be in decline, there can be little doubt that a powerful residuum remains, particularly in established churches like the Church of England.[5] The Church of England is, in its own right, a major landowner and investor on the Stock Market, giving it a vested interest in the capitalist system. It is within this view of the church as broadly a legitimating institution for the ruling class that I shall examine the place of clergy in the Church of England, who dominate in numbers, time, and influence in hospital chaplaincy of all kinds.

A number of features can be cited to justify the assertion that clergy essentially form a dependent group of the ruling class in English society and are therefore likely, albeit unwittingly, to act in ways which are consistent with the interests of that class. First, in terms of social origins, a majority of clergy come from the higher and middle social classes, while only 5 per cent come from social class 5. About 50 per cent come from social classes 1 and 2, while about one third attended public schools.[6] Amongst the higher clergy, 88 per cent of the diocesan episcopate were found to be educated at Oxbridge, a further indicator of upper class origin or assimilation.[7]

Secondly, the professional nature of the clerical occupation suggests that clergy will share many of the assumptions and behaviour patterns of professional groups as a whole. These tend to emphasise a particular kind of education, training and

[5] See Peter Matheson, *Profile of Love*. Belfast: Christian Journals Ltd, 1979, pp. 34–7.
[6] For these figures see Stewart Ranson, Alan Bryman, and Bob Hinings, *Clergy, Ministers and Priests*. London: Routledge and Kegan Paul, 1977.
[7] See Kenneth Thompson, 'Church of England Bishops as an elite' in Philip Stanworth and Anthony Giddens, eds., *Elites and Power in British Society*. Cambridge: Cambridge University Press, 1974. In 1992 68 per cent of the episcopate had been educated at Oxford or Cambridge. See David Fanning, 'Letter to the editor', *Church Times* 18 December 1992.

socialisation, one-to-one relationships and putative political neutrality.[8] Professions depend for their influence upon legitimation from powerful social groups. Professional status also has significant implications for how a group sees itself in society as well as for who can belong to it (professional training requires education and financial resources, so it may not be readily available to people from lower social classes). On the whole, professions have not been groups radically committed to the socio-political needs of lower-class people. They have been firmly dominated by the interests and values of the upper classes which do well from the present order of society.

Prima facie, clergy, like other members of the upper and professional classes, act as 'organic intellectuals' for the ruling classes, disseminating, albeit unconsciously, ideas and practices which buttress and legitimate the claim to rule of the governing class.[9] If this assertion that clergy serve as basically part of the ideological control and promotion apparatus of the ruling class within contemporary society seems improbable and arbitrary, the history of the clerical profession should be recalled.

In the past, clergy of the Church of England acted quite willingly as agents of social control. George Herbert, for example, reflecting the *rapprochement* between church and state in the seventeenth century, devoted much of his time to ensuring that his parishioners were well-disciplined and conformed to the social norms and state laws of the time.[10] In the eighteenth and nineteenth centuries, Anglican clergy were closely linked to the ruling and landed classes who were often responsible for their appointment. They frequently served as Justices of the Peace and were an effective and valued part of the local social control apparatus. Many clergy were active and overt politicians, usually on the side of the Tory party.

---

[8] For more on the individualist and ostensibly apolitical nature of professional work see Anthony Russell, *The Clerical Profession*. London: SPCK, 1980; Wilding, *Professional Power and Social Welfare*.

[9] For the idea of intellectuals and professionals being in the service of ruling-class hegemony, an idea derived from the Italian Marxist thinker Gramsci see, for example, James Joll, *Gramsci*. Glasgow: Fontana, 1977, ch. 9; Paul Corrigan and Peter Leonard, *Social Work Practice Under Capitalism*. London: Macmillan, 1978, pp. 151ff.

[10] See further Pattison, *Critique*, ch. 4.

They were regarded as bastions of the established order over against the revolutionary egalitarian ideas percolating into England from France. While the nineteenth century saw clergy withdrawing from a direct and overt role in politics in favour of the ideal of neutrality associated with professionalism, their work in education and poverty relief enabled them to remain effective agents of social control and influence on behalf of the ruling classes.[11] There clearly have been, and are, individual clergy who are politically radical in the sense of displaying active commitment to the poor and oppressed. However, this is in reality a minority voice within a dominant tradition of conforming to, and affirming, the values and norms of the *status quo*. In this connection it is worth bearing in mind Miliband's assertion that:

It would not seem unfair to suggest that the reason why the Churches in advanced capitalist countries have been so willing to serve and support the state is not ... so much because of its 'democratic' character, but because of the governments which have had an ideology and political bias broadly congruent with that of the Churches themselves.[12]

There is little real evidence to suggest that the churches and clergy are on aggregate essentially more critical of the established order of capitalist society than they have ever been.

This would seem to be borne out in general terms in the case of chaplains within mental health. By asserting their much-valued independence, universal concern, and availability, chaplains avoid confronting real differences in class, status and power, allowing the prevailing order to continue unchallenged. By attempting to remain neutral, chaplains are in fact, siding with the powerful against the powerless. Freire encapsulates this point in relation to churches thus:

When they insist on the neutrality of the church in relation to history, or to political action, they take political stands which inevitably favour the power elites against the masses. 'Washing one's hands' of

---

[11] For all of this see Russell, *The Clerical Profession*, especially chs. 11, 12, 13, and 15.
[12] Miliband, *The State in Capitalist Society*, p. 184.

the conflict between the powerful and the powerless means to side with the powerful, not to be neutral.[13]

In relation to chaplains in particular, this point is confirmed by the fact that some of them seem prepared to cross picket lines in strikes by low-paid workers, the justice of whose cause they may well acknowledge. There can be no social and political neutrality in such a situation.

The focus on individuals and small groups prominent in the work of many chaplains can also be seen as implicitly affirming the *status quo* and the power of people who already have power, both in the mental health services and in wider society. By emphasising the locus of pathology as lying within the individual, the family, or small group relations, chaplains divert attention away from larger social structures and forces in society and hospital, turning possible social evils into personal problems.

Chaplains who emphasise the importance of the spiritual, transcendent, and liturgical may be regarded as deflecting attention away from the ills of the present with their social and historical causes and context to an ahistorical, invisible realm where historical conditions of pain and suffering are individualised and abstracted from any kind of historical struggle for justice and equality. Liberation theologians have pointed out that in Latin America the sacraments can perform this ideological or reality-disguising function which leads to the devaluation of social and historical activity.[14] This point is amplified by the Sri Lankan theologian, Tissa Balasuriya, who demonstrates how the Eucharist, which expressed Christ's mission of human liberation and opposition to oppression and injustice, has become a tool of social domestication. The Eucharist is individualised, privatised, and made ethereal so that the appearance of unity can be maintained at any price.[15]

Chaplains can be seen as having a legitimating function

---

[13] Paulo Freire, 'Education, liberation and the church' in Kee, ed., *A Reader in Political Theology*.

[14] Segundo, *The Liberation of Theology*, ch. 2.

[15] Tissa Balasuriya, *The Eucharist and Human Liberation*. London: SCM Press, 1979, ch. 1.

within the mental health services, both to patients and to the outside world. The presence of white, well-educated, independent, and responsible upper-middle-class people who work as chaplains is reassuring. It allows society to believe that there can be nothing very much wrong with the mental health services if such people are happy to work in them without protest. At the same time, chaplains can help to convince patients that the services they are receiving are benevolent and legitimate. This apologetic function is made explicit by Grainger's assertion that 'From the point of view of the hospital, (the chaplain) justifies his [*sic*] place within the institution as its advocate and interpreter, explaining the hospital to the patient.[16]

The chaplains' legitimating function is matched with a palliative or analgesic function. Simply put, this is the matter of making people feel a bit better about the situation in which they find themselves, so they will not attempt to leave it or change it. The chaplain can act as an 'oiler of the machine' so people do not get so angry or frustrated that they demand major structural changes for themselves or others. Thus Longbottom:

it may be that the most important role of the chaplain is to act as the carer of those who care, especially in high stress areas ... So we must expect and be available to act as a listening post for individual carers' grumbles, troubles, hopes and fears. We don't have to give advice, rather to listen. How many people drop out because there is no listening post.[17]

By this kind of individualised 'holy' listening which leads to no action, the chaplain may well help to make the intolerable acceptable and the insufferable bearable. This function may be exercised with all types of groups in the hospital, and it can be conceived as reconciliation rather than the anaesthesia, which it might appear to be in some situations.

Halmos would describe this palliative function as one of therapy, by which he means that it is part of a process whereby individuals are helped to adapt and change to suit social rules,

[16] Grainger, *Watching for Wings*, p. 3.
[17] Longbottom, 'Paper on chaplaincy', p. 89.

norms, and roles, rather than those rules, norms, and roles themselves being changed which would require what he would see as political activity.[18] Halmos points out that the personalist, therapeutic orientation which is common in society (and, as we have seen, amongst chaplains) is very different from the political, social reformist orientation. More radical theorists have warned that the whole concept of 'care' in relation to individuals is implicitly politically conservative because it focusses on changing individuals rather than the conditions and society which contribute to their problems.[19] Many of the therapeutic methods used in mental health are oriented towards individual change not social change, thus implicitly affirming the social order. In using individualistic, personal therapeutic methods and concepts, chaplains may unwittingly fall into the same trap.

Chaplains are not bound to be socio-politically conservative and supportive of the established order. Sometimes, their activity may have some socio-political effect for justice and change. For example, counselling activities may build up the confidence and self-esteem of individuals so that they feel more able to assert their own autonomy and power.[20] I certainly do not want to suggest that chaplains should never ever give any care and attention to individuals. None the less, the general assertion that they perform a broadly socio-politically conservative function within the mental health services and in society at large still stands. If this were not the case, it is unlikely that mental health chaplains, in common with military and prison chaplains, would remain such a welcome part of a politicised and underfunded NHS as they do.

SOCIO-POLITICAL CONSTRAINTS IN PASTORAL CARE

I have tried to show that chaplains, the main official providers of pastoral care in the mental health services, play a basically functional, conservative, and facilitative role. They are oilers

[18] Paul Halmos, *The Personal and the Political*. London: Hutchinson, 1978, ch. 2.
[19] See, for example, Mike Simpkin, *Trapped Within Welfare*. London: Macmillan, 1979.
[20] Cf. Peter Selby, *Liberating God*. London: SPCK, 1983.

of the wheels, providers of care and solace for individuals and small groups, apparently largely oblivious to the socio-political issues surrounding mental illness and the care of mentally ill people. Their practice tends not to be socially and politically aware and committed to the poor and oppressed, i.e., mentally ill people themselves and those who work most closely with them. At its nadir this can mean that they acquiesce inaudibly to the *status quo* in the face of poor and inadequate social conditions in and outside the caring services. They thereby unwittingly ensure the perpetuation of those conditions and contribute, at least passively, to the long-term unnecessary suffering of those for whom they (sincerely) profess to care. They tacitly and largely unreflectively help to keep the system going with little apparent regard for the important issues of injustice, inequality, power, and social structure which were identified above as having an important bearing on the well-being of mentally ill people. On meeting a hospital chaplain who was interested in the structural issues confronting the NHS, Margaret Kane, a theologian of work and industry was very surprised for, 'Hospital chaplains along with prison chaplains, which have strong establishment support from the state, tend to focus on the traditional pastoral approach.'[21]

It may be that some readers will be unperturbed by this diagnosis, even if they accept its validity. It can be argued that the business of addressing and acting upon social injustices is not the job of chaplains who are precisely there to perform a personalised, vaguely therapeutic pastoral role, giving comfort and respect to those whose individuality is constantly threatened. Others, however, may now be feeling that chaplains are benighted moral blackguards who actively and personally assist in the oppression of the poor by their blindness and collusion with the forces of injustice. Society and the care professionals may metaphorically 'throw the stones', but chaplains hold their coats and look on, approving or indifferent, while this is done (cf. Acts 7. 58–8. 1).

In organisations, it is common to find individuals being

---

[21] Margaret Kane, *What Kind of God?*. London: SCM Press, 1986, p. 104.

blamed and held responsible when things go wrong. This often happens when abuse or neglect is discovered. The cry goes up that someone must be found personally responsible for whatever evil has come about. Often a person is found and they are either disciplined or dismissed. This approach is not, I think, a relevant or helpful one in trying to understand how chaplains think or act in the mental health services. The point is that they, like the mental health services and mentally ill people, are constrained and influenced by complex socio-political factors.

Like anyone else, chaplains are situated in a capitalist social order, which expeditiously emphasises individualism, and hides from itself the social roots of many of its ills, and has set itself against resolving fundamental inequalities and poverty.[22] (I write on the day when the British government issued a White Paper, 'The Health of the Nation', which seeks to reduce mental disorder, amongst other illnesses, but steadfastly rejects any strategy of tackling poverty and inequalities in health.) This same society finds it consonant with its dominant values to employ methods of understanding illness in terms of individual pathology, prescinding from socio-political context. Further, it places little value upon mentally ill people, who are regarded as an unproductive, disruptive, and stigmatised group. It is hardly surprising that chaplains, as members of professional classes who largely support the existing social order, should have internalised an implicitly conservative world view in relation to mental disorder.

There is quite a lot of psychological evidence to suggest that religion performs a conservative function in Western society, and that religious people tend not to be politically radical.[23] Chaplains are members of churches which have performed a largely conservative social function, supporting the ruling class implicitly if not explicitly. The theologies of these churches have been individualistic and hierarchical, supporting the dominant values of society:

[22] For more on individualism in capitalist society see Steven Lukes, *Individualism*. Oxford: Blackwell, 1973.

[23] Michael Argyle and Benjamin Beit-Hallahmi, *The Social Psychology of Religion*. London: Routledge and Kegan Paul, 1975, ch. 7.

In our urban/industrial society a few models: Lord, Master, King, Father, dominate our conception of God. These models have seemed to make sense of and to validate our particular kind of society . . . [I]t is clear that religion is a factor in creating and supporting the values of an industrial society: hierarchical organization, obedience to external authority, paternalism, dependence on the benign domination of the *male* 'Father' figure . . . The qualities these models stress contradict the most creative insights of today: participation, the reponsibility and power of human beings, human solidarity, the equality of men and women.[24]

Institutionally, the churches have shown relatively little interest in fundamentally changing the injustices of society or in the situation of mentally ill people. No major denomination has yet published a policy statement on the latter, and if it did it is unlikely that that situation would be presented in terms of the need for social change and justice. In general, churches seem content to nominate or approve chaplains for appointment in mental health services, and then to forget about them, simply being grateful that the state is paying their salaries. It is almost as if the churches actually want to have only a token and ineffectual presence in mental health services. This demonstrates a certain amount of concern without requiring anything further of the churches in terms of action or financial commitment. There is thus little active, critical support for chaplains in their pastoral work which might help to radicalise their perspectives and practice.

Training and socialisation into the clerical profession is individualistic ('my' vocation) and makes much of personal, therapeutic techniques such as counselling at the expense of a wider vision of pastoral practice.[25] From the beginnings of clerical life, students are taught to see the world primarily in terms of persons and small groups, and they are not taught skills of social and political analysis. This tendency is highly congruent with the dominant therapeutic ideas in other 'caring' professions, and is reinforced if a minister starts to work in the health care services.

[24] Kane, *What Kind of God?*, p. 120.
[25] See Selby, *Liberating God*; Alan Billings, 'Pastors or counsellors?', *Contact* 108, 1992, 3–9.

The situation and conditions of chaplains in the mental health services are profoundly unconducive to becoming socio-politically radical in analysis and action. Chaplains are a tiny minority group; often, they are part time or only have part-time colleagues. This means there is often little opportunity to build up a chaplaincy group culture which may be different from that of other groups within the service. The churches outside the services are frequently indifferent to the work of chaplains, seeing them as competent professionals who should simply be left to get on with their jobs. This means that chaplains have to develop a way of existing on their own in their work. It is not surprising in these circumstances that they tend to identify with other professional groups in order to obtain a sense of value and belonging, hence the enthusiasm for joining the therapeutic team or engaging in counselling. While this endears chaplains to their colleagues, and meets their own needs for significance and belonging, it can easily mean that chaplains 'go native' and cease to have the possibility of being truly independent critics. Chaplains are responsible to the service managers who hire and fire them, not to Christian communities or to service users. Again, this is a disincentive to radical questioning or socio-politically controversial action. He who pays the chaplain chooses the hymn, or at least influences the kinds of hymns that can really be chosen. In the light of all this, it is much easier to get on with a task of socially acceptable therapeutic benevolence to individuals which provides some personal satisfaction and reward, than to face being a con-troversial, possibly ostracised, voice in the wilderness.

The conclusion to this part of my analysis must be that chaplains cannot be blamed personally for failing to be socio-politically aware and committed in their pastoral practice. If they appear to be blind or indifferent to wider factors, this is probably not due so much to personal wickedness as to a sense of isolation, powerlessness, and ignorance in the face of massive prevailing customs and structures. Given their background and structural situation in society, church, and hospital, it would be somewhat surprising if they were in any way radical. For chaplains easily to appropriate a socio-politically aware and committed pastoral care, a vast amount of change in institutions and society would have to occur. Such change would involve individuals, groups, organisations, and churches far beyond the narrow confines of local mental health services. Having acknowledged that the circumstances conducive to adopting such a role demand wide change beyond the influence of individual chaplains to avoid narrowly blaming that group for complacency, however, it is still possible to begin to sketch out a role for chaplains in bringing such change about. But before doing that, it is important to consider to what extent socio-political analysis and commitment on the side of the oppressed might be an appropriate imperative for pastoral care.

CHAPTER 15

Liberating pastoral care

The recent majority tradition in pastoral care suggests that pastoral care is essentially a matter of giving good personal care to individuals. Frank Wright, a pastoral theologian with considerable sympathy for a socially committed approach to pastoral care, still asserts that

Under the compulsion of the Kingdom, the pastor will never settle for impersonal, but always seek the welfare of the person. There, at least, is pastoral distinctiveness.[1]

Healing, sustaining, guiding, reconciling and nurturing, the core elements of pastoral care, have been directed mainly at individuals and small groups.[2] For many people, pastoral care is synonymous with personal counselling and a therapeutic role.

I will argue here that, while giving care and respect to individuals is certainly an important part of the pastoral task, this is too limited. Pastoral care has fallen into the trap of thinking too narrowly about how people's welfare might be sought and their potential developed. In so doing, it may actually inadvertently work against its intentions to promote well-being; it may also collude with some of the social and political forces which create and maintain human suffering. I will outline briefly how pastoral care has become trapped in apolitical individualism. I will then discuss why it should have a wider sphere of vision and action in relation to the pastoral

---

[1] Frank Wright, *The Pastoral Nature of the Ministry*. London: SCM Press, 1980, p. 73.
[2] Cf. Howard Clinebell, *Basic Types of Pastoral Care and Counselling*. London: SCM Press, 1984, ch. 2 for a discussion of these elements.

task. This provides a rationale, if not an imperative, for pastoral carers to adopt a socio-politically aware and committed pastoral care in whatever situation they work. In the particular case of professional pastors working with mentally ill people, there is an urgent need to advance beyond models of ministry and pastoral care focussed on individual needs to undertake the kinds of socio-political perspective and action outlined in the next chapter.

PASTORAL CARE IN THERAPEUTIC CAPTIVITY

One of the most important insights of liberation theology is that all institutions and ideologies, including ecclesiastical and theological ones, have a human and social context which helps to shape them. The theory and practice of contemporary pastoral care is no exception. Pastoral care is influenced by, and congruent with, the social order in which it is situated. It is with this presupposition in mind that it is possible to ask how and why pastoral care has made individual care its focus and priority, to the almost complete exclusion of the social and political dimension of existence. A number of relevant factors can be identified here. The first, and perhaps most important, influence is the individualistic nature of Western capitalist society, generally. The emphasis upon the fundamental importance of the atomised individual finds expression in Margaret Thatcher's reputed dictum that there is no such thing as society, only individuals. The dominance of individualist ideas of the person over against a more corporate view of life is consonant with the nature of capitalist society which depends on people being able to enter freely into contractual relationships in the market and being able to sell as many different things to as many different people as possible, thus requiring multiple units of consumption. Individualism masks the class structure of society and makes people think of themselves as independent monads with little in common with others, rather than as partakers with them in a common class position:

The existence of classes is hidden by the individualisation of all operations within the capitalist market ... the political process with its rights of citizenship and individual ballots, also masks the class structure of capitalist society.[3]

If individualism provides the social background and matrix of understanding for pastoral care (along with other forms of professional care such as medicine and nursing), it has nurtured and been amplified by correlative individualism in religion and theology. Sölle writes

> We ... reduced our symbols and confined them to ourselves, to our personalities. We used religious concepts and images for one purpose only: they had to serve the supreme value of middle-class culture – individualism ... Religion becomes a tool of the ruling classes, and only continues to function in order to comfort the sad, enrich personal life, and give the individual the feeling of significance. Sin then becomes personal transgressions ... The cross then becomes my unique suffering, and the resurrection my individual immortality.[4]

A futher factor leading to the individualistic captivity of pastoral care probably originates in the professionalisation of the clergy in the last century. Along with developing a fairly narrow, specialised, 'religious' and 'spiritual' role, clergy adopted many appurtenances of nascent professions, such as specialised training and professional journals. Most significantly in this context was an emphasis on the one-to-one relationship between the professional and the client. This provided a background for pastoral care which is individually, spiritually, and psychologically oriented. Russell notes that

> The notion that the clergyman is 'above politics' may be taken as a significant indicator of the degree to which clergy (have) accepted (the professional) ideal; for the concept of neutrality – affective, emotional and political – is of central importance in the professional model.[5]

Within the context of the factors described so far, it comes as no surprise that individual counselling should be such a popular model for pastoral care, and that it has had such a powerful influence upon it. From the influence of Freud, with

---

[3] Gough, *The Political Economy of the Welfare State*, p. 25.
[4] Dorothee Sölle, *Choosing Life*. London: SCM Press, 1981, p. 82.
[5] Russell, *The Clerical Profession*, p. 228.

his discovery of individual 'talking cures' in the first part of this century, counselling has mushroomed both inside and outside the churches, particularly since the Second World War. Individual counselling chimes in nicely with the professional role of clergy working for socially conservative churches informed by individualistic theologies, and looking for a new sense of purpose and efficacy in a secular context where many people's main welfare needs are met by non-religious agencies. Individual care seems possible, desirable, and satisfying in a milieu in which the church and clergy have felt that they are losing their social significance and influence. It is, of course, socially and politically non-controversial, being consonant with dominant social values.[6]

Commenting on the narrowing of pastoral care down to looking after individuals in a 'tenderness trap', Campbell writes

The literature of pastoral care becomes largely a re-stating of the tenets of good counselling in a religious context; the activities of the pastoral carers become narrowed down to the refinement of one-to-one and small group interactions; the development of the individual's capacity for self determination according to the values he chooses for his own life become the epitome of the Gospel hope and promise. Somewhere in the by-going the prophetic edge of Christianity is lost and the pastoral care movement becomes dangerously like a new version of Marx's 'opium of the people'.[7]

SUBVERTING THERAPEUTIC INDIVIDUALISM

Although the dominant tradition in contemporary pastoral care has been one of asocial, apolitical therapeutic individualism (as witness, for example, the volumes in the SPCK 'New Library of Pastoral Care' which mostly deal with issues in personal counselling) there are critical voices and traditions suggesting that this ideological standpoint is not adequate in the face of human need. Leech, for instance, writes

---

[6] Cf. Paul Halmos, *The Faith of the Counsellors*. London: Constable, 1965; Bernice Martin, *A Sociology of Contemporary Cultural Change*. Oxford: Blackwell, 1981 pp. 190ff.
[7] Alastair V Campbell, 'The politics of pastoral care', *Contact* 62, 1979, 2–15, at p. 6.

Christian theology needs to ask questions about the politics of therapy and counselling. What are therapy and counselling actually doing about the problems confronting human society? Are they in fact simply helping people to be well adjusted in a society whose fundamental values and assumptions remain unquestioned?[8]

Following the lead of Leech and the liberation theologians, it is possible to create a critique of privatised pastoral care from a number of different angles, which suggests that this activity must be seen in much broader terms if it is to nurture human well-being in its fullness.

The first critical element which must be considered is that of the implausibility and counterfactuality of individualism. Donne's assertion that 'No man is an *Island*, entire of it self' has attained the status of a gratifying platitude. Taken seriously, however, it affirms the reality of the fundamentally social nature of human existence. We are what we are because of the society in which we live. Without other people, we could not be born, fed, use language, or share ideas and values. Jenkins asserts that

'the individual' is a myth and a dangerously dehumanizing myth. We are not individuals, we are persons ... The process of the development of the potentialities of the image of God which is the process of being and becoming human is the process of developing community ... We cannot be human until all are human.[9]

Even the idea that we are individuals is a socially formed and sustained one. Any line drawn in pastoral care theory and practice which suggests that it is possible to think of individual good or ill, without having regard to matters social and communal, is arbitrary. It may even be dangerously misleading. Furthermore, it can be argued that if one truly values individuals and seeks to make sure that all can exercise and develop their individuality, the only way to make this a reality is to become involved in social action which will make it possible.[10] There is a sense, then, in which individualistic approaches are subverted from within by their own contradictions.

[8] Kenneth Leech, *The Social God*. London: Sheldon Press, 1981, p. 80.
[9] Jenkins, *Contradiction of Christianity*, p. 102.
[10] Lukes, *Individualism*, p. 157.

The biblical and theological tradition provides a further element of critique. Although modern Christians may tend to regard salvation and religious experience as essentially a personal matter, this understanding would probably not have been comprehensible in biblical times. The Old Testament is a testimony to the corporate response of a whole people to the will of God, and right social relations which manifest justice and peace are the priority, not the salvation of the individual soul. The shepherds of Israel, mentioned for example in Ezekiel, are not kindly therapists, but, rather, the rulers of the nation engaged in tasks of leadership. The prophets likewise were concerned with the ordering of the nation. Arguably, this basically corporate, social, and political view of religion and well-being is continued into the New Testament, where Jesus preaches about a kingdom of God in which the poor have a prominent place, and where Paul concerns himself with the whole people of God. As the liberation theologians have shown, it actually takes a good deal to find a rationale for attending to individuals in terms of biblical religion. Even the miracles of Jesus can be seen as having more to do with making a social and theological impact, rather than with seeking the welfare of individual people – they are public, critical acts with a corporate context and implication.[11] The individualism of the Reformation, itself a product of wider social change and the growth of individualism in society as a whole, has blinded us to the corporate nature of salvation and religious life.[12]

Some trends in contemporary theologies are also questioning the hegemony of a privatised, individualised world view in religion. The work of the liberation theologians has already been extensively discussed, but even within Europe there is growing awareness of the social and political dimensions of reality. Theologians like Moltmann, Metz, and Sölle seek to transcend the world of personal consciousness and individual need to reassert the need for public, critical theologies. The

---

[11] See further Pattison, *Alive and Kicking*, ch. 4; R. A. Lambourne, *Community, Church and Healing*. London: Arthur James, 1987.

[12] See further, for example, Krister Stendahl, *Paul Amongst Jews and Gentiles*. Philadelphia: Fortress Press, 1976.

split between 'public' and 'private' is being challenged in the name of a universal God who must be found everywhere if anywhere.[13] Confining God to the realm of personal existential need, as pastoral theorists have tended to do under the influence of aspects of the thought of theologians like Paul Tillich, is beginning to be perceived as a fundamental and significant theological error which has radically distorting consequences for theory and practice.[14]

At a more empirical level, the nature and causes of human need and suffering interrogate the assumption that individual therapy should be the definitive model for pastoral care. As we have seen in the analysis of the situation of mentally ill people above, the locus of suffering may be the individual, but some of the factors that cause the individual to suffer lie far beyond any individual's control or influence. Poverty and unemployment, for example, are essentially social problems which have severe consequences for individuals, but actually require social and political solutions. If such solutions are excluded by those who claim to seek the welfare of individuals, then present suffering is perpetuated and a replication of such suffering for other people will be inevitable in the future.

This brings me to a very important point concerning the fallacy of socio-political neutrality in adopting an exclusively individualistic model of care. To choose such a model is to adopt a very particular political solution. No set of actions is without a set of implicit values and a particular socio-political commitment. To act as if individuals and their problems are not affected by the social order is to support the *status quo* and to leave social and political structures unchallenged by a kind of therapeutic quietism. In this sense, the personal is very definitely political, if only tacitly and implicitly. Adjusting people to unsatisfactory social conditions so they can live more contentedly in them may provide pastors and counsellors with a sense

---

[13] See further Selby, *Liberating God*.
[14] For more on the influence of Tillich on pastoral theology see Clinebell, *Basic Types of Pastoral Care and Counselling*, p. 106; Seward Hiltner, *Preface to Pastoral Theology*. New York: Abingdon, 1958; 'A descriptive appraisal, 1935–80', *Pastoral Psychology* 29, 1980, 86–98.

of agency and job satisfaction but it prescinds from questioning the injustice of the present social order. Thus Leech remarks

It does seem, in fact, that therapy and counselling have one of the lowest levels of political awareness among the various disciplines ... There seems to be a growing danger of the misuse of therapy and counselling in order to dodge and evade fundamental social and political issues ... It is at this point that the Christian prophetic tradition of asking fundamental questions about justice in society is extremely important.[15]

The final element of critique which should be mentioned comes from the pastoral care tradition itself. While this provides a good deal of evidence for helpful acts for, and with, individuals, for example, auricular confession, it also furnishes evidence for communal and socio-political emphases. I have noted the corporate dimensions of St Paul's thought. One does not need to look far for other examples of socio-political elements within the history of pastoral care. St Augustine, for example, used the secular forces of the Roman Empire to unite the schismatic Donatists with the true Catholic Church in fourth-century North Africa. Calvin, in sixteenth century Geneva, tried to found a theocracy in which public discipline was a primary pastoral goal. He also tried to manipulate secular political forces in other countries to ensure the well-being of Calvinist churches. More recently, the example of Anglican clergy, such as George Herbert, suggests that a large part of pastoral care consisted of a kind of social control in helping people to conform to the laws of the land and fit into the church community. Clergy of the eighteenth and nine-teenth century had few qualms about involving themselves in the wider community in social and political roles, such as being medical officers of health, almoners, public health officials, magistrates, or local politicians.[16] Even auricular confession can be seen as having a social and political content; it allowed the church to maintain corporate discipline and control over its members.[17]

---

[15] Leech, *The Social God*, p. 80.
[16] For more on thse examples see Pattison, *Critique*, ch. 5.
[17] Mike Hepworth and Bryan S. Turner, *Confession*. London: Routledge and Kegan Paul, 1982.

There is evidence from the pastoral care tradition itself that it can contain all manner of actions which respond to human need or social necessity. The personal good and well-being of the individual for his or her own sake (as opposed to the good of the community) has only been an exclusive defining priority in pastoral care for a relatively short time. In general, diverse human, ecclesiastical, and social needs have provided the motivation, imperative and shape of pastoral care, rather than any notion of the primacy of the individual or the efficacy of individually focussed techniques of care. This leaves a question mark against the dominance of this focus in the present century.

The conclusion of this cumulative critique is that the narrowly individualistic understanding of pastoral care which has come to dominate in the present century is socially conditioned and somewhat arbitrary. The onus is on those who would limit pastoral care to a therapeutic model to show that it is more authentic, beneficent, and appropriate than pastoral care which has a wider perspective and range of action. I would argue that pastoral care must be allowed to grapple with real, concrete, priority human need, and not become 'spiritualised' or individualised, thus devaluing present experience and suffering. If the imperative to meet human need is to be determinative, pastoral care must be reconceptualised. Seeing it as being mainly and narrowly concerned about individuals is an unhelpful misrepresentation which colludes with, and perpetuates, circumstances of injustice and oppression. Pastoral care has socio-political implications and consequences. Sometimes the only appropriate pastoral action is social or political action.

REMODELLING PASTORAL CARE

To respond to the critical elements highlighted above and to allow pastoral care to escape from its ideological captivity, it is helpful to propose the following definition:

Pastoral care is that activity, undertaken especially by representative Christian persons, directed towards the elimination and relief of sin and sorrow and the presentation of all people perfect in Christ to God.

There are many aspects of this definition which I have discussed elsewhere.[18] In the present context these are: First, unlike many definitions of pastoral care, this one does not focus on individuals. If anything the focus is upon shaping and forming a community, though care of individuals is not in any way excluded. Secondly, the elimination and relief of sin and sorrow is intended to denote all the things which make people suffer and keep people suffering, whether they be material or psychological (the only way that God can appear to a starving man is in a loaf of bread, not in prayers or words of comfort). Thirdly, the positive notion of presenting all people perfect in Christ to God suggests a prophylactic or preventive role for pastoral care. It is not enough to assist people when they are in a state of sin, sorrow, suffering, and urgent need. The point is to maximise their potential and to prevent unnecessary suffering occurring. The 'Good Samaritan' model of picking up individuals when they are down may provide a sense of power, goodness, and satisfaction for pastors involved in this work, but doing something about the robbers on the road from Jerusalem to Jericho might be of greater long-term benefit to more people! Finally, pastoral care is not confined to the needs of church members and would-be believers. Following the liberation theologians, it allows for universal care through all areas of life. Christians and the church may be a focus for providing pastoral care, but meeting the needs of the world and of all people should be the aim of the church and its carers.

Pastoral care is a rich and variegated activity. It is no use narrowly prescribing what it should do in all circumstances. If history teaches anything, it is that almost everything has been done within the scope of pastoral care. The point is not to decree that social and political activity should always and everywhere inevitably be a part of all pastoral care, but to create a permissive space in which it must be considered as a possible part of pastoral action, depending on the priority

[18] See further Pattison, *Critique*, ch. 1.

given to different kinds of human need. However, in some circumstances not to have socio-political awareness and commitment in pastoral care is to ignore important concrete human needs. An individualistic, therapeutic approach in this context is inappropriate, 'fiddling while Rome burns'. Occasionally, even often, it must give place to wider understanding and action which will do more to promote human flourishing and to diminish suffering.

The notion of developing a more socio-politically aware, critical and committed pastoral care has gained some prominence over the last few decades. In Britain, R. A. Lambourne was a pioneer of the communal and corporate dimensions of existence, launching a considerable onslaught on the dominance of professional counselling as a model for pastoral care. His associates Michael Wilson and James Mathers have taken these anti-individualistic ideas further. Mathers wrote a particularly important paper highlighting the importance of privileging the leadership and corporate dimensions of pastoral care over those of caring in situations where the well-being of a group or organisation is threatened.[19] The work of Campbell and Leech has been mentioned already, but the fullest and most credible plea for politically informed pastoral care has come from Selby. His book *Liberating God* points decisively to the need to integrate private care and public struggle:

To presume to care for other human beings without taking into account the social and political causes of whatever it is they may be experiencing is to confirm them in their distress while pretending to offer healing.[20]

A number of writers in the USA have also contributed to a wider understanding of the communal and political challenges facing pastoral care. Bonthius, for example, writes

---

[19] James Mathers, 'The pastoral role: a psychiatrist's perspective', in M. A. H. Melinsky, ed., *Religion and Medicine* 2. London: SCM Press, 1973; Lambourne, *Community, Church and Healing*; Michael Wilson, ed., *Explorations in Health and Salvation*. Birmingham: University of Birmingham Institute for the Study of Worship and Religious Architecture, 1983; *A Coat of Many Colours*. London: Epworth Press, 1988.

[20] Selby, *Liberating God*, p. 76.

Now we are open as never before to a reform of the idea of pastoral care. In one sentence, the situation as we see it is that persons are so much products of structures that we must change structures in order to help persons ... In Christian terms it is a 'structure', an ideal community, that we are taught to pray for and asked to work for. Ministry to structures is not simply subordinate to ministry to persons ... Ministry to persons is ultimately for the purpose of enabling them to serve a structure: the Kingdom of God.[21]

Browning, Kemp, Hulme, Seifert, and Clinebell have also pointed up the importance of community, justice, social action, justice, prophecy, and paying attention to the needs of the poor. Combatting outward injustice is seen as a necessary accompaniment to overcoming inner conflicts.[22] Clinebell developed a holistic model of pastoral care which reaches out to the community, to society, even to the ecosphere.[23]

The literature referred to above was mostly produced some years ago now. Interest in the social, political, and communal in pastoral care may now be on the wane. A recent book by American pastoral theologian Charles Gerkin, promisingly entitled *Prophetic Pastoral Practice*, deals with hermeneutic and ethical problems within the Christian community, rather than with changing structures of injustice.[24] Socio-political perspectives on pastoral care have by no means successfully challenged or supplanted the hegemony of more socially conservative individualist, therapeutic orientations in church and society.

CONCLUSION

If pastoral carers are truly interested in promoting human well-being in all its aspects, it is arguable that they need to be prepared to look beyond the individual to action in wider

21 Robert H. Bonthius, 'Pastoral care for structures – as well as persons', *Pastoral Psychology* 18, 1967, 10–19, at 11.
22 Cf. Browning, 'Pastoral care and the poor'; Charles F. Kemp, *Pastoral Care with the Poor*. Nashville: Abingdon, 1972; William E. Hulme, 'Concern for corporate structures or care for the individual?', *Journal of Pastoral Care* 23, 1969, 153–63; Harvey Seifert and Howard J. Clinebell, *Personal Growth and Social Change*. Philadelphia: Westminster, 1969, p. 11.
23 Clinebell, *Basic Types of Pastoral Care and Counselling*, ch. 2.
24 Charles V. Gerkin, *Prophetic Pastoral Practice*. Nashville: Abingdon, 1991.

social structures. There may be circumstances in which a refusal to do this could ensure or institutionalise present and future suffering which could be prevented. However, it is one thing to recognise that socio-political awareness and action should be a possibility or even an imperative in pastoral care. It is another to see what the principles and practicalities of this might be. It is to this that I now turn.

CHAPTER 16

What is to be done? Towards a socio-politically aware and committed pastoral care

Social and political liberation from oppression and injustice is not something which is done to or for people, but by people themselves. If they are prone to it, pastoral carers should probably resist the temptation to see themselves as individual liberators of others along the lines of the kind of radical personal heroism displayed by, for example, Camilo Torres in South America. This type of action on behalf of others is extreme, and may be neither helpful nor realistic. It could be unhelpful, because it fails to recognise the need for people to work together with many others in complex, organised ways to achieve their own liberation and empowerment. It is likely to be unrealistic because of the context and social, institutional, and personal constraints within which most pastors work in the Western world. Pastoral workers, particularly when they work professionally in churches or the NHS, are heirs to a predominantly conservative tradition which prizes order and authority. They are often valued, and may value themselves, because of the rewards of an individually focussed ministry. They may have chosen their profession because of their skills with people. These workers cannot reorient themselves overnight to become social and political 'liberators', even if that aspiration were not dubious on other grounds.

For this reason I do not argue for direct social and political action on the part of every pastoral carer, but for growing social and political awareness and commitment on the part of all pastors (though more direct action may be desirable for some, particularly in situations of extreme suffering where social and political causes are overt and uppermost). Whatever the focus of pastoral care and the particular skills, strengths, and preferences of a pastor, whether it be counselling, group-work, or organisation, it is possible to be socio-politically aware of the situation one is in, and of the implications of the activities which one undertakes. Above all, one can try to ensure that any kind of action is undertaken in such a way that it is in solidarity with oppressed people, however indirectly. It may not be possible for pastors to contribute directly to others' struggle for liberation; women, for example, may not welcome the active participation of men in their activities for empowerment. However, it should be feasible to cease being an obstacle to this process, and even to become a catalyst for it through understanding and solidarity. Thus, commitment in the cause of oppressed people is possible for those who are institutionally or temperamentally constrained from taking action more directly in the social and political arena.

Following on from my argument that pastoral care has been arbitrarily confined within an individualistic paradigm, and that there is a case for developing elements of socio-political awareness and action in this activity to avoid the creation and perpetuation of avoidable suffering, I shall now outline some guidelines which lead in this direction. These are very general, needing interpretation in the concrete circumstances of pastoral care of various kinds. It is not possible narrowly to prescribe what pastors should do in particular contexts. All I hope to do is to set up some preliminary guidelines leading to a deepening of socio-political awareness and commitment. These will need development, criticism, and correction in the light of others' experience. Clearly, it makes sense to exemplify the implications of the principles here from the situation of pastoral care with mentally ill people. It should be noted, however, that they are useful and applicable in other situations, for examaple, in thinking about pastoral care with women (the subject of the next chapter).

There are six basic principles which might inform those pastors who seek to develop a socio-politically aware and committed pastoral care:

1 It must be based on a thorough analysis of the socio-political context in which pastoral care is exercised.

2 There must be an option for the oppressed.

3 Pastoral carers should seek to become 'organic intellectuals' of oppressed groups, exercising an educative, consciousness-changing role.

4 There must be a preparedness to belong to, and co-operate with, groups of all kinds seeking desirable social and political change.

5 An 'unfinished' model for social and political action is required.

6 Appropriate pastoral care of individuals is not in any way proscribed, but this must not be allowed to act in an ideological, reality-disguising, and oppression promoting way.

Each of these precepts will now be examined in more detail.

1 Analysis of the social and political context of pastoral care

If pastoral care in any situation is to become appropriately socially and politically aware and committed, the starting-point has to be a careful analysis of socio-political context. Such an analysis will help to make clear who the oppressed people and groups are in a particular situation or institution, and will suggest relevant stances and modes of action which might be pursued. Using the tools of the social sciences as well as beginning to listen to the voices of oppressed people themselves, it is likely to be time-consuming and complex. However, failure to undertake it may lead to misidentification of groups and to over-hasty, inappropriate, or ineffective action.

The analysis of the situation of mentally ill people under-taken above may be regarded as paradigmatic of the kind of activity advocated here. This kind of analysis is useful and revealing; it is also difficult and complicated. It is important to realise that while examination of the socio-political factors surrounding another institution or type of pastoral situation might employ different tools and sources of information, the exercise itself cannot be avoided.

To understand the position of the oppressed and the reasons for it within the social and economic situation they live in is the essential preliminary to the practice of a socio-politically aware and committed pastoral care.[1]

2 *The option for the oppressed*

Liberation theology has as one of its own primary principles that the starting-point for theological activity and reflection should be a concrete option for the oppressed. A conscious option for the oppressed should also be the fundamental basis for a socio-politically aware and committed form of pastoral care, whether within a particular institution or setting or in society in general. In any situation where there is a substantial conflict of interest, and where there are large differences in class, status, and power between groups (as, for example, between doctors and service users in mental health), it behoves pastors to make an option for the weaker, poorer side. This principle is posited on the assumption, discussed above, that, if there is a situation of conflict and inequality, it is impossible to be neutral. Neutrality in this case will mean being partisan, if only inadvertently and passively. There are, however, a number of practical and theoretical difficulties which flow from the assertion that neutrality should be eschewed in favour of a concrete option for oppressed people and groups, and these need some discussion.

First, prevalent conceptions of reconciliation need to be revised. There is a long tradition in Christianity and among its pastors of attempting to bring together groups and individuals who are in conflict with each other. Underlying this assumption is some kind of notion that in Christ all people are united and so all division and disunity is contrary to the will of God. In practical terms, pastors have attempted a role of recon-

[1] See Roy Bailey and Mike Brake, 'Social work and the welfare state' in Roy Bailey and Mike Brake, eds., *Radical Social Work*. London: Arnold, 1975, pp. 1–12 for further consideration of this principle as it is applied to social work.

ciliation on the basis of neutrality and mediation. This kind of attitude is apparent in the much vaunted and valued neutral and non-partisan stance self-consciously adopted by pastors in mental illness services. It may, therefore, seem that advocating a partisan stance here in situations of inequality and conflict threatens the ministry of reconciliation. However, the aim of seeking to unite people and effect reconciliation remains the same in socio-politically aware and committed pastoral care as it is in ordinary ministry. It is the means which must differ. A partisan stance is commended here because, in the past, all too often what has passed for reconciliation has in fact meant cooling out opposition, adjusting people to oppression, and disguising the fact that injustice is rife. Writing to the biblical traditions of reconciliation, justice, and mercy married together in the action of God Stendahl notes,

for him [*sic*] who has and for him who is comfortable, reconciliation is very attractive – the sooner the better, so we can give up as little as possible. That is what reconciliation has come to mean, in stark contrast to the Christian tradition's sign of reconciliation, the cross where Christ gave all in order that reconciliation might be had. Judgement and mercy. We must resist all homogenizing, neutralizing, dialecticizing and balancing acts with these terms. There is little mercy except the chance of repentance for those of us who sit in judgement; but when judgement comes upon us, there is much mercy for the oppressed.[2]

True reconciliation, as opposed to the appearance of 'cheap' reconciliation, can only be achieved by the pursuit of liberty, justice, and equality for all people. Where these things do not exist it is necessary to strive actively for them. This may well mean throwing one's influence, power, and knowledge into the conflict on the side of the oppressed. It is not a question of loving the oppressed and hating the oppressors. The true freedom and reconciliation of both groups can only be realised when the oppressed are freed: 'Liberation . . . has to take place before reconciliation of the two sides is possible – without liberation there is not reconciliation but conciliation.'[3]

---

[2] Stendahl, *Paul Among Jews and Gentiles*, p. 107.
[3] Davies, *Christians, Politics and Violent Revolution*, p. 184.

A second, related, problem is that pastoral carers seeking to identify themselves with, and opt for, the oppressed may find themselves unpopular with their own churches and colleagues. British mainstream churches generally adopt a fairly positive and quiescent attitude to the prevalent social order and to eschew radical social change. Those who would challenge that order to take a critical, active, and positive stance with the oppressed may not receive much support or acclaim from the church's leaders and members. It must be clearly recognised that socio-politically aware and committed pastoral care which opts for the oppressed may challenge vested interests inside the church and other institutions. There is, therefore, a risk of alienation from the institutional church as well as from powerful groups in institutions such as hospitals and homes.

Finally, there is the problem of actually discerning who the oppressed groups who should be 'opted for' are in a particular situation. In the analysis of the socio-political context of the mental health sector above, for example, many different types, degrees, and levels of powerlessness, inequality, and injustice were identified. So, although it seems safe to conclude that mentally ill people themselves are the most impotent group within the service, there is an argument for seeing, for example, junior nurses, as also relatively powerless. Similarly, while doctors within the mental health sector are relatively powerful, the whole sector is discriminated against and unequally treated within the NHS generally. This kind of complexity and contradiction warns against arriving at naive and over-simple stances in pastoral care. Two things are then demanded of the pastor who seeks to make an option for the oppressed. First, there must be a willingness to analyse situations and institutions without minimising or evading ambiguities and complications. Secondly, there must be the possibility, in the light of such analysis, of developing a modulated and differential response to the various issues of injustice and inequality exposed. So it might happen that in the context of the hospital ward a chaplain would identify primarily with the patients over against the medical staff, while at the level of external social reality he or she might actively co-operate with professionals to

try and get a better financial deal for the mental health services
as a whole in terms of finance and resources.

3 Becoming 'organic intellectuals' of oppressed groups

This principle embodies the insight of the Italian Marxist
thinker, Antonio Gramsci, that clergy basically as members of
the intellectual and professional classes in society, legitimate
the rule of the powerful in society but can, if they will to do so,
reject this role to put their intellectual and other resources into
the service of oppressed people and groups.[4] As educated
professionals, clergy and other pastoral workers have considerable resources in terms of understanding and the ability to use
and manipulate information. This can be of use to those who
may have little access to tools for understanding and changing
their own situation in the face of the ideological and other
forces ranged against them.

This kind of activity is clearly exemplified in the life and
thought of the liberation theologians, considered earlier, who
use their intellectual skills to help poor people to empower and
express themselves. It can also be found in the sort of example
described in this country by pastors like Laurie Green.[5]
Writing of the real contribution made to change by critical
reflection, Gutiérrez comments

all reflection is a way of exercising power in history. It is only one
way, of course, but it is a real way. It makes a real contribution to the
transformation of history – to the destruction of the system of oppression and the construction of a just and humane society.[6]

To some extent, the mere fact of having been educated to a
high level furnishes pastors with the equipment they need for
this role which requires analysis, understanding complex information, interpretation, and effective communication.
However, this can be enhanced by training in the social
sciences and in liberation theology, which will make the possibility of clear analysis and social insights into inequalities,

[4] See James Joll, *Gramsci*. Glasgow: Fontana, 1977.
[5] See Green, *Power to the Powerless*.
[6] Gutiérrez, *The Power of the Poor in History*, p. 101.

injustice, and action more likely. By using theological, socio-logical, and other intellectual skills and insights to help power-less people understand their situation more clearly, pastors can act as effective and appropriate catalysts for desired social and political change.[7]

4 Working with other groups

Individuals on their own will find it almost impossible to preserve and develop a radical analysis, critique, and practice. They can have only a limited impact for change on particular situations and institutions, or on society in general. Pastors seeking social and political amelioration for those for whom they care must, therefore, be prepared to work closely with other groups and organisations, for example, pressure groups, political parties, to obtain fundamental social changes. This principle applies at all levels of pastoral activity.

Unfortunately, such a principle challenges one of the key features of contemporary pastoral practice. Unlike many other professional groups, clergy have tended to stick very closely to a model of individual activity. Even today, the normal pattern is for clergy to work on their own in parishes, exercising a great deal of autonomy over their own activity.[8] Close co-operation with other groups, particularly non-religious groups, may demand a degree of compromise and surrender of indepen-dence quite alien to many pastors. However, it is quite clear that, if pastors insist on adopting a posture of 'rugged indi-vidualism', there will be little scope for systematically address-ing the causes of sin and suffering which lie beyond the indi-vidual. This is, therefore, an important principle in seeking to evolve a socio-politically aware, committed, and effective pas-toral care.

Not all the groups with which pastors may need to co-operate will consist entirely, or even predominantly, of prac-tising Christians, and this may pose a further deterrent.

---

[7] For more on this kind of role see Peter Leonard, 'Towards a paradigm for radical practice' in Bailey and Brake, eds., *Radical Social Work*.

[8] See further Russell, *The Clerical Profession*, chs. 17 and 18.

However, if the insights of the liberation theologians are correct, it is not only, or even mainly, Christians who are used to make real the kingdom of God on earth. This should provide an incentive and imperative to wider co-operation.

5 Using 'unfinished' models for social and political action

The root of much avoidable sin and sorrow lies in unjust social and political structures. The relief and prevention of these things therefore depends on some kind of action to change those structures. Often, this kind of action must be oriented towards long-term fundamental change; its planning and execution is likely to take a long time to get under way. If major social changes at a national level are required, for example, many years may elapse before they can occur. At the same time, however, people at a local level will continue to have short-term needs of various kinds, and will continue to experience the effects of the way things actually are at the present moment. This poses several difficult dilemmas for pastoral carers. Should short-term, fundamentally ameliorative action be undertaken, or is it more important to concentrate on long-term aims? Is it more appropriate to work for small immediate reforms, or to look towards the radical transformation of the whole social order in the future. There is a tension in creating priorities for action between local, proximate 'reform' which may benefit a few people immediately, and what might be called social transformation or 'revolution'.

In the face of this kind of tension, an 'unfinished' model of social action for change is helpful and illuminating. Proposing this, social theorist Stanley Cohen suggests that it is necessary to obtain both short-term reforms within the constraints of the present social order and long-term change in the totality of that order. It is unhelpful to opt for one mode of action to the exclusion of the other. The option for future total change alone leads to the neglect of the immediate needs of those who are oppressed, while the exclusive option for immediate reform can easily lead to co-option to the *status quo* and the loss of fundamental long-term change. This model is useful to those who seek to sort out priorities and appropriate action in the context of a socio-politically informed and committed pastoral care.[9]

The question also arises of which issues and which needs most need to be tackled as a matter of priority. No pastor or pastoral group can hope to act effectively in all directions. Hessel offers the following criteria for congregations seeking to prioritise and select their social concern priorities. Some of them may be helpful, with appropriate adaptation, for helping pastoral carers to determine their priorities:

Serious and pervasive condition
Demands Christian ethical attention
Neglected by powers and authorities
Most urgent to poor and vulnerable
An opportunity for empowerment
Has concrete and manageable handles
Chance to make a systemic difference as well as to meet a service need
Available modes of response.[10]

6 Appropriate pastoral care of individuals

It is important to emphasise that there is still room for care of individuals within a socio-politically informed and committed pastoral care. Individuals remain ends in themselves, and not all their needs can be met by making changes in the wider social order. For example, people will continue to suffer bereavement in any social order, and this can best be ministered to within a personal frame of reference and care. That the care of individuals is a very significant part of the pastoral task is not in question here. However, it is questionable whether it should have the exclusive dominance at all times and in all situations that it has tended to have in recent times in Western society.[11]

From the perspective of the socio-politically aware and com-

9 See further Stanley Cohen, 'It's all right for you to talk: political and sociological manifestoes for social work action' in Bailey and Brake, eds., *Radical Social Work.*
10 Adapted from Dieter T. Hessel, *Social Ministry.* Philadelphia: Westminster Press, 1982, p. 191.
11 Individual emotions and character may be influenced by wider social factors. See further Rom Harré, ed., *The Social Construction of the Emotions.* Oxford: Blackwell, 1986.

mitted pastoral carer, individual contacts can contribute to
understanding and working on wider issues. They allow a
pastor to keep in touch with the constituency he seeks to serve,
helping to provide a picture of needs and desires. Personal
contacts also reduce potential distrust that can easily exist if
pastors become involved in a social and political approach
which alienates some individuals and interest groups – as most
social and political approaches are bound to do.

Beyond this, radical therapists from various professional
groups have suggested that it is possible for individual therapeutic encounters to form part of socio-politically aware and
committed action for change. Banton et al. point out that the
'individual' is constructed and shaped by a particular social
order. By paying close attention to the contents of an individual's consciousness and seeing it in a social context, it is
possible to work with people to uncover and make conscious
the discourses of power and the roots of socio-political oppression as they manifest themselves in people's consciousness. This
can enhance their understanding and empower a capacity for
social, as well as personal, change.[12]

From a medical perspective, Waitzkin suggests principles for
working in therapeutic encounters which write back in the
social context removed from such encounters when they are
used to control, normalise, and socialise people to the standard
(harmful) expectations of capitalist society. He suggests that
doctors should fight against conservative medical dominance
which serves an ideological function by (i) encouraging both
participants in a medical encounter to try and overcome the
domination, mystification, and distorted communication
which comes from asymmetric technical knowledge; (ii)
encouraging explicit analysis of the connections between social
structure and individual distress; (iii) avoiding the medicalisation of non-medical problems which need social solutions;
(iv) trying to change the ideological foundations of medical
practice. This approach profoundly challenges practices such
as treating the depression of a person who has become

---

[12] Ragnhild Banton, Paul Clifford, Stephen Frosh, Julian Lousada, Jo Rosenthall,
The Politics of Mental Health. London: Macmillan, 1985.

unemployed as just a personal problem needing symptom relief, or colluding with the idea that being able to fit into the workforce is the main indicator of good health. Using it, there is some prospect that isolation and individualism can begin to be converted into corporate resistance and action for change. A progressive therapist–patient relationship which refuses merely to treat the symptoms of social processes as if they were a matter of individual pathology fosters social change, 'Otherwise, the medical encounter dulls the pain of today, without hoping to extinguish it in the future.'[13]

Similar principles can inform the work of those who are inclined towards individuals in pastoral care. In a paper written for pastoral counsellors interested in situating their practice within a quest for social justice, I outlined the following guidelines

First, I do not want all counsellors to abandon their consulting rooms to 'man [sic] the barricades'. There are different ways of being committed to justice and of being in solidarity with poor people. Some kinds of psychotherapy are directly useful in this. I think particularly of womens' therapy centres run on feminist lines where people can think and work through their experiences of social and personal oppression.

Second, I would affirm the search of counsellors to uncover the springs of oppression in individuals, families, and groups. This is parable and paradigm of an archaeology which needs to take place at all levels of existence, and it is directly useful to people.

Thirdly, I would encourage counsellors to situate their perceptions of oppression and alienation within wider social structures and the wider socio-political order.

Fourthly, I would ask counsellors to actually *see* social injustice where it exists. Seeing injustice being done is an indispensable prelude to seeing justice done.

---

[13] Waitzkin, *The Politics of Medical Encounters*, ch. 11.

Fifthly, I ask counsellors to eschew reductionism and stereo-typing of social and political action and activists which invalidates or weakens attempts to create a just social order.

Sixthly, counsellors might like to reflect upon the social and political significance of their own practice and activity. Who can use therapy? Who can pay for it? Are the paradigms used in therapy such as to build up community and corporate solidarity, or are they such that they collude with the idea that there is no such thing as society, only individuals?

Finally, counsellors have much to contribute to the analysis of social and political behaviour in our society. It seems to me of cardinal importance that they should embrace the social and political dimension, rather than eschewing it, with a view to creating a more just society and better intermediate structures between the individual and the state.[14]

The fact that committed social and political action on the part of pastoral carers creates unhappiness and alienation amongst some individuals and groups should not be allowed to deter pastors from moving in this direction. While overt political activism may tend to estrange pastors from some members of the Christian community or the institutions in which they work, it can increase their acceptability and credibility with others who had previously rejected the ministrations of a conservative church.[15] Individual care remains, even though the constituency of the 'flock' may change. The question, as always, is, with whom do you want to be identified, whose interests do you want to promote, and to whom do you wish to be acceptable?

PASTORAL CARE IN THE MENTAL HEALTH SECTOR

Having outlined six principles of socio-politically aware and committed pastoral care in a rather abstract form applicable to

[14] Stephen Pattison, 'Seeing justice done', *Counselling* 2, 1991, 95–7.
[15] For more on this see Gill, *Prophecy and Praxis*, ch. 4.

many different situations, it behoves me to exemplify what these principles mean practically in the mental health sector. The first principle of analysing social and political context in the pastoral situation has been adequately illustrated in this book. I will, therefore, start by discussing the meaning of an option for the oppressed within the context of pastoral care with mentally ill people. What does it mean to make a concrete option for the oppressed in the mental health sector?

The answer to the question is that it might mean all manner of things depending on who are identified as being oppressed and what their needs are. To the extent that mentally ill people and the mental health sector as a whole suffers from an unjust social order, the option for the poor at its widest might mean a clear commitment to trying to change the whole social order so that it becomes more just. In concrete terms, this might mean joining and working hard for a left-wing political party which works for radical social change. Within the NHS, a pastoral worker may want to use his or her influence and contacts to see that resources are funnelled into mental health services rather than elsewhere, by mobilising ecclesiastical and other political opinion in this direction.

The analysis of the mental health sector undertaken above suggested that the least powerful group in the mental health sector tends to be the users who suffer from economic deprivation, social discrimination, stereotyping, and many other social and political disadvantages. This suggests that the primary identification of the pastoral worker within the health sector should be with users or patients. As we have noted, patients are not, on the whole, themselves militant and effective promoters of their own liberation cause (though there are some militant and effective social and political lobbying groups made up of mainly ex-patients). Patients are unlikely to be self-consciously seeking social and political liberation and justice. So what does it mean to make an option for this group?

The first thing that it means is that pastors must listen very carefully to users, and take their perspective on life and the hospital very seriously indeed. There is a pervasive tendency in hospitals to stereotype patients and to regard their views as

symptoms of a disordered mind. Ex-patients talk of the frustration of never being believed or taken seriously. One manifestation of the option for the oppressed is to try and see the world
from their point of view, and to promote their views rather
than some kind of 'official' or professional view of reality. The
users' definition of the reality of life in mental health services is
often disparaged in favour of the views of relatively powerful
professionals. One implication of this is that pastoral workers
may need to distance themselves from the shared therapeutic
language of the professionals to see life from the patients' point
of view. Another implication is that they may need to dis-
identify themselves with the 'therapeutic team' with its shared
view of patienthood which may be very different from the
patients' own views. Pastoral carers need to spend their lives in
the patients' space, physically and psychologically, if they are
to understand their perspective and gain their trust. To this
extent, it is probably unhelpful, strongly and publicly to
identify with the staff perspective by, for example, attending
ward meetings or case conferences unless asked to do so by
patients themselves. Maybe, then, pastors should not want to
be included in the 'therapeutic' team unless patients are also
recognised as members of it.

To the extent that it is possible and desired by mentally ill
people, pastoral carers need to work with them to help them
understand their situation and to promote empowerment and
equality. This might mean helping to bring about structures in
which patients can have a greater voice in shaping their own
care and institutions. It could mean defending or advocating
the patients' point of view on policy issues or when important
decisions are being made about a particular individual, for
example, whether they should be treated against their will. It is
easy for staff to arrive at an opinion of what would be in the
best interests of a patient, without the person themselves being
consulted in such a way that they feel their perspective can be
articulated or taken seriously.

Chaplains in the mental health sector might also like to take
a particular interest in the most demoralised parts of the
service, where patients are not articulate and there is a lack of

resources. As I have said, doctors and others tend to spend a disproportionate amount of time and resources working with younger, acutely mentally ill people, while the elderly, those suffering from dementia or chronic mental disorder, are neglected in, for example, the back wards of hospitals. It could be appropriate, in the interests of making a concrete option for the oppressed, for pastors to have exactly the opposite bias in their own work. By the same token, they may find it appropriate to pay particular attention to the views and needs of those working at the bottom of the nursing hierarchy, who can also easily feel that their views and perceptions are ignored or derided. Being independent of the nursing hierarchy, a chaplain can do much to encourage junior staff in retaining a sense of vision and purpose when the odds are against them. *Prima facie*, there would seem little excuse for not supporting those who, in the interests of their patients, raise the alarm or 'whistle blow' about inadequate conditions and abuse.

Turning to the principle of becoming an 'organic intellectual' of the oppressed in the mental health sector, this is a role which should not be minimised. Chaplains enjoy a certain amount of independence of hierarchies in the hospital and are not bound to adopt the language of therapy or management in their dealings with people. As skilled users of critical concepts and words, and as representatives of another organisation (the church), chaplains who have conducted a full analysis of the socio-political context of their pastoral care can throw a very different light on the situation than their therapeutic counterparts. They can help both patients and staff to a more critical evaluation of their situation and role. It is vital that people should have a realistic appraisal of the social system and the location of power within it if they are to maximise the chances of changing it. Chaplains can also use their communication skills to ensure that the perspective of the oppressed is heard in policy making and ecclesiastical arenas and is clearly presented. They can demythologise and politicise the situation of mentally disordered people within the NHS as a whole and beyond, by their work with individuals, public speaking, and writing:

radicalising mental health can mean making public what is hidden, making open and generous what is confined, and making political what has been reduced to personal, silent pain.[16]

It was suggested as a general principle of socio-politically aware and committed pastoral care that co-operation between pastoral carers and different kinds of groups would be necessary to attain desirable social change at all levels. In the context of the mental health services this might mean working with groups of patients, fellow workers, with unions, and with hospital committees and sub-committees. Outside the mental health services themselves there are lobbying groups such as MIND, the National Schizophrenia Fellowship, and Survivors Speak Out which aim to bring pressure on government and other organisations to produce change. Churches and church groups have a role to play here which has been very undeveloped. So far, no major Christian denomination in Britain has produced a policy or position statement about the care and treatment of mentally ill people. The church could form a powerful lobby group in changing views, perceptions, and policies in favour of mentally disordered and other poor and oppressed groups, as well as in transforming capitalist society. Similarly, professional groups, like the College of Health Care Chaplains which represents full-time chaplains, could become more engaged in political lobbying. Pastoral carers should not forget the potential significance of joining together in political solidarity with other groups seeking a better deal for the poor in society, by becoming members of political parties or trade unions. To remain isolated and 'neutral' may ensure the perpetuation of injustice and the hegemony of ruling class values in capitalist society into the far distant future.

The principle of adopting an 'unfinished model' of social and political action needs little further exposition in theory. However, it is around this principle that some of the most difficult practical dilemmas for pastoral carers will arise. Should a pastoral worker help to keep an old, decrepit, hospital open by continuing to offer his services in it for the sake of

[16] Banton et al., *The Politics of Mental Health*, p. 196.

those who have to continue to live there (a short-term goal) or would it be better to withdraw from it, thus delegitimating its existence and drawing attention to the need for fundamental long-term change? Should chaplains facilitate the transfer of patients from hospital settings into the community, drawing upon the voluntary energy, resources, and good will of local churches (a short-term practical goal), or would it be better not to participate in this kind of activity on the basis that community care will be inadequately funded by government and, in the long term, is bound to fail, thus increasing, rather than ameliorating, the plight of mentally ill people? There are no cut and dried answers to these complex questions. However, it is important that pastoral carers do not reject the option of radical long-term social change for short-term apparently ameliorative solutions without careful thought.

Finally, the pastor attempting to develop a socio-politically aware pastoral care within the mental health sector will find that there is no shortage of opportunity to work with individuals. As people come to realise that a pastor is really on their side and not part of the apparatus of institutional legitimation, they will be prepared to share themselves and their perceptions in a way in which they are not willing to do with other professionals. Those who are working for desired change will value the support and solidarity which pastors can provide, and there will be opportunities to build up networks of change, support, and resistance which can oppose personal and corporate dehumanisation. While some individuals may be alienated and argue that pastoral care should be about saving people's immaterial souls, others, who have mistrusted the church for years, may draw near. Again, it all depends on who a pastor wants to identify with and be useful to.

CONCLUSION

There has probably never been a time when a socio-politically aware and committed pastoral care was more needed within the mental health sector, nor a time when it is more difficult to contemplate its being possible. In the early 1990s we face a growing economic depression which is likely to bring a greater incidence of mental disorder at the same time as cuts in public expenditure are required. The gap between need and provision is likely to grow. At the same time services are being reordered, with the pace of resettlement into the community increasing.

Chaplains are having to face enormous changes in their institutions and roles, becoming much less independent and far more accountable to a new breed of managers, whose job is to manage limited resources while claiming to provide excellent services on pain of losing their jobs. The culture of the NHS is becoming less tolerant of criticism, appearing to insist that all is for the best in the best of all possible worlds.[17] All this is overlaid by a rhetoric of consumer power and choice which is, in fact, an illusion in the face of severely rationed resources and centralised control.

Somehow, at the very moment when social and political factors are most clearly and directly influencing the well-being of mentally ill people, the demanding roles involved in trying to practice a socio-politically aware and committed pastoral care seem most difficult to contemplate. It is necessary to reiterate that to fail to develop some kind of socio-political critique and activity is to ensure complicity in the perpetuation of avoidable sin and sorrow for mentally ill people. It is equally important to say that individual pastoral carers cannot be expected to bear the burden of working for social change on their own. Churches and others need to play a supporting role in making a socio-politically aware and committed pastoral care a real possibility.

[17] Cf. Stephen Pattison, 'Glossing over the facts', *Health Service Journal* 102; 5319, 1992, 19.

CHAPTER 17

Bringing it all back home? Pastoral care with women[1]

> Feminist theology challenges liberation theologians to
> take their preferential 'option' for the poor and oppressed
> seriously as the option for poor and Third World women
> because the majority of the poor and exploited today are
> women and children dependent on women for survival.[2]

A main aim of this book is to establish the relevance of
liberation theology to pastoral care in the Western world. This
kind of theology can be regarded as fascinating but irrelevant
in Britain; however, examining the specific example of pastoral
care with mentally ill people has shown that its insights and
methods are of considerable illuminative and practical value.
Although mentally ill people are a large group within society,
some readers may feel that they cannot really see the relevance
of this kind of approach for ordinary congregationally based
pastoral work. To counter this tendency, I now turn briefly to
another oppressed group to ask the question, what difference
should a liberationist approach (such as the one outlined in the
last chapter) make to pastoral care with women? This preliminary and suggestive excursion will extend the critical relevance
of the liberationist stance; it will also reveal some of its limitations.

There are many oppressed minority groups apart from mentally ill people which might seem obvious candidates for a

---

[1] This chapter was written with a lot of help, criticism, and support from Sue Spencer,
a Methodist minister in West Bromwich. It is based to some extent on her work,
Susan E. Spencer, 'Enough to Make My Wings Droop: Women, Self-esteem and
Christianity'. Unpublished M.Phil. thesis, University of Birmingham, 1989.
[2] Elisabeth Schüssler Fiorenza, 'For women in men's worlds: a critical feminist
theology of liberation', *Concilium*, 171, 1984, 32–9, at p. 35.

liberationist approach, for example, prisoners, gay and lesbian people. Women comprise half the population, and so cannot be described as a minority group. It may then appear absurd to highlight this very diverse group, spread throughout society, and to suggest that this approach is necessary here. Women are just women. They contribute to the economy and human relationships. They are the givers and recipients of pastoral care; surely no more needs to be said than that. Problematising pastoral care with women here may seem superfluous, particularly if it is believed that such oppression as women experienced in male dominated societies is now on the wane through equal opportunities legislation and other emancipatory action. Most adult women can now vote. An increasing number are able to enter, for example, the spheres of higher education and employment. It may seem that the women's movement has achieved many of its aims, so there is no need to talk of the oppression of women or to seek women's liberation in pastoral care. Mainly for the benefit of male pastoral carers and those brought up in the patriarchal tradition of pastoral care, I hope to show that a liberationist approach in pastoral care with women is apposite. That so little attention has been paid to this topic before is indicative, not of lack of injustice and oppression, but of these things being so well institutionalised and entrenched that they are not noticed; like women themselves, they are assumed and made invisible.

I shall proceed by, first, outlining some of the ways in which women are generally oppressed in patriarchal society. For the sake of continuity and convenience the concrete implications and consequences of this oppression are exemplified in relation to women and mental health. Turning to the collusive and oppressive role of religion and pastoral care in the lives of women, it is asked how the principles of socio-politically aware and informed pastoral care can point ways forward for this activity. In pastoral care, as elsewhere in society, women's needs, perceptions, and gifts are ignored. One does not need to go to South America or to work with mentally ill people to find oppression. Injustice is in our own back yard, in our own homes (often the *locus* for much of the exploitation of women).

The oppressed situation of women should bring home the message that liberation theology is of great relevance for everyday pastoral care, even if the position and analysis of women's socio-political place cannot be uncritically homogenised into a liberationist perspective.

THE CONTINUING OPPRESSION OF WOMEN

Feminists and others claim that we continue to live in a patriarchal society where women are oppressed. Patriarchy is

the manifestation and institutionalization of male dominance over women and children in the family and the extension of male dominance over women in society in general. It implies that men hold power in all the important institutions of society and that women are deprived of access to such power. It does *not* imply that women are either totally powerless or totally deprived of rights, influence, and resources.[3]

The origins of patriarchy and male domination are obscure, as are the reasons for its gaining supremacy.[4] Similarly, there is a complex and disputed relationship about whether capitalism is the primary engine of oppression or whether sexual oppression comes first and is predominant.[5] Suffice it to note here that capitalism and patriarchy seem in many ways inextricably bound up in the present social order; women are often used by capitalism to provide a cheap, fluid, and ready labour market to fill gaps in the production process, for example. The reality of women's oppression (understood as the unjust imposition of economic, sociological and other constraints which prevent women from attaining their potential) within the current capitalist–patriarchal social order is clearly discernible, and many books give accounts of it.

In one of the most recent of such works, Marilyn French outlines 'the war against women'.[6] French documents with

---

[3] Gerda Lerner, *The Creation of Patriarchy*. Oxford: Oxford University Press, 1986, p. 239.

[4] See further Lerner, *Creation of Patriarchy*; Marilyn French, *Beyond Power*. London: Sphere Books, 1986.

[5] See further Jaggar, *Feminist Politics and Human Nature*.

[6] Marilyn French, *The War Against Women*. London: Hamish Hamilton, 1992.

searing clarity the ways in which women world-wide are systematically subordinated and discriminated against. For example, economically

women do between two-thirds and three-quarters of the work in the world. They also produce 45 percent of the world's food. But they are still granted only 10 percent of the world's income and 1 percent of the world's property.[7]

Women have a gigantic task in reproducing, supporting and maintaining the human race, yet their work is not actually considered to be 'real' work; much of it, such as child-rearing, is unpaid. They are forced into economic dependence on men who exclude them from positions of influence in organisations and pay them less than they would male members of the workforce. Politically, women have been similarly subordinated, having some influence in the domestic sphere, but being almost entirely excluded from public life. Women have even been written out of history which is mostly presented as an account of the doings of ruling class men.[8] This legitimates their exclusion from the contemporary political and economic arenas. Women's reproductive functions have been ordered and determined by men in the interests of promoting the patrilinic family. It has been argued that they are biologically inferior to men. Women continue to experience systematic discrimination and lack of equal opportunity, both as contributors and recipients, in spheres such as education, the legal system, the workplace, and the medical system. They are blamed for failures in parenting, subject to physical violence from men in and outside the home, and they are often deprived of essential financial support by their male partners. All of which constitutes an ongoing, real, and vicious war by men, individually and as a group, against women.

These global assertions can be localised within contemporary Britain. Women are substantially under-represented in the 'higher' reaches of social and economic life (there are very few women MPs or chairs of major public companies, for

[7] French, ibid., p. 24.
[8] See further Lerner, *Creation of Patriarchy*; Bonnie S. Anderson and Judith P. Zinsser, *A History of Their Own*. London: Penguin, 1988.

example). Lewis, in a study of women in Britain since 1945, reports the following trends. First, more women are now engaged in paid employment. However, many of them are only employed part time (thus losing out on pension and other benefits) and often they are involved in low paid, low-status work. On average, there is still a pay differential of 30 per cent between men and women reflecting, perhaps, the still dominant assumption that women will not be the primary wage-earners in a household. Secondly, although women are now expected to do more work outside the home, there has been no diminishment in the expectation that they will discharge their unpaid domestic and caring responsibilities towards children and other dependants. Men have not increased their share of unpaid work in the domestic sphere. Thirdly, although there are now many more female heads of households living without a male partner, but often with children, social policy largely continues to assume that women are dependent upon employed men for financial support. The consequence is an increase in the number of women and children living in poverty. Many women, one can safely assume, live lives of massive responsibility in quiet desperation trying to look after dependants while balancing this against the need to provide financially for themselves and for their families.[9] As a group they continue to suffer considerable disadvantage, economic and other. Lewis notes

Many ... women feel that their range of choices is greater than that of their mothers with regard to work, marriage and reproduction. Yet gender inequality in terms of low pay and sexual segregation in the labour market, unequal power and control over resources in marriage, and unequal responsibility for contraception, to name but three, persist ... While middle-class and professional women in particular have been able to make gains in the post-war period, those gains are remarkably fragile. For example, divorce may significantly diminish the income of the professional woman with children. Progress has been remarkably uneven and for individual women can also be subject to reversal.[10]

9 See further Jane Lewis, *Women in Britain Since 1945*. Oxford: Blackwell, 1992.
10 Lewis, ibid., p. 10.

The injuries of gender discrimination and patriarchal oppression concretise themselves in many ways, not least in the sphere of women's mental health. The circumstances of women's lives sideline them into responsible and demanding productive and caretaking roles which are not highly valued in society. Baker Miller writes

Women's tasks are essential, but outside of the 'real world', and so women work with a pervasive sense that what they do does not matter as much as what men do.[11]

This external factor is consonant with, and promotes, a psychology of insignificance and low self-esteem. Rowbotham memorably refers to women's 'neurosis of nothingness', a pervasive feeling of emptiness, of being nothing, not existing except as someone who is needed by husband and children.[12] Self-images of dependence and attitudes of self-abnegation, self-blame, and helplessness are nurtured in women from a very early age.[13] The socially acceptable but very negative image of womanhood in our society is one of passivity, docility, dependence, lack of initiative, and inability to act, to decide, or to think. Women are required to adopt these attitudes for themselves while being capable carers and nurturers. At the same time, they are encouraged to put the needs of others before their own at all times, so they never have their own needs met. Thus, women give to others out of the deep well of their own unmet needs.

Turning specifically to mental disorder, it has been shown that actually to exhibit the qualities of femininity is to be seen as more likely to be suffering from psychiatric illness. Broverman and colleagues demonstrated that what is regarded as the healthy adult conforms to the social stereotype of masculinity.[14] Thus, women who demonstrate archetypal feminine

[11] Jean Baker Miller, *Towards and New Psychology of Women*. Harmondsworth: Penguin, 1976, p. 79.
[12] Sheila Rowbotham, *Woman's Consciousness, Man's World*. Harmondsworth: Penguin, 1973, p. 76.
[13] See further, for example, Luise Eichenbaum and Susie Orbach, *Understanding Women*. London, Penguin, 1985.
[14] K. Broverman, D. Broverman, F. Clarkson, P. Rosenkrantz and S. Vogel, 'Sex role stereotypes and clinical judgements of mental health', *Journal of Clinical and Consulting Psychology* 34, 1970, 1–7.

qualities of passivity, conformity, less aggression, and lower achievement motivation are seen as psychologically unhealthy anyway. However, if women show more stereotypically masculine qualities then they are also more likely to be regarded as deviant or mad:

Although masculinity is associated with more positive mental health, it seems that this is only for men; and women who are adventurous, competitive, sexually active, independent, women who reject the role of wife and mother, to name but a few examples, may be at risk of being designated psychiatrically ill.[15]

With these contradictions bearing upon them, as well as difficult external circumstances such as confinement in the household looking after young children, caring for dependant relatives, or bringing up children single-handedly in relative poverty, it is not surprising that many women often have a sense of low self-esteem, helplessness, and hopelessness:

Satisfaction of self-esteem needs generates feelings and attitudes of self confidence, self-worth, strength, capability and the sense of being useful and necessary in the world. The thwarting of these needs leads to feelings and attitudes of inferiority, ineptness, weakness and helplessness, which in turn lead to discouragement, futility and hopelessness in dealing with life's demands.[16]

The sense of helplessness and hopelessness is indicted in research which shows that women have higher rates of mental disorder than men, especially in the diagnostic categories of depression and anxiety disorders. Brown and Harris, in their study of working-class women in London, suggested that feelings of hopelessness and lack of self-esteem, induced by a variety of socially conditioned agents and provoking factors such as lack of employment and other stresses, were key factors in the formation of clinical depression.[17] Other studies have shown that married women have more mental illnesses than married men, and that, while women's self-esteem may be enhanced by employment, this produces a role stress as women

---

15 Ussher, *Women's Madness*, p. 168.
16 Spencer, 'Enough to Make My Wings Droop', p. 17.
17 Brown and Harris, *Social Origins of Depression*.

try to combine their domestic responsibilities with being good employees.[18] The net conclusion is that women as a group have to face social conditions and attitudes which make them vulnerable to mental disorder in a way that men are not, in patriarchal society.

Not only do social and socio-psychological factors appear to increase women's liability to mental illness, ironically, women also have the job of caring for society's dependants and casualties:

when nursery places, hospital beds and old people's homes disappear, it is women at home who pick up the pieces. If you are mentally ill in the community you are likely to be a woman or be looked after by a woman, or you will be alone ... The alienated and fragmented social relations of capitalism are made manageable by the fact and fiction of the caring family.[19]

As government continues to transfer the human and financial cost of caring for people out of the public sector and into the nuclear family, the bill will be picked up mainly by women. Stress and pressure on them will thus increase as they try to juggle their various commitments and roles while having limited capacity to earn outside the home. The consequences for women's mental and physical health of this familist ideological assumption are likely to be increasingly deleterious.[20]

The exploitation of women in patriarchal society dominated by the ideology of the caring nuclear family (for which read, the unsung and unpaid caring of women) is increasingly well documented and understood, particularly with the rise of feminist research and insights. Mental health is just one area in which women are disadvantaged over against men, whose interests are still largely protected by dominant ideologies, assumptions, and practices. It is taken as a concrete example here because of its relevance as a subject to the rest of the book. However, in almost any area of social life, for example,

[18] For a résumé of this evidence see Agnes Miles, *Women, Health and Medicine*. Milton Keynes: Open University Press, 1991, ch. 7. For women and mental disorder see Elaine Showalter, *The Female Malady*. London: Virago, 1987.

[19] Banton et al., *The Politics of Mental Health*, p. 176.

[20] For more on this transfer of responsibility and on familist ideology see Dalley, *Ideologies of Caring*.

employment, income, career opportunities, there is systematic discrimination against women which exploits them and limits their potential. It is, therefore, appropriate to ask where religion and pastoral care fit in to this scenario. Do these things encourage or question the victimisation of women, and how should a liberationist approach to pastoral care with women be construed?

WOMEN AND RELIGION

Marilyn French reserves some of her severest condemnation for the religions of the world, including Christianity. For her, as for many other feminists including some theologians, religion has systematically sacralised, legitimated, and encouraged the subordination of women and stunted the development of their potential:

All major world religions are patriarchal. They were founded to spread or buttress male supremacy – which is why their gods are male.[21]

Like other patriarchal institutions, religion has made women invisible, both historically and in the contemporary world. While absorbing women's energy over the centuries, it has encouraged women to take an inferior social place. It has hallowed their role as mothers and carers in the family, discouraging them from taking an active role outside the domestic sphere. Religious ethics have been used to control women's reproductive processes and to teach women subordination within marriage. Now, the rise of fundamentalist traits in most religions threatens to reverse some of the progress women have made in finding their own voice and potential in the world.[22] Not surprisingly, many feminists regard religion as irredeemably sexist and a threat to women's liberation.

Looking at contemporary practice within British Christianity, evidence can be found to substantiate these global claims. Although many churches are supported largely by female members, the public organisation of the church is

[21] French, *War*, p. 46.   [22] Cf. ibid., pp. 46ff.

dominated by men. In some churches, women cannot be ordained to the ministry and, even when they are, they may not be allowed to attain positions of influence commensurate with their abilities. The mainstream churches continue actively to support the ideology of the nuclear family as the norm for full human existence. (Despite Jesus' own rather negative teaching about the family and the fact that only a small minority of people live in conventional nuclear families, many churches make their main service a 'family' service.) Some Christians continue to idealise motherhood and domestic life as the most fulfilling role for most women. Even liberal Christians fail to criticise a model of monogamous marriage in which women are encouraged to give up their own ends to meet the needs of others. There is little questioning of women's primary caring role, and no telling men to stay at home to look after their wives, children, and dependent relatives.

Christian theologies and liturgies reflect the concerns of the men who have formulated them without input from women over the centuries. The traditional hierarchical order with God at the top, then men, then women beneath them is incarnated in much theology. Language is shot with notions of domination and submission in most liturgies. These continue to speak of a male God, while readings selected from scripture treat of the doings of men and talk of brothers and fathers almost to the complete exclusion of women. This strongly reinforces the idea that men are the normal mode of human being and women are some kind of sub-species who represent a curious type of 'otherness' which is mostly to be despised or rejected. Where women are mentioned at all, they are mostly either idealised mothers, like the Virgin Mary, who exemplify a maternal caring role for women, or they represent the embodiment of despised carnality, evil, and temptation, like Eve. The Christian tradition can furnish few well-known examples of strong women living autonomous, interdependent lives which do not focus on supporting men. Even the reality of the nurturing, caring roles of women in everyday life is devalued and parodied in many denominations by the fact that it is men who call themselves pastoral carers and who, donning quasi-female dress, 'make' and distribute the liturgical meal of the eucharist (probably the only meal preparation and service that many men undertake).

Recently, attempts have been made by feminists in the churches to discover liberating memories about women within the Christian tradition. Jesus' apparent egalitarianism towards women and the excavation of powerful women in leadership roles in the church down the centuries, for example, have been taken as hopeful signs that Christianity is not irredeemably sexist. Efforts are also being made to reinterpret aspects of Christian tradition and doctrine so it reflects and validates women's experiences and needs.[23] However, the attempt to write women in to historical and contemporary Christianity, so making them visible and validating their existence, is proving difficult. It is often actively opposed by many of the men who still dominate the leadership of the churches, as well as by some women who support this domination. Women have a long way to go in achieving recognition of their place within the normal life, liturgy, and theology of the mainstream churches. For some, like theologians Mary Daly and Daphne Hampson, the struggle appears vain, so they, like many others, have left the churches to develop their spiritual potential elsewhere.[24]

The failure to validate and make visible the existence of women in all aspects of church life has serious implications for the liberation of women from oppression. Sexist liturgies downgrade women's sense of significance. Theologies which emphasise servanthood and the ideology of motherhood may play on women's guilt, encouraging a position of submission and servitude which limits their potential. While men may have a problem with over-assertion and *hubris*, women's problems in attaining their potential often revolve around not being assert-

---

23 For introductions to these trends see Susan Dowell and Linda Hurcombe, *Dispossessed Daughters of Eve*. London: SPCK, revised edn., 1987; Ann Loades, ed., *Feminist Theology: A Reader*. London: SPCK, 1990; Rosemary Radford Ruether, *Sexism and God-Talk*. London: SCM Press, 1983. For more on re-reading the Bible see, for example, Elisabeth Schüssler Fiorenza, *In Memory of Her*. London: SCM Press, 1984. For reinterpretation of a basic Christian doctrine, atonement, see Mary Gray, *Redeeming the Dream*. London: SPCK, 1989. .

24 Mary Daly, *Beyond God the Father*. London: The Women's Press, 1986; Daphne Hampson, *Theology and Feminism*. Oxford: Blackwell, 1990.

ive and independent enough.[25] Moralities which encourage women only to be active in the reproductive, domestic, and private spheres collude with the ideological familism of late twentieth-century capitalism, and prevent women from offering their gifts in the 'outside' world presently dominated by men. Altogether, everyday Christian practice does little to enhance women's self-esteem and sense of efficacy. Far from being liberating, it probably contributes positively to the subordination of women (and, incidentally, to their mental ill health). What, then, of pastoral care in relation to women?

PASTORAL CARE WITH WOMEN

Women remain socio-structurally oppressed within patriarchy and within Christianity. One might hope that pastoral care, with its historic interest in promoting human flourishing and freeing people from sin and sorrow, would represent a locus of hope and liberation within this broad picture. This is, unfortunately, not the case. The literature of pastoral care until very recently contained almost no material about the specific pastoral needs of women, so contributing to the invisibility of women and a practice of normative androcentricity. The place of women as themselves agents of pastoral care, contributing much of the everyday care which both men and women require, has been usurped by male professionalisers of that activity. These men set themselves up as authorities in this area, organising themselves hierarchically, and used pastoral care as one of the methods of controlling women. The historical and contemporary insignificance of women is reflected in a continuing dearth of female pastoral theologians. Counterfactually, pastoral care has ignored and implicitly minimised the needs and agency of women, confirming them in a subordinate role, and contributing to the failure to deal justly with them within church and society.

Vital areas of pastoral need for women – questions of abortion, contraception, sexuality, violence and sexual abuse – only began to

[25] See further, Loades, *Feminist Theology*, p. 81f.; Anne Borrowdale, *A Woman's Work*. London: SPCK, 1989.

feature as legitimate pastoral concerns once women achieved greater visibility and entered positions of leadership in the churches. Women's unequal position in society has also gone unchallenged by the churches because pastoral theology has never been sufficiently 'client-centred' to allow such critical positions to be articulated.[26]

Fortunately, the liberation of women from oppression does not depend upon male pastoral carers waking up to their responsibilities in this area. The women's movement has made considerable strides in raising awareness over the needs and contribution that women can make to their own liberation, especially amongst the more wealthy, educated classes in Europe and North America. Many women, outside and inside the church, are beginning to take their own experience seriously, and are determined to become the subjects of their own existence. They are no longer prepared to be abnegated within patriarchal society and institutions. Women's liberation is something which women can, and will, only achieve for themselves. However, as with mentally ill people, there would seem to be a role for male or patriarchally conditioned pastoral carers to take up a position of conscious solidarity with women in their struggle to cast off various yokes and injustices. It is appropriate here, therefore, to try and see how the principles of a socio-politically aware and committed pastoral care might begin to illuminate and affect pastoral care conducted in a way to further the cause of the liberation of women in church and society.

Analysis of the social and political context of pastoral care

Most pastoral workers will be in a situation where they will be working with women. Often, women will comprise a majority of any Christian group. The universality of women's presence in almost all situations throws into relief the extent to which they have been specifically ignored in the theory and practice of pastoral care. However, largely thanks to the women's movement and the analytic literature produced under its impetus, it also means that there are plenty of resources to

[26] Elaine Graham, 'The sexual politics of pastoral care' in Elaine Graham and Margaret Halsey, eds., *Lifecycles: Women and Pastoral Care.* London: SPCK, 1993.

draw on to analyse the social and political context of pastoral care with women. There is now a large literature, written from a variety of different analytic perspectives, for example, social-ist, Marxist, liberal-reformist, which deals with the oppression and injustices faced by women in all situations ranging from housework and childbirth through to social policy and national government.[27] It is necessary to define the parameters and nature of any pastoral context and to select analytic tools and perspectives carefully. However, the resources exist to do this in a much fuller way than they do when trying to analyse the socio-political context of a group perceived as more margi-nal, such as mentally ill people. As important as reading the analytic literature about women's oppression in general, and the factors which bring it about and sustain it in a particular situation, is listening to women's own stories about their lives and what oppresses them.

The option for the oppressed

Amongst women some are more oppressed than others (for example, working-class women, black women). Women are oppressed in different ways in different circumstances; some women may not think of themselves as being oppressed at all. The complexity of women's oppression must not, however, be allowed to obscure the fact that women as a group over against men in almost all circumstances have least of what there is to be had and have to fight hardest to get it. There is every reason for pastoral carers to have a bias towards women and their inter-ests. According to context, this bias might range from cam-paigning to ensure that social security benefits are not cut in such a way as to increase women's poverty, to ensuring that locally there are proper child-care facilities so women can take full-time jobs, to ensuring that within the church women are not given all the 'menial' and caring jobs which assume that they are only capable of taking a quasi-domestic supportive role in church life. It will almost certainly mean being pre-pared to enter into conflict with men and women who wish to

[27] For the scope and nature of this literature and references to analytic sources see Sheila Rowbotham, *The Past is Before Us*. London: Penguin, 1989.

protect the patriarchal *status quo*. The most important thing is to try to start looking at reality through the eyes of oppressed women, to believe what they say about their lives, and to help them to make the changes which will empower them for greater freedom and opportunity. One aspect of this may be accepting that women do not want men to be involved in any way in their struggle, and offering the service of sympathetically keeping out of the way as women establish their own identities and plans. Allowing a space to be opened up in a patriarchal institution and then keeping out of it can be a valuable service in making a useful option for oppressed people. Men can also become more conscious of how they treat women generally, and of how they refer to them when talking to other men; does their discourse affirm, denigrate, or question negative stereotypes of women?

Becoming 'organic intellectuals' of oppressed groups

Part of the impetus for the present day women's movement has come from raised expectations engendered by more educational opportunities for women in the 1960s.[28] There is a substantial intellectual cutting edge to the women's movement and, arguably, many women would not want males, especially from the clerical caste, to regard themselves as 'organic intellectuals' of the women's movement. Women can do their own leading and thinking for themselves, and this is part of women's liberation. However, there may still be a role for men in positions of leadership and responsibility to ensure that they put their skills at the service of a feminist viewpoint. For example, many women in churches are so used to being brainwashed by sexist liturgy and readings from scripture, exalting heroic men at the expense of 'weak' women, that they have become convinced of their own inferiority before God and men. Changing liturgies and images and exploring other ways of thinking about self and God can be a valuable and validating consciousness-raising activity, helping both men and women see that the world does not have to be the way it is now.

[28] See ibid.

Oppressed people may need help to feel that their perceptions are valid and that they do not have to live and think in the ways that they do. Sometimes, male pastors may be able to help women to take themselves more seriously and to understand more of the kind of situation that they are in. They can at least prescind from perpetuating myths and stereotypes which are likely to keep women in a position of domesticated inferiority. They can supportively keep out of the way when women try to do their own thinking and conceptualising about their situation rather than trying to impose some kind of orthodoxy or norm of thought. And they can remember that consciousness-raising is a two-way process in which they need to learn more than the people they are working with, and to have their own assumptions and knowledge bases formed by an abstracting patriarchal educational system challenged.

Working with other groups

There are many kinds of groups at all levels of society working against women's oppression, for example, equal opportunities groups, women's groups, poverty action groups. The institutional churches have been slow to encourage and develop such groups, but most have some women's groups working on issues like ordination and liturgy, and it is important that these should be supported. There are also established, if often conservative, groups like the Mothers' Union which can be supported and affirmed. It is equally important, however, to support and work with groups outside the churches, as this is where much of the impetus for change arises, and where concrete changes can be made which could affect the lives of all women for the better. Even if groups cannot change society for the better, at least they can stop it getting worse and losing gains which may have accrued for women over the last few decades. In one of the very few essays written by a man about the implications of a liberationist perspective for pastoral care with women, an Anglican bishop, Peter Selby, tells how he felt it was important to be involved in an intra-ecclesiastical group, the Movement for the Ordination of Women, and in a secular men's self-help group which was trying to help men to respond appropriately to the women's movement.[29] These are just two kinds of example of the sort of group pastors might become involved in in their active solidarity with women trying to overcome oppression.

Using 'unfinished' models for social and political action
'Liberation is not some finally achievable situation; instead, it is the process of eliminating forms of oppression as long as these continue to arise.'[30] Here, as with mentally ill people, there needs to be a recognition that everything cannot be achieved at once. There will be conflicts between putting energy into long-term or short-term projects and about whose side to be on in particular situations. So, for example, some English Anglicans argued for the ordination of women to the priesthood because they saw this as an achievable short-term goal which gives women their rightful place in the church. Others argued that the church is such a sexist institution that it needs to be reformed in far more radical ways (no priests or ministers at all, perhaps); in their view, ordination of women simply disguises the continuing inequality and corruption of the institution. There are other, perhaps more important, issues where decisions about priority and energy have to be made. One thing is certain: decisions about how to spend time and where to deploy energy in the cause of solidarity with women's liberation are bound to arise.

Appropriate pastoral care of individuals
A key insight within the women's movement is that 'the personal is political'. This phrase has a double significance. On the one hand it is a statement that the domestication of women and their exclusion from public life dominated by men has political, structural significance and causes; it does not just happen by magic, because nature decreed it, or by luck. On the other, it is an affirmation that women's experience of their own personal

---

29 Peter Selby, ' "They make such good pastors" ', in Richard Holloway, ed., *Who Needs Feminism?* London: SPCK, 1991.
30 Jaggar, *Feminist Politics and Human Nature*, p. 6.

lives has political significance; women can find and examine in their own lives the roots of oppression, and in so doing can prepare themselves to enter into and shape human society more directly. This second perception in particular has enormous significance for pastoral care with individuals. If women are appropriately listened to, attended to, and learned from, this in itself can help them to appropriate a fuller existence and greater subjective agency. They can be listened into existence and helped to learn to value their own experience and perceptions. The experience of many counsellors working with women is that initially they find it difficult to take themselves seriously and to think that it is worth finding out more about themselves (a symptom of worthlessness, low self-esteem, and the wrong kind of altruism).[31] Only gradually is it possible for them to realise that they are valuable human beings, and that they can have a life of their own, acknowledging some of their own needs and gifts. From this, it is possible for them to make more demands upon society and to gain self-respect. The process of paying attention to women and taking them seriously is thus an act of social and political significance which can allow both listeners, and those listened to, to grow in awareness of oppression and confidence to change it. Perhaps there is no more important piece of initial advice which could be given to pastoral carers who wish to radicalise their practice than this: listen to women![32] Borrowdale writes

It is essential that men should actually spend time *listening* to women, and trying to understand what it has meant for women to be subordinate. Without that understanding, the 'New Man' is likely to construct himself in a role that is equally oppressive.[33]

CONCLUSION

A critical consciousness about the contribution of pastoral care to the oppression of women is beginning to arise within the

[31] See further Joan Woodward, *The Uses of Therapy*. London: Macmillan, 1988.
[32] Ussher, *Women's Madness*, p. 306.
[33] Anne Borrowdale, *Distorted Images*. London: SPCK, 1991, p. 41. Emphasis original.

churches.[34] The ideology of family and home, for example, is starting to be questioned. So Joann Garma writes

Pastoral carers must recognize the reality that the most violent group to which women and children belong is the family. Pastors and church members view the family unit as a place where Christian values are taught and lived. They want to see the family as a haven for security, love, and joy. Nevertheless, the fact is that the family is a place where violence and tragedy can and do occur.[35]

Anne Borrowdale points out that male pastors themselves often model sexist behaviour and assumptions, putting their own home lives last (i.e., leaving them to their partners and children) while engaged in the work of pastoral care out in the 'real' world.[36] Realisation is dawning that the personal is political. Pastoral care must take account of this if it is not to contribute to the oppression of women.

There is a long way to go in developing a pastoral care and church community in which women are heard and recognised, and their needs attended to. Equally, pastoral care will need to reform itself radically if this is to happen. Feminists themselves have been sceptical about adopting the kind of paradigm suggested by liberation theology. Although they have found the concept and inductive method of liberation an empowering one, which validates women's experience and human struggle, they have been critical of the intellectualism and dualism embodied in this basically Marxist approach to reality. Above all, they have deplored the blindness of liberation theology and its authors to women and women's situation.[37] It may be that, as women shape and become subjects of their own lives and pastoral care, the concepts and methods associated with liberation theology will appear partly or wholly inappropriate to this enterprise.

[34] See, for example, Carroll Saussy, *God Images and Self Esteem*. Louisville: Westminster/John Knox Press, 1991; many articles in Rodney J. Hunter, ed., *Dictionary of Pastoral Care and Counselling*. Nashville: Abingdon, 1990.

[35] Joann M. Garma, 'A cry of anguish: the battered woman' in Maxine Glaz and Jeanne Stevenson Moessner, eds., *Women in Travail and Transition*. Minneapolis: Fortress Press, 1991, p. 126. Cf. Borrowdale, *Distorted Images*, ch 10.

[36] Ibid., p. 46.

[37] See Beverley Wildung Harrison, *Making the Connections*. Boston: Beacon Press, 1985, pp. 235ff.

One group working with prostitutes, for example, found that 'liberation' was not the key theological concept for working with women on the streets. A woman worker with this group writes of the struggle to find appropriate theological language to work with thus:

As part of the struggle to make our initial theology accessible to a wider group I needed a key word to make our theology accessible to a wider group. At first the word 'liberation' seemed a possibility. Liberation theology sprang from a response to the oppression of people in South America and we had defined prostitutes as oppressed. Liberation is a process from one state to or towards another and in this context has normally been the experience of communities rather than isolated individuals. However, prostitutes are isolated individuals. Certainly, they are part of a sub-culture that is closed to the average citizen, but it is hard for the women to work together for mutual benefit. Their experience of oppression reduces the ability to co-operate. Trust is a luxury and friendships may prove false. Apart from physical violence from men who would resist women's power and independence, women themselves accept fairly traditional roles and personal relationships with macho men whom they mother. The danger was that 'liberation' led us back to the rescuing fallen women idea and that other people would be confirmed in their assumption that we were saving fallen women, liberating poor, powerless creatures and turning them into respectable women. Instead, the key term was 'Justice' which recognised the complexity of women's situations in ways that other people could grasp. Rather than liberating women from a particular lifestyle so that we could feel more comfortable, quest for justice could be seen to go in many directions at once, in relation to police, courts, boy friends, punters, family, neighbours, access to resources and so on. Just because a woman earns her living through prostitution does not mean that she has forfeited her humanity and thus her human rights. Women themselves often rebelled, verbally at least, against the unfairness of the system in which they lived. They wouldn't have defined themselves as being in need of liberation but they did recognise their need to be treated fairly and with respect. Justice more than liberation fitted women's own definition of their own situation and spoke to the anger we sometimes felt on their behalf.[38]

Whether or not the insights and methods of liberation theology prove to have long-term relevance and value for women

[38] Barbara Hayes, 'Working with prostitute women', unpublished paper, nd.

finding their own voices and modes in pastoral care, the case for regarding women as a structurally oppressed group is one which must be taken seriously. The approach outlined here should have some value for raising awareness of the need for a socio-politically aware and committed pastoral care with women in a preliminary way. It is to be hoped that it will not be long before far more is heard about pastoral care from women themselves.

The challenge of women to pastoral care does not ... simply require their inclusion in a tradition that remains otherwise unchanged. Instead, it is a programme for reconstituting the nature of pastoral values and the theological understandings which underpin Christian practice.[39]

To which one can only respond, 'Amen'.

[39] Graham, 'Sexual politics'.

Conclusion

Can the insights and methods of liberation theology originating in Latin America usefully be put to work in reorientating the theory and practice of pastoral care in the Northern hemisphere? This was the question with which this book started. After considering the nature, insights, and methods of liberation theology I drew out some critical questions which might be pertinent in examining pastoral care. The suspicion was formulated that pastoral care might have social and political implications of which it is ignorant, and which lead it to unwittingly side with the powerful over against the oppressed. To test this suspicion, I then turned to the example of pastoral care with mentally ill people.

Following the methods of the liberation theologians, I examined the social context and factors surrounding mental disorder and mentally ill people both within and outside hospital settings. Using a broadly Marxist perspective, it was shown that there are many significant issues of conflict, injustice, and inequality bearing upon the situation of mentally ill people. Much of the suffering and oppression which mentally disordered people experience is owed to social, rather than to individual, factors. It is in principle avoidable by social and political change. This finding led me to look again at the role of pastoral care with mentally ill people, asking to what extent pastoral workers acted as critics and activists against the sociopolitical factors which enthral people in suffering. The answer to this appeared to be that, for a variety of constraining reasons, they were not aware of these factors. While elderly patients were being abused and neglected in the back wards of the old psychiatric hospitals due to lack of interest, status, and resources, for example, chaplains focussed mainly on individual care and counselling.

I then argued that pastoral care has become confined within an individualistic therapeutic paradigm which largely prescinds from concerns of social and political justice, inequality, and oppression. This is a distorting phenomenon which allows the perpetuation of avoidable suffering. I therefore proposed that concerns of justice and inequality should have a much more important part in a reconstructed socio-politically aware and committed pastoral care, some principles for which were outlined. These were exemplified in relation to mentally ill people, the central test case for trying to see how liberation theology might relate to pastoral care.

The need for a socio-politically aware and committed pastoral care was extended beyond the specific case of mentally ill people to show that this kind of approach is relevant (with modifications) to looking at pastoral care in many situations, specifically with women who, like mentally ill people, have been historically ignored and exploited. With this example I suggest that socio-political awareness and commitment must be a central and critical part of *all* pastoral care if that activity is not to fall almost automatically into promoting the interests of the powerful against those of the powerless.

The case that a creative, practical, hermeneutic relationship between liberation theology and pastoral care is possible has, I hope, been established. While some may disagree or have reservations about which insights and methods have been adopted from liberation theology, the Marxist perspective in general, the interpretation of material drawn from sources in the social sciences, or the possible nature of a socio-politically aware and committed pastoral care, it should be clear that the insights and methods of liberation theology do have something to contribute to the theory and practice of pastoral care. Using the methods and insights of the former opens up new perspectives on the latter. It also enriches its reservoirs of theory by drawing attention to the resources of social sciences other than the psychology which has had such an influence on pastoral care in this century. Although the Marxist, conflict perspective on society and social relations only provides one particular cross-section through the nature of reality, it is a powerful corrective to the consensual view of the social order which tends to reign unexamined in conventional pastoral care.

The insights and methods of liberation theology do something more than suggesting a new critical standpoint for analysing pastoral care in general terms. They also offer a challenge, even an imperative, for pastoral carers to examine their action and practice with a view to orienting it towards a quest for socio-political justice and equality. If my analysis of the situation of mentally ill people and women has even a grain of accuracy in it, then there is a clear case for pastoral carers to adopt different priorities. Preventable suffering with social causes cannot be just a phenomenon of academic curiosity. It is a summons to action for justice.

Pastoral workers cannot, as lone individuals, change the social order which allows mentally ill people and women to be neglected and ignored. They cannot, by themselves, set the oppressed free or liberate the exploited. However, they can try to ensure that their practice is socio-politically aware so that, at the very least, it facilitates and does not hinder people's attempts to liberate themselves. For generations, pastors have appeared to support the forces of domination, exploitation, authority, and power. In the light of the critique provided here, it should no longer be possible to do this unselfconsciously. The veil has been removed, and what has always been true has now been made explicit; the pastoral is political. Whether pastors choose to use methods and support values which serve the interests of the powerful or the powerless is up to them. However, they can neither avoid nor ignore this choice. There is no such thing as neutrality. As a practical religious activity, pastoral care should recognise and welcome the need for self-conscious critical commitment.

The first British edition of Bartholomé de Las Casas' *A Short Account of the Destruction of the Indies* has recently been published as a sobering corrective to the celebration of Columbus' 'discovery' of the Americas in 1492.[1] Las Casas, a sixteenth-century *conquistador* turned Dominican bishop, is sometimes hailed as the fore-runner of the liberation theologians. He gives eloquent testimony to the bestiality and savagery of the Spanish conquerors of the Americas as, in their search for gold and land, they laid waste the largely peaceable, gentle, and unwarlike native peoples. These were regarded as irrational, sub-human savages undeserving of life, respect, or love by their conquerors, who called them 'dogs', but treated them as insects to be trodden underfoot at will. Almost any page of Las Casas' moving account records events which are literally sickening, especially to anyone who stands in the Christian tradition which was used as the great 'gift' bequeathed to the 'savages' in exchange for their wealth, land, and lives. On Cuba, for example, when some local people had travelled to bring the *conquistadors* food and gifts,

the Christians were suddenly inspired by the Devil and, without the slightest provocation, butchered before my eyes, some three thousand souls – men, women and children – as they sat in front of us. I saw that day atrocities more terrible than any living man has ever seen nor ever thought to see.[2]

A local Cuban chief called Hatuey thought that he had got the Spaniards' number and could fend off destruction for himself and his people:

'They have a God whom they worship and adore, and it is in order to get that God from us so that they can worship Him that they conquer and kill us.' He had beside him . . . a basket filled with gold jewellery and he said: 'Here is the God of the Christians. If you agree, we will do *areitos* . . . in honour of this God and it may be that we shall please Him and He will order the Christians to leave us unharmed.' . . . And after they had danced before this god . . . Hatuey addressed them once again, saying: 'Mark you: if we keep this God about us they will kill us in order to get their hands on Him. Let us throw him into this river' . . . And . . . so they threw the god into a great river nearby.[3]

---

[1] Bartolome de Las Casas, *A Short Account of the Destruction of the Indies*. London: Penguin, 1992.
[2] Ibid., p. 29. [3] Ibid., pp. 26–7.

Unfortunately, Hatuey was captured and burned at the stake. Before being incinerated, a Franciscan friar tried to convert him to Christianity so he would go to heaven. Upon learning that Christians went to heaven, Hatuey concluded that he would prefer to go to hell so that 'he would never again have to clap eyes on those cruel brutes'.[4]

Las Casas himself was no revolutionary. He was a loyal subject of the Spanish crown and a former land and slave owner. Despite his vociferous pleas and writings, his protests at the exploitation and genocide committed against the native people were in vain. As almost a lone voice his chances of changing anything were almost non-existent. However, two significant things can be said of Las Casas. First, he persistently refused to be silent or self-deceived in the face of the dehumanisation he saw, constantly bearing witness to it before those who had the power to stop it. Secondly, the example of Las Casas, 'Defender and Apostle to the Indians', is one of the few things which lends Christianity any historical credibility as a benevolent and liberating force in Latin America. Despite his lack of success, he remains a sign of hope, as the many statues to his memory in South America bear witness.

The post-Christian Europe of the 1990s may seem light-years away from the pre-Christian Latin America of the sixteenth century or from the Latin America of today with its extremes of wealth, poverty, power, and exploitation. There is, nonetheless, extensive dehumanisation and injustice in our own society. Reading about the abuse of patients in receipt of psychiatric 'care' in hospitals is no less nauseating than reading of the abuse of American native peoples 500 years ago. The deification of gold and greed may be less overt now, but the subordination of human need to personal acquisition is a no less powerful force under late capitalism than it was when the colonialists first sighted America. Justice, understood as distribution according to need, is not presently a fashionable concept. We are asked to believe that there is no such thing as society, only individuals who should look after themselves and

---

[4] Ibid., p. 27.

their own while the needy are made invisible and held responsible for their own plight. In the face of the dehumanising
social and political forces shaping and distorting human well-
being at all levels in society, we need a socio-politically aware
and committed pastoral care. We can at least open our eyes to
what is going on and to our part in it. And, like Las Casas, we
can bear true witness to what we have seen.

If my analysis is correct, social and political analysis, reflection, and action lie at the heart of appropriate, responsive, and
responsible pastoral care in Western countries today. Pastors
need to self-consciously choose where they are going to situate
their care in the conflict of interests between powerful and
powerless. My hope is that we will choose justice and life
through a socio-politically aware and committed pastoral care,
rather than inequality and endless, avoidable suffering.

Index of Names

Subject Index

Cambridge Studies in Ideology and Religion

A Theology of Reconstruction: Nation-Building and Human Rights
CHARLES VILLA-VICENCIO

Christianity and Politics in Doe's Liberia
PAUL GIFFORD

Protestantism in Contemporary China
ALAN HUNTER AND KIM-KWONG CHAN

Politics, Theology, and History
RAYMOND PLANT

Christianity and Democracy: A Theology for a Just World Order
JOHN W. DE GRUCHY

Pastoral Care and Liberation Theology
STEPHEN PATTISON

Religion and the Making of Society: Essays in Social Theology
CHARLES DAVIS